Dedicated to their future:

JAINISM

AND THE

NEW SPIRITUALITY

Vastupal Parikh, Ph.D.

Peace Publications
Toronto, Canada

Peace Publications

National Library of Canada Cataloguing in Publication Data

Parikh, Vastupal, 1930-
Jainism and the new spirituality

Includes bibliographical references and index
ISBN 0-9689863-0-7
1. Jaina Philosophy 2. Spiritual life--Jainism I. Title

B162.5.P37 2002 181'.044 C2001-903788-0

Published by:
Peace Publications
685 Merton Street.
TORONTO,
Canada M4S 1B4
peacepub@hotmail.com
Design & Production
ABSTRACT B /02 Siddha Chakra Apts.
Ellisbridge Ahmedabad - 380 006.INDIA
abstractvp@icenet.net

Special Educational Discount (20 copies or more): For use in schools, colleges, universities, *pathshalas*, and for *prabhavana* distribution at religious and social functions, please contact the publishers.

ISBN 0-9689863-0-7
9 780968 986301

Price
USA: $ 19.95
CANADA: $ 29.95
INDIA: Rs. 600.00

ACKNOWLEDGEMENTS

Writing a book like this depends upon the good will of a large number of friends and family members who have provided me with encouragement, advice, and admiration as well as criticism. A large number of youth curious to know about this ancient religion and its relevance to the modern times have provided the inspiration. To all of them my sincere thanks!

Mikal Radfod, Monali Varia, Laura O'Brien, and my daughter Rita served as youthful critics questioning many of my statements, providing a broader secular perspective, suggesting several topics for inclusion in the book, and generally ensuring the readability and clarity of my writing. My wife Nalini a critic totally devoted to the project would not let by any page unless it meets her absolute standards of logic, clarity, design and aesthetics. The devoted contribution of all these well-wishers is evident on every page of this book, and is gratefully acknowledged

Years ago Mr. Lalit Shah invited me to write this book. His constant prodding, and his kind words kept me going. Without his help this project would not have even started. Some of my closest friends deserve a special mention, because discussions and correspondence with them have influenced the quality of this book. I am deeply indebted to Dr. Jitendra Shah of L.D. Institute of Indology, Dr. Shekharchand Jain, Dr. Lonn Friese, Dr. Premchand Gada, Dr. Pravin Shah, and Prof. Joseph O'Connell and several of his students at the University of Toronto, for providing valuable guidance.

My special thanks to Mr. Parmanand Dalwadi of "Abstract" for excellent photographs have enriched both quality and purpose of this book.

My special thanks to Mr. Viren Zhaveri of "Abstract" for the tasteful designing of this book . His imaginative use of Jain art has added beauty, and enhanced the usefulness of the book as both a textual and visual resource.

Digamabras portray Tirthankara in mediation mood.

Svetambaras portray Tirthankara as a King.

Table of Contents

Preface

Jainism is an ancient religion, but also has a great deal of relevance for the modern societies. I find its emphasis on rationality, nonviolence, simple living, and openness to differing ideologies to be both appealing and contemporary. When I reflect on the 20th century's record of world wars, holocaust, unsustainable growth, environmental degradation, and nuclear weapons I must ask: "What does the new century hold? Is it going to be a repeat of the past? Will we ever have peace and serenity?" Jainism offers me a rationale for optimism for the future - a future built on peace, mutuality, community, and trust.

For most people modernity represents an age of logic and reason, not of dogma and 'blind faith'. With the advent of modern educational systems, we tend to be reluctant to accept any statements that lack logical support. We seek rational explanations for many of the concepts that past generations mostly accepted on mere faith -- a faith that has been largely undermined through modern systems of inquiry. Jainism, on the other hand, can offer a different perspective on these questions of faith in relationship to modernity. Jainism is a unique spiritual system that has always demanded that the practitioner question 'blind religious faith'. In other words, ancient Jain philosophers did not require a 'leap of faith,' but on the contrary, applied logic and rationality to satisfy their quest for spirituality. It is within this context that I would suggest Jainism's classical approach to spirituality is what the world could use to satisfy the spiritual needs of the 21st century. I think that the Jain system of personal commitment to peace and ecological stewardship, and its emphasis on rationality holds out a promise for the construction of a more sustainable way of life rooted in justice, hope, and equity.

Currently there are many Western theologians and scholars who view the trend of modernity - the trend away from dogma or faith, and towards reason and rationality - with great concern. In sounding the alarm, Houston Smith writes in *Beyond the Post-Modern Mind* [2]

---

[2] Smith, Houston, *Beyond the Post-Modern Mind*, The Crossroads Publishing Company, New York, 1992, p. 145

A defining feature of modernity is loss of transcendence. The sense of the sacred has declined. Phrases like "the death of God" and "eclipse of God" would have been inconceivable in early days... the chief assailant has been modern science.

In addition, as early as 1979 Edward Norman said in *Christianity and World Order* [3].

"There is no doubt that into developed societies education has contributed to the decline of religious belief."

I believe that such statements could be simply a reactionary position to the current turmoil and confusion created by the crumbling of old power structures. They imply that the contemporary mind is no longer interested in spiritual values, and that science and education are to be blamed for the loss of spirituality. In reality, the spiritual quest is still well and alive, and a wonderful pattern of global spirituality is emerging. Its focus is shifting from old spirituality, based on the dogma and orthodoxy, to a new spirituality that is not necessarily emanating out of the temples, mosques, and churches of the world. This new spirituality is growing out of the grass-roots movements of the streets, cities, and forests, and is manifesting itself in the form of human rights, animal rights, pacifist movements, and environmental concerns. The high priests of the new spirituality are today's activists. Many religions are responding to this shift by de-emphasizing the rituals and obedience to authority, and are tending to highlight love, justice, mutuality, and human rights as a means to spirituality. While such a change in focus is desirable, the old power struggle between institutional religions and the sciences - a struggle that usher in an era of human rights -- are not easily forgotten.
The late astro-physicist Carl Sagan[4] suggested that:

A religion old or new, that stressed the magnificence of the universe as revealed by modern science, might be able to draw forth reserves of reverence and awe hardly tapped by the conventional faiths.

That is, for the modern mind spirituality is neither just faith nor pure materialism. To draw forth the "reserves of reverence and awe," a revitalized spirituality must be multi-dimensional and multi-layered. It must blend a 'new faith' with logic, and must cast a more critical eye toward the relationship between humans and all other living beings. It must not only stress the magnificence of the universe but also the means of preserving our universe. Above all, it must address the nexus of individual behavior and global peace.

---

[3] Norman, Edward, *Christianity and the World Order*, Oxford University Press, New York, 1979

[4] Sagan, Carl, *Pale Blue Dot: A Vision of the Human Future*, Random House Canada, *1994*

My spiritual journey began within this new spiritual framework - a framework that took me to Jainism. I found that a possible answer to the 21st century's quest for spirituality lies within the Jain philosophy. It blends together an experience-based worldview of the universe as reality with a soul-based spirituality, and incorporates a rational cause and effect-based theory of *karma* with a code of conduct that reveres all life, and promotes peace by focusing on transforming personal behavior.

Jainism, and the New Spirituality is an attempt to explain how Jainism has managed to root faith in logic, and how concepts formulated in an ancient tradition can be applied to a modern quest for spirituality. The format used in this book is that of personal narrative, rather than a heavy philosophical treatise. I hope that such a narrative would make interesting reading not only for the scholars but also for college and high school students interested in a religious spirituality that is particularly compatible with our modern 'era of logic.'

Chapter 1 begins, therefore, with my personal quest for spirituality. This quest, combined with my concern for the injustices of the 20th century, first took me to the Jain literature. It was the arguments provided in these texts, which drew me deeper into its rich tradition. Frankly, this journey has been an amazing one - filled with surprises, discoveries, and excitement, as well as periods of internal peace. What follows is an attempt to share these experiences.

The remaining chapters are grouped into five sections. The first three sections detail the Jain lifestyle, worldview, and knowledge (*samyak-charitra, samyak-darsana* and *samyak-jnana* respectively). **Section I** deals with the core principles of Jain conduct, the path Jains follow to live up to these principles, and their struggle for personal perfection and the tangible rewards. **Section II** explores the worldview and philosophy that guides the Jain lifestyle. The Jain worldview is based on logic and knowledge. Jain philosophers have therefore written volumes on the theory of knowledge, and the mechanism through which we gain knowledge. **Section III** offers a brief summary of the voluminous work by these scholar-monks and their discussions on the topic of 'knowledge'. These three sections provide an overview of the Jain principles and practices, and therefore provide a background to understanding how these can be effectively applied to contemporary global problems. Anyone - whether a Jain or non-Jain -- actively involved in attempting to resolve current issues such as violence, war, poverty, globalization, fundamentalism, etc. would benefit from this overview.

Section IV is an attempt to reflect on the principles and practices of Jainism in light of the contemporary 21st century mindset. This section deals with topics such as the 'new spirituality,' nonviolence, peace, vegetarianism, and science. Admittedly, readers may find such reflections somewhat nontraditional, and therefore controversial. They are offered, however, in the typical Jain spirit of *anekantavada* (multiple viewpoints), and *ahimsa*, (nonviolence). My intention is simply to stimulate thinking and to promote activism. Should my comments offend you, I ask for your pardon in a traditional Jain style, "*michhami dukkadam.*"

Section V explores the history of Jainism and Jain sacred literature. Unfortunately, the written records of ancient Indian periods are scarce. As in many of our oldest civilizations, much of India's varied and rich history has been captured in a detailed oral tradition. The history of Jainism is therefore a combination of Jain lore and extant texts, references cited in early Buddhist and Hindu literature, and the work done by Westerners in the 19th and the 20th centuries. Conclusions drawn from such wide sources can be very confusing because of incomplete information and misinterpretations. Fortunately, recent archaeological research by Western scientists in Northwest India, Pakistan, and Afghanistan provides a more concise picture of early Jain history. In this section I draw largely from this contemporary research. It contradicts much of the misinformation presented in earlier history books, and although it confirms parts of Jain tradition and lore, it contradicts others. However, this must not be construed in anyway as an attempt to negate Jain beliefs about their past, but rather, to encourage an active and ongoing inquiry into their history.

Vastupal Parikh — February 2002

1

1. Introduction: One Person's Journey

My spiritual journey into Jainism began earnestly in Canada some 35 years ago. At that time I was teaching chemistry at a university in Canada. One day a professor from the Religious Studies department asked me to speak to her class on Jainism. She had heard that I was a Jain, and knew that I was a vegetarian, showed an extra sensitivity to the plight of plants and animals, and that I treated the ecosystem around me with a rather unusual reverence. By the North American norms of the mid-1960s this was considered to be odd behavior. To me, however, this was simply the way I had been raised.

The invitation to speak on Jainism gave me an opportunity to explore the philosophical and ethical basis of my own lifestyle. Until then I had never read anything on Jainism. In other words, I had very little understanding of the religious and ethical principles that had shaped my life. Indeed, with my scientific, logic-based education, I was a skeptic as far as any religion was concerned. Therefore, it was within a context of a scientist's curiosity, skepticism, and critical analysis that I tackled my first book on Jainism.[5] To my great surprise this particular text was a treat for the logical and analytical mind of a scientist!

The book was an 11th century commentary on a 2nd century text on Jain practices and principles. It did not demand a blind faith, promise mercy for the faithful, or threaten the infidel, nor was there any assertion of a singular truth. Instead, this text warned against accepting anything as a gospel. Its advice was to treat human understanding of reality, regardless of its emotional appeal, as only a partial and relative truth.

---

[5] *Dravya Sangraha* by Nemichandra Siddhantdeva, ca. 11th Century A.D., English translation by S.C. Ghoshal, (1917), republished in 1956 by Delhi Jain Samaj, New Delhi, India.

Absolute truth, it maintained, is beyond human comprehension. It was a reasoned, logical appeal to the intellect, insisting that only those arguments that meet the reader's highest intellectual and critical scrutiny be accepted. To me this sounded like a two thousand year-old affirmation of modern scientific thinking. The basis for much of my behavior and world-view was explained in this 2nd century philosophical treatise.

What I first learned was that Jainism, like all the great religions, is about liberation of the soul, and that Rikhava (later called Rishabha), the first *Tirthankara* (spiritual teacher), showed a path towards this liberation many thousands of years ago. Rikhava realized that every living being suffers; however, when *jiva* leaves the body, the dead body no longer experiences suffering. Therefore, it is not the body but an entity within the body called *jiva* (the soul) that experiences pleasure and pain. He taught that all suffering is a result of the *jiva's* entrapment in the material body. The entrapped *jiva* gets even more entrapped in a cycle of repeated death and birth due to its activities (*karma*). However, every soul has the potential to liberate itself from this painful cycle and attain a pure state (*moksha*) in which the soul establishes its omniscience, omnipotence, and enjoys eternal bliss. He taught that one could reach *moksha*, by winning complete victory over oneself -- over one's emotions, passions, desires, and weaknesses. Such a victory is gained by practicing self-discipline through meditation, inquiry and austerity. Jains believe that Rikhava himself achieved *moksha*, and regard him as their first *Jina* -- one who achieved total victory over the self. He advised that *moksha* is the ultimate goal for every soul, and that all humans should try to reach this goal.

Jains have absorbed his message and follow his code of conduct even today. This code of conduct, the book explained, is prescribed through a set of principles. The book began by saluting the Jain teachers for revealing that everything in the universe is either *jiva* - the soul or spirit - that embodies bliss, energy, and infinite consciousness; or *ajiva*, which refers to all that is non-living. In fact, *ajiva* is a group term referring to five non-living elements namely matter, space, time, the medium of motion, and the medium of rest. Thus, together with *jiva* there are the six fundamental and eternal elements of the universe. All living beings, for example, are souls (*jiva*) entrapped in a material (*ajiva*) body, a result of the interaction between these two. Being eternal, both *jiva* and *ajiva* can neither be created nor destroyed, but mutual interaction can change their forms. It is this understanding of the nature of the universe that underpins all Jain philosophy.

With terms like matter, energy, time, and space, and with discussions of motion, inertia and their interactions, this ancient religious scripture read more like a 20th century scientific treatise. In addition, the book discussed the principles, which govern the interactions between the six fundamental elements of the universe. These principles, such as the *Principle of Karma* (the law of cause and effect), are the "operating principles" of the universe! According to the Jains, this then is how the universe works. I had to read the book repeatedly; each time I was awed by its scientific insights.

The text went on to summarize the central themes governing the Jain code of conduct as: nonviolence (not hurting other souls or universal love to all living beings), non-absolutism (exploring and respecting many-sided viewpoints), and, non-possession (limiting one's material possessions). In addition, it offered the philosophical supposition that life, in any form, shape, or size, has a soul that is essentially the same whether it exists in a human being, animal, or plant. That soul unit not only sustains every life but is also eternal and potentially blissful, omniscient, and omnipotent. Since all living beings are potentially the same entrapped souls, every life - whether human, plant, or animal -- must be preserved, respected, and revered. This Jain concept of soul as the essential element of all forms of life strengthens the autonomy of life of every being and has made nonviolence, or a*himsa*, the central Jain doctrine. Here, finally, I found the basis for my own vegetarianism explained.

TERMS TO REMEMBER	
Ahimsa	Doctrine of non-hurting, non-killing
Ajiva	Non-living
Anekantavada	Doctrine of Multiple viewpoints
Aparigraha	Doctrine of Limiting possessions
Jina	One who has achieved total victory over the self
Jiva	Soul, infinite consciousness energy and bliss
Tirthankara	Liberated one who shows path to liberation.

Beyond prescribing nonviolence, the Jain text also advocated practices of inquiry and asceticism. It was this Jain promotion of inquiry through non-absolutism, that I found resonated most with my choice to become a scientist. Reading almost like a contemporary lesson in post-Modernism, the text stated that according to the principles of non-absolutism or *anekantavada*, all knowledge (except omniscience) is only one viewpoint, and thus only a partial truth. The basis of this Jain doctrine is that only the liberated soul (omniscient) is capable of perceiving absolute truth, and in the entrapped state all of us are affected by our own biases or perceptions. The doctrine of *anekantavada* does not suggest that every viewpoint should be accepted as valid, nor does it allow outright rejection of differing viewpoints without exploring and examining them as holistically as possible. It encourages Jains to be patient and respectful of their adversaries. Upon careful examination, should an individual find a differing viewpoint unacceptable, the doctrine encourages one to explain why they find it so. Thus, non-absolutism strengthens the autonomy of thought of every individual, and promotes investigation as a means of broadening one's knowledge, understanding, exploration of truth, and peaceful resolution of potential conflicts.

Here, then, was a basis not only for understanding a scientific mind, but also for finding hope for some of the gravest issues plaguing our planet. Non-absolutism was a tool to ensure against dogmatism -- which, to my mind, is the root cause of many human conflicts. The days that followed my professor friend's request launched me on the path of a personal spiritual quest that was to awaken me to the issues of the day such as the environment, the conflict in Vietnam, flower power, and the dropping out of the 'rat-race'. It also helped to create in me an awareness that the world was warming up to the messages of peace, nonviolence, racial equality, and human dignity. The morality of 'blind faith' in the name of nationalism, religion, or ideology was now being questioned, and I was finding these 'modern' issues addressed prophetically in the old Jain scriptures.

For example, the Jain doctrine of limiting ones possessions (*aparigraha*) helped me to understand the environmental consciousness I had observed within the Jain community. This doctrine asks Jains not to seek the acquisition of material goods, but rather, to limit one's possessions and live harmoniously in a state of interdependence with all in the ecosystem. As early as 600 BCE, Mahavira, one of the last liberated teachers (*Tirthankaras*) of Jainism, stated:

He who knows what is bad for himself knows what is bad for others, and he who knows what is bad for others knows what is bad for himself. One whose mind is at peace and who is free from passions does not desire to live at the expense of others. He who understands the nature of sin against earth, water, air, fire, plants, and animals is a true sage and understands karma. For, all these elements are truly alive (possess soul energy) and those who harm them harm themselves by bonding their souls firmly with non-liberating karma.[6]

By choosing to live humbly, one frees the mind from the ever-nagging desire of wanting more, greed, and jealousy. It allows one to live in harmony with nature according to Jainism's basic code of nonviolence by limiting one's impact on the environment and demand for material goods. In the atmosphere of the early 1960,s consumerism, living humbly in harmony with nature and vegetarianism may have

6 - Mahavira quoted in the *Acharang-sutra*, ca. 600 BCE

seemed odd, but it appears that now there is a greater appreciation of this lifestyle. Though Jainism is still little known, more people around the world are being exposed to the Jain way of living. The West is realizing that Jains believe in nonviolence towards all beings, show unusual sensitivity towards the plight of plants and animals, and treat the ecosystem with reverence. They are beginning to understand that this is a philosophy of mutual respect and peace. In the West it is no longer an odd belief !

Twenty-six hundred years ago, Mahavira, (the last of 24 *Tirthankaras)* preached that practicing Rikhava's principles of nonviolence, non-absolutism, and non-possession was the path to personal peace. In the years since I began my personal journey into Jainism, I have realized that this philosophy has an even greater and more inclusive relevance in that it can offer a path to global peace. The world has changed much since Mahavira's time. Technological innovations in communications, travel, industry, trade and investment patterns have created a 'global village' and heightened an awareness of the interdependence of all world citizens. Nevertheless, deadly acts of war, economic exploitation, and environmental degradation are threatening to destroy our planet in the 21st century. A fundamental change in our mind-set is needed to avert this threat. I have realized that Jain principles and practices could bring about such a basic change and provide potential solutions. In such solutions, there is hope !

This hope has made me pro-active - not to proselytize Jainism as such but to promote its values, values that Jains have lived by for several millennia. Now, is the time to inform the rest of the world about these values ! Death and destruction by wars, bigotry, and greed has taken a heavy toll on humanity and our planet during the 20th century. A new concept of spirituality, defined in terms of humanity and environmental awareness is emerging around the world.

Jain values offer excellent tools for promoting this new spirituality. Jains need to work with other faiths, and use these tools to resolve the problems facing our world. In doing so they can truly live up to their principles, help the world, and regain the lost glory of their ancient religion.

Jains may not be actively seeking converts to their religion, but they certainly hope that one day the world will adopt Jain values as template for all human values, and that in so doing, they will help all realize the promise of a peaceful 21st century.

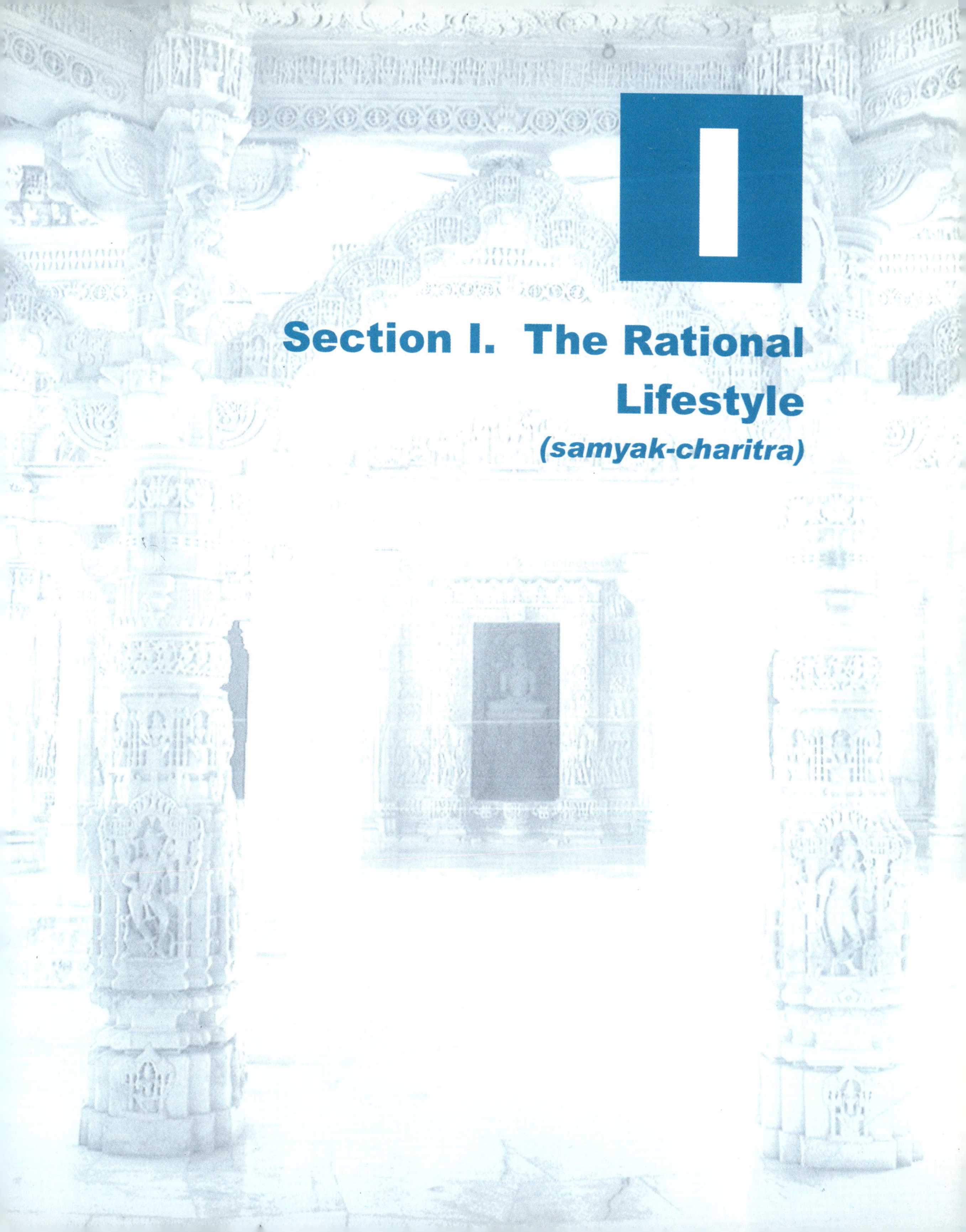

I

Section I. The Rational Lifestyle

(samyak-charitra)

SECTION PREVIEW

Whereas some religions seek salvation through God, the Jain path to salvation depends essentially on our rational behavior aimed at purifying our soul. The key elements in rational behavior or rational conduct are: universal love for all living beings, respect for all viewpoints, and minimizing wants and possessions. These require self-control and discipline because our emotions tend to work against these three.

Jain masters have devised a code of conduct and have charted a path to help us achieve self-control. They suggest that this path would lead us to absolute self-control, but progress along the path is gradual and requires a goal-focused lifestyle and daily practice. In other words, one must find the goal, understand it, study it, and choose a rational lifestyle to help achieve the goal through daily, disciplined practice. Section 1 explains how this can be achieved through rational lifestyle or Rational Conduct (samyak-charitra)

Finding the goal means, 'to awaken' to the reality, and to understand the rationality of it. Chapter 2 deals with these two issues. Once the goal is fixed, progress towards it depends upon our determination. Jain masters suggest that a series of pledges or vows would fortify our resolve to achieve the goal and remain focused on it. Practicing these vows, as a routine not only helps us gain self-control but also reduces the stress associated with it. Chapter 3 explains the introductory vows for the beginners to progress along the path to liberation. Chapter 4 explains the path. It illustrates that there are many steps to climb and many stages to pass through before we are able to reach the goal. The Jain path recommends an austere, ascetic and demanding lifestyle but the ultimate goal is well worth it. In chapter 5 we look at the practical benefits of this lifestyle. Not everyone would want to, or be capable of, living an ascetic life. Nevertheless, the practical benefits to be accrued to our mental and physical health, by following Jain practices in a less rigorous manner, are well worth the attempt. Furthermore, the survival of this planet may well depend upon how seriously the world takes these principles and practices. I urge that, at least for this practical reason, the world needs to understand and adopt a rational lifestyle.

2

2. Awakening

I had just finished my talk on nonviolence at a peace conference when a young member of the audience asked, "How does one become Jain? Do I go to some Jain priest and ask to be converted to Jainism? Do I have to visit a Jain temple regularly? Must I attend regular religious services?"

So, how does one become a Jain? I had never given much thought to this question. Am I a Jain just because I am born one? Would I still be Jain even if I never went to a Jain temple? What would my status be if I never studied anything about Jainism or never attended a Jain sermon? What would it mean if I took up hunting and fishing as sport? If I ate meat, would I still be a Jain? Is a particular religion to be taken as a birthright?

"Everyone here is interested in peace and nonviolence. Does that mean that they all are Jains?" the young person said, putting me on the spot. "Just being interested is not enough. Lifestyle, conduct, one's goal, and the path one follows to achieve that goal are the key", I replied. In effect, I was telling him that anyone could be Jain by adopting its lifestyle, regardless of culture or birth. However, simply adopting a particular lifestyle is not enough. A rational lifestyle (*samyak-charitra*) in the Jain sense of the word cannot be achieved without faith in its philosophical system - a rational world-vision (*samyak-darsana*) - with the fortification of faith by rational knowledge (*samyak-jnana*). After all, a religion is a belief system, and Jainism stresses a belief system based on logical inquiry.

According to the Modernist theories of the social critics, the modern educational systems have weakened the dogmatic religious entrapments that kept us in a particular faith. The new era encourages us to be rational and knowledgeable in choosing our faith. Jainism also has the same message. The key elements in the Jain life style are: universal love for all living beings, respecting all viewpoints, and

minimizing wants and possessions. If these resonate with our values, we may simply adopt the lay Jain lifestyle, understand Jain worldview, and fortify our faith in it by critical and rational study. We need not be formally baptized or be enlisted into a Jain congregation. However, we all need some support system - particularly when changes in lifestyle and goals are involved. Jain places of worship, meeting-places, temples, and their scholars and monks can provide us the moral support, inspiration, knowledge and understanding needed to keep our new-found faith. Therefore, though not mandatory, a frequent visit to such places and congregations nurture a sense of belonging to the community and can encourage our progress along the spiritual path. Formal initiation comes only if we choose to be a monk or a nun. A formal welcome then awaits us - not into Jainism - but into the order of the ascetics that we may have chosen for guidance along our chosen path.

To be a Jain does not necessarily require a Jain birth or an induction into the Jain fold by a priest or religious order (unless one wants to be initiated into an order of Jain monks or nuns.) Anyone, who is awakened to s*amyak-drsti* (rational understanding), and decides to follow a specific path to reach the goal, is a Jain. What then is this goal, and what path must one follow to reach it? The goal is simply to attain a state of everlasting happiness, perfect bliss. However, how does one define happiness?

Happiness

Similar questions were asked of me at a gathering of young high school students, but in a different context. When I asked, "what would make you most happy"; here are some of their immediate answers:

Power,	*Good Job,*	*Millions of Dollars,*
Sex,	*Good Health,*	*Getting high on Drugs*
Cars	*Big House*	*Becoming Famous*

I countered by asking a few more questions: "Does that make the world's most powerful person - the president of United States - the happiest on earth? "Are billionaires the happiest of people?" "What happens when you are no longer 'high' on drugs or alcohol?" How long would that happiness last?

I think they got the point! They realized that permanent happiness lies beyond these temporary pleasures, and the external things do not necessarily make one permanently happy. They understood that there is something within the body, which experiences joy and happiness. Some call it spirit, soul, life force, or *atman.* Jains say it is *jiva.* Perhaps, the realization that there is a soul or *jiva* within everybody was the beginning of the 'awakening' for these students.

Jains believe that we may experience temporary joy and happiness, but cannot be permanently happy as long as our *jiva** remains trapped within the body. Does death release it from this imprisonment? Jains don't think so. They believe that, at death the *jiva* simply transmigrates and takes rebirth. It thus remains bonded, and shall remain entrapped in the cycle of rebirth and death until it is liberated.♦ Permanent happiness or infinite bliss is the basic quality of the liberated soul, and every soul longs to be liberated to regain bliss. Until then, *samsara* (the cycle of birth and death) is an unhappy and painful state. Jains believe that liberation should be the ultimate goal of human life, and the goal is achievable through the Jain path of self-purification.

Before Awakening

The Jain path to liberation is a fourteen-stage (*gunasthana*) spiritual development(page19). Jains believe that the awakening occurs at the fourth stage. The first stage is a state of delusion, misconceptions, and aimless drifting. Unaware that there is a way out of our misery, we remain entrapped. At this stage, our mind has a definite dislike and repulsion to truth and reality; we have absolutely no idea of the true reasons for our misery and suffering, and we are not even ready to seek out or listen to any advice in these matters. When this attitude changes, the dislike turns into indifference towards reality. Even after getting an opportunity to understand reality, we fail to seize the opportunity. This is the second stage in our spiritual progress. At the third stage, the desire to know more about reality is still not there, but, there are a few fleeting moments when we become curious about the nature of truth and reality. In these fleeting moments our intuition is mixed with delusion and error, but we are curious about our spiritual progress.

If curiosity is not sustained with an effort to discover truth, we may slip back into the second stage and 'awakening' escapes us. This third stage is similar to early dawn when one just wakes up, becomes barely aware of light, and slips back into the darkness of sleep. It is not a real awakening. Those at this stage are likely to refuse to acknowledge that they encountered a glimpse of reality and of the path leading towards its realization. Unable to look critically upon their lives and behaviors, people in this stage doubt their ability to control destiny, and thus continue to be in the cycle of eternal suffering in *samsara* (cycle of reincarnation).

* Details in Chapter 6. The Western or even Hindu concept of soul is not the same as *jiva*. *Jiva* is not a part of some divine force that remerges with the whole. *Jiva* is an entity with its own unique qualities and characteristics. Consciousness and bliss are some of its characteristics. There are infinite numbers of individual *jivas*, each imprisoned in a body until liberated. Each retains its identity, both in liberated as well as in the non-liberated states. For the convenience of the reader, however, we will continue to use the words soul and *jiva* interchangeably.

♦ Details in Chapter 9.

The Awakening

The real awakening occurs at the fourth stage. Why and how does it happen? Jains have an explanation for this in their *Theory of Karma*. We will study it later. For now, let us see what happens when we reach the fourth stage. Are we suddenly different when we reach the fourth stage (*avirati gunasthana*)? Do we suddenly change our behavior? The awakening certainly brings about changes in an individual but they are gradual, and initially entirely internal.

According to Jainism, our journey on the path to liberation begins at the very moment when we realize that life has an ultimate goal that of liberation. We then emerge from the depths of delusion and entrapment (a state of *mithya-drsti* - incorrect understanding of reality) and are at the fourth stage (*avirati*) of our spiritual progress. Progress from the fourth to the sixth stage of our spiritual life as a layperson is somewhat like climbing an eleven-step ladder (*pratima*). These steps lead to the ascetic life essential for reaching the pinnacle of freedom for our soul. Jains call this stage of awakening., *samyak-drsti,* or rational understanding."

Awakening may occur through intuition, study, and contemplation, or simply through an accidental event in our life. We may then begin to wonder about philosophical questions such as: Who are we? What is life? Is this universe real? Who made it? What is the purpose of my life? Why am I happy/unhappy? Our sustained curiosity and faith in such an awakening then launches us on the path towards liberation.

The hallmark of this stage is 'awareness'. We become aware of the true self. We realize that "*me*" is not this body but it is the soul within it. We accept that soul is a real entity and that it interacts with a number of other eternal entities (we will study these in the next section). With the recognition of our own soul and its interactions with other entities, we begin realizing that these entities are universal. They interact with one another strictly according to a set of natural operating principles (*navatattva,* Chapter 8). The mystery of the universe suddenly begins to unfold and we understand that there is nothing irrational or mysterious about it. No mystical or supernatural power is playing with our lives. We, and we alone are responsible and we must take our fate in our hands. This realization, this trust in our own ability to better our future, marks our 'awakening.'

We now become aware of our soul, its true nature, and its goal of liberation. We become aware also of other factors and realities that affect and influence our soul. This awareness changes our focus from physical pleasures to the knowledge of innate and pure qualities of the soul. This shift away from external objects brings about a change in our attitude whereby we realize that materialism is not the basis for our happiness. Disenchanted with such objects, we begin to control our passions. We experience peace of mind, tranquility, and extraordinary internal happiness. This experience has another wonderful effect on us. We begin to develop compassion and empathy for all souls that have been suffering because of their entrapment in this painful cycle of birth and death. We resolve to refrain from inflicting any pain on other living beings.

Fourteen Stages of Spiritual Progress

(fourteen gunasthanas)

	Gunasthana	Behavioral and Psychological Characteristics at that Stage.	Level
1	*Mithyatva*	Lowest stage, Ignorance, delusion, negative attitude towards reality	Ignorance
2	*Sasadana*	Indifference to reality vague memory of spiritual insight	Confused
3	*Misra*	Fleeting moments of curiosity towards reality	Mixed
4	*Avirati*	Awareness of reality; positive attitude and trust in it combined with willingness to practice self-discipline	Awakening
5	*Desa-virati*	Introductory vows, 11 - step climb of *pratima* ladder begins	Lay vows
6	*Pramatta or Sarva-virati*	Ascetic vows; renunciation of possessions and firm resolve to control passions;may fail their vows due to lack of full control over their passions or due to carelessness (*pramatta*)	Starting ascetic life
7	*Apramatta Virati*	Intense practice of vows has increased self-control and virtually replaced carelessness with spiritual vigilance and vigor (*aprammatta*); passions are under greater but not total control.	Determined effort for self-control
8	*Apurva-karana*	Near total self-control over actions, higher control over mind, thought and passions ready for suppression or annihilation of the conduct-deluding *karma*.	Self-discipline
9	*Anivritti-karana*	Intense spiritual activity, higher control over passions; suppression and elimination of conduct-deluding *karma* begins.	Increased self-discipline
10	*Suksma-samparaya*	Almost complete suppression or elimination of all four passions except for subtle degree of attachment (greed) e.g. attachment for life; conduct-deluding *karma* virtually eliminated.	
11	*Upasanta-moha*	Suppressed passions and lingering conduct-deluding *karma* may rise to drag the ascetic to stage 9 or even down to 1. Fleeting experience of equanimity.	
12	*Kshina-moha*	This is the point of no return. All passions as well as conduct-deluding *karma* are eliminated. Permanent internal peace achieved. No new bondage.	
13	*Sayoga-kevalin*	All residual knowledge and perception obscuring *karma* eliminated. Omniscience achieved, *Arhat* stage reached. Perfected soul.	*Arhat*
14	*Ayoga-kevlin*	Liberation and bliss. *Siddha* stage reached. Purest soul.	**Moksha**

These are the gradual changes occurring internally at the stage of awakening. We are now aware that we can gain control over our destiny and reach our goal of liberation by following the right path. We now begin to search for the right path. How does one know which path to liberation is "right"? Is the Jain path the correct one? No answer, verbal or written, will convince us fully until we personally go through the experience. We have to touch ice, taste sugar, and listen to music to accept their qualities. Nevertheless, we routinely accept certain statements because of the expertise and the authority of the people who may have direct experience of the event. Daily, we hear and accept news although we may be miles away from the event. We may try to verify it, but in the final analysis we do accept the event as a fact without having direct experience of it. Such is the case also with the path to liberation.

TERMS TO REMEMBER

Charitra	Conduct, behavior, lifestyle
Darsana	Intuition, worldview
Gunasthana	Stage of spiritual progress
Jnana	Knowledge
Mithya-drsti	Incorrect understanding
Ratnatraya	Three jewels, threefold path
Samsara	Cycle of transmigration, birth and death
Samyak	Rational, logical, correct, right

Through years of meditation, experimentation, and practice, *Tirthankaras* have developed a spiritual path to liberation. The twenty-four *Tirthankaras* continued to live after achieving omniscience, to teach us the path they followed and the bliss they experienced. Since then thousands have followed their example, have made spiritual progress, and have written about it. These people have claimed omniscience for themselves, and judging from the fact that very little in the philosophy and science that these monks have claimed over the millennia is incompatible with the theories of 20th century science, I would suggest that it is hard to dispute their claims.*

These omniscient ones are the experts in the art and science of liberation. Consequently, as we do in other fields, we may decide to follow the path suggested by these spiritual experts and verify if we too can actually experience the bliss promised by the *Tirthankaras*. Reaching the fourteenth stage may take a lifetime or more, but by faithfully following their suggested path, we can certainly experience at least some degree of peace and tranquility as we progress through the fifth and the sixth *gunasthana*. A true Jain is one who trusts and follows this path, and works for his/her liberation. Consequently, anyone who does not trust such a path is not really a Jain, even if born of Jain parents. In practice however, most Jains, though not strictly on the path to liberation, trust the Jain view of reality and do

* See Chapter 14.

try to follow the basic principles of the Jain code of conduct to the best of their ability.

The Rational Understanding

Earlier we talked about our search for the right path to follow 'awakening'. We suggested that it is safe to explore the Jain path because it is taught by the omniscient ones. Similarly, we also suggested that the stage of awakening marks our understanding of reality. We begin to trust that 'reality' consists of soul and its liberation. We accept that five other fundamental entities exist and interact with one another according to the nine 'operating principles' of the universe. However, accepting such a path or reality simply because *Tirthankaras* taught it would amount to 'blind faith'. Our faith in such reality or path should not be a blind faith. Faith, which results in spiritual progress, is positive faith, and that which results in dogmatism and orthodoxy is blind faith. *Tirthankaras* have warned against blind faith and preached that we must know ourselves, try to understand reality, analyze the path leading to it, examine it, test it, verify it, and then, if satisfied, if convinced of its efficacy, build our faith on the foundation of this correct understanding of reality. If we awake and extricate ourselves from ignorance and delusion, we are the masters of our own destiny. This is *samyak-drsti* (rational understanding). Such rational understanding is essential as we embark on a journey to liberation.

The Journey

Awakened by *samyak-drsti*, Jains now continue their fourteen-stage journey on a three-fold path based on the so-called "Three Jewels - *Ratnatraya*" viz.:
samyak-charitra (rational conduct or lifestyle)
samyak-darsana (rational world vision), and
samyak-jnana (rational knowledge).

Most lay Jains believe that they are at the fourth stage of the fourteen-stage journey. Each subsequent stage has several intervening steps, but progress along all three fronts must be achieved for liberation. Progress transforms our outlook towards the surrounding world. It forces us to re-examine our short-term goals and relationships, and generates love, respect, appreciation, and compassion for others. A renewed respect for all life generates harmony with our eco-system. A feeling of indifference to physical pleasures, praise or criticism, and antipathy, takes over. Living becomes a peaceful experience filled with self-confidence, inner bliss, and a purpose defined by the understanding of the reality.

At peace with oneself, one begins a serene journey towards liberation. At the far end of the path lies freedom -- a freedom, which at last, liberates the soul from the seemingly endless cycle of birth, suffering and death. One, who undertakes this journey and follows the path, regardless of where, when or how one is born, is truly a Jain! One needs to be truly awakened to be able to begin this journey.

3

3. The Journey

To be a Jain does not necessarily require a Jain birth or an induction into the Jain fold by a priest or religious order (unless one wants to be initiated into an order of Jain monks or nuns.) Anyone, who is awakened to s*amyak-drsti* (rational understanding), and decides to follow its rational path, is a Jain. Our rational understanding at the fourth stage of the 14-stage spiritual progress involves the realization that the entire universe consists of only six fundamental and eternal entities, which are *jiva*, and the five *ajivas* (matter, space, time, the principle of motion and the principle of rest).* We also become aware that for our soul to regain its innate state of permanent happiness, it must be liberated from its entrapment in *samsara* - the cycle of rebirths and death. We then begin our search for a path to liberation. What is liberation?

Most religious systems are concerned with the afterlife. They preach that our life today should be such that we attain permanent happiness after death. For some, permanent happiness is 'admission to heaven', for others it is merging of their soul with a super consciousness. For the Jains, it is the freeing of the soul from its bonded *karmic* material so that it can regain its innate qualities of infinite consciousness, bliss, and energy. Different religions prescribe different paths to achieve permanent happiness. Religions which believe that God created and governs this universe preach that we must seek God's grace and His mercy, or we must so behave to endear ourselves to God that He will grant us an admission to heaven. The path they therefore recommend is to be good, accept Him in your life, and seek his mercy and grace.

Jains believe that the universe is eternal, made of the six eternal entities listed above, governs itself according to its own operating principles, and therefore, there is no creator or governing God. Thus, their concept of liberation is not

---

* Details in Chapter 6

constructed around the idea of seeking the mercy and grace of God. They believe that God does not make us happy or unhappy, nor should one depend on His grace and mercy for permanent happiness. Our soul has somehow become impure or polluted and thus entrapped in this unhappy cycle of rebirth and death.* The Jain path to permanent happiness therefore, involves purifying the polluted soul so that it is liberated and regains its innate quality of infinite bliss. Jains call this liberated state, "*moksha*". We ourselves are responsible for our destiny, and *moksha* can be achieved only through our own efforts and actions.

Salvation, Nirvana and Moksha

We have been using the terms such as salvation, liberation, nirvana, bliss, and moksha somewhat loosely and interchangeably. These terms are religion-specific and differ in their finer understanding as well as in the ways to achieve these states. The dictionary meaning of the term 'bliss' is simply the highest degree of happiness, gladness, exalted felicity, heavenly joy, etc. All the other terms mentioned above are supposedly able to deliver us that bliss.

Salvation - the Christian path to bliss is the deliverance from the shortcomings of the human condition. They believe that human misery is caused largely by their own weaknesses and that the world, to some extent, is dominated by evil forces. God is still ultimately in control, however, and would one day send the Messiah who will conquer the forces of evil, the dead would be resurrected and all would be judged -- salvation for the righteous and damnation for the rest. According to Christian doctrine one must believe that Christ is both fully divine and fully human. One must believe in the doctrine of Trinity, which holds that God consists of three aspects -- God the Father, Jesus Christ the Son, and the Holy Spirit -- who are at the same time one God. The Jewish concept is to know God in his true form. They believe that this can be achieved either through correct practice from moment to moment, or, through rigorously following thirteen principles of Jewish theology (Maimondes), or with the heart through love (Kabbalah and Hasidism).

Nirvana - This Sanskrit term literally means 'blowing out' or 'extinction' and is used by Hindus and Buddhists, as well as by Jains. *Nirvana* for Hindus is emancipation from ignorance and the extinction of all attachments except for God. In this state (*samadhi* or *sthitpragna*) one is believed to be truly in union with God. It is a state of transcendence in this life, which enables us to live fully in the

* Details in Chapter 9.

human condition with an underlying state of joy and tranquility. According to Hinduism there are three paths to achieve the state of *nirvana.*

(1). The Path of Dharma *(karma-marga)* is to follow one's ethical duties, observe household rituals, and conform to religious laws in personal and social life. "Following one's *dharma* without any attachment or expectations of the fruits of action leads one to the union with God," advises a Hindu Scripture.[7]

(2). The Path of Devotion *(bhakti marga)* is to offer unconditional love and reverence to one's chosen deity - a reincarnation of God. Total surrender to this deity takes one into a state of extreme joy and ecstasy. This path is mostly based upon Ramanuja's (c. 1137 A.D.) interpretation of the Upanishads.

(3). The Path of Knowledge *(jnana marga)*. This path, based on Shankara's (c. 850 A.D.) interpretation of the Upanishads, emphasizes the attainment of the knowledge of the true nature of reality through meditation and profound contemplation. True reality, according to Hinduism is only one -- the Brahman -- the indescribable, impersonal supernatural power. The rest of the universe is just a cosmic illusion. The realization of the true knowledge of Brahman liberates the soul and merges it with the supernatural. Hindus maintain that any one of these three paths could lead to liberation.

For the Buddhists also, Nirvana is a form of transcendence in this life. Since they do not believe in the existence of souls or a creator God, their Nirvana is not a union of a soul with God. Buddhists describe Nirvana as the ineffable ultimate in which one has attained disinterested wisdom and compassion. It is an ideal condition of rest, harmony, stability, and joy. For a Buddhist, Nirvana is simply the extinction of individuality in an undifferentiated final state.

Moksha: Jains do use the term *nirvana* but their use of this term is generally to describe 'blowing out' or 'extinction' of all impurities from the soul. For the exalted state of liberation, the real Jain term is *moksha. Moksha* does not involve the union of soul with the supernatural, or receiving any judgment for salvation or damnation by God. The worldview of Jains is based on the eternal existence of an infinite number of souls and their pure and impure states. For the Jains the pure, liberated soul has bliss, but this characteristic is marred by the impurities in a defiled soul. Purifying the soul and liberating it from this entrapment is therefore the main goal of human life. How do we achieve this goal?

[7] *Bhagavad-Gita, 2.47*

We learnt of the Hindu belief that their goal of *nirvana* can be achieved by *any one* of the three paths namely; *dharma*, devotion, or knowledge. The parallels in Jainism are rational conduct, rational worldview, and rational knowledge. The Jain unified path to *moksha* requires all three. The Hindu state of liberation is a form of transcendence in this life, and union of the soul with Brahman. The Brahman itself may, from time to time, take rebirth on the surface of this earth. For the Jains on the other hand, *moksha* is complete liberation of the soul from the painful cycle of birth and death. The liberated soul regains its fundamental quality of eternal bliss, and of course, no more rebirths - not even as an *avatar*!

The Jain Path

What path do we follow for Moksha? At the fourth stage of the fourteen-stage spiritual development, i.e. at the 4th *gunasthana*, (see spiritual progress chart,page 19) we become just aware of the need to liberate our soul. However, the journey is yet to begin and life is still without any self-restraint (*virati*). This *gunasthana* is therefore called *avirati* (non-restraint). Now, the goal is known, the path is decided and the journey is to begin, but progress depends on determination and self-discipline. Taking vows helps our determination and helps us develop self-discipline. Therefore, laypersons are advised to take introductory vows and practice self-restraint. One reaches the fifth *gunasthana* when partial self-restraint (*desa virati*) is achieved and the sixth *gunasthana* when total self-restraint (*sarva virati*) is achieved. Climbing eleven steps of the spiritual ladder through these two stages was hard. However, even harder journey is yet to come as we enter the ascetic life. Understanding the vows will give us an insight into the daily lifestyle of a Jain layperson, or a monk and nun.

The Introductory - Vows

Life is short, and the goal (liberation) lofty. One must be fully motivated and disciplined if the destination is to be reached. The Jain teachers - *Tirthankaras* - have recommended a motivational tool of 'taking vows' *(vrata)* to launch oneself on a path to *moksha*. A casual attitude without vows, of course, would achieve very little progress. Beginners start with twelve introductory-vows. More rigid observance of vows is prescribed for the monks and nuns who are seriously progressing along the path. The main goal of beginner vows is to help people meet their obligations to the family and society, and to overcome the emotional stresses of passion, desire and greed, and of day-to-day materialist living. As we achieve a degree of self-restraint and equanimity, more vows are taken to gain greater control over other weaknesses. The twelve introductory vows are normally taken in three steps of increasing intensity. These are:

Five *anuvratas* - the basic vows
Three *gunavratas* - designed to reinforce the five *anuvratas,* and
Four *sikshavratas* - the spiritual exercises.

The Basic Vows *(anuvratas)*

The journey begins with five basic vows *(anuvratas).* These five are called:
ahimsa vrata (nonviolence),
satya vrata (being truthful),
achurya vrata (non-stealing, or not gaining anything by illegitimate means),
shila vrata (keeping the mind and thoughts as pure as possible), and
parigraha-parimana vrata (limiting ones needs and possessions).
Usually, a layperson declares his/her vow in front of a monk (or nun). The first *anuvrata* - the vow of nonviolence - for example, would be:

> *"I will refrain from injuring living beings having two or more senses (animals), with a deliberate act of my mind, speech or body, and will avoid killing one sensed beings (plants, microbes) unless unavoidable".* [8]

This, in fact, is a less intense vow of the extremely severe vow required of the ascetics. The vow for the ascetics is as follows:

> *"I renounce all killing of living beings, whether subtle or gross, whether movable or immovable. Nither shall I myself kill living beings nor cause others to do it, nor consent to it. As long as I live, I confess and blame, repent and exempt myself of these sins, in the threefold way, in mind, speech and action"* [9]

Note that this vow goes far beyond the Judeo-Christian concept of never hurting one's neighbor. It extends to all living creatures, even spiders and mosquitoes. It means that not only must one forego all Meat (for which the animal had to be killed), but also involves foregoing eggs which is an animals way of reproducing life. It also means avoiding consumption of any plant whose cultivation involves killing the plant itself (potatoes, garlic, onions, etc.). Note also that the vow includes not just the *action* of hurting or killing but also harmful *thoughts* or *will.* In there lies the true Jain meaning of *ahimsa.* Although, a mere thought or ill will may not hurt or kill another being, it pollutes our soul. The vows emphasize these because our motive here is to achieve equanimity (inner

TERMS TO REMEMBER	
Nirvana	Death of holy person, reaching ecstasy
Moksha	Absolute purity of soul
Pratima	Steps for spiritual progress for lay persons
Siddha	One who has achieved omniscience
Sravaka	A lay man
Sravika	A lay woman
Vrata	Vows

[8] - - Ratnakaranda Sravakachara. 3/53

[9] - Acharang Sutra Book II, Lecture 15, i, 4

peace), respect for all life, and self-restraint. One can achieve these only by disciplining one's own mind and thoughts. In fact, the Jain definition of a*himsa* extends beyond actual killing or hurting, it also means refraining from any act - physical, verbal, or mental - that could possibly lead one to violate ones avowed path towards liberation. In this context, all other vows are but an extension of this fundamental code of *ahimsa.*

The second vow *(satya-vrata)* demands that one must not tell lies or resort to false speech, action, or thought. Once again, note the focus on 'thought'. This focus enables lay Jains to resolve intellectually any conflicting situation one might inevitably encounter (for example, one might conceivably tell a lie that was certain to save someone's life and not, therefore, suffer the same consequence as a lie instigated with malicious thought).

The third vow *(achurya vrata)* demands that a Jain must not acquire anything by illicit means (e.g., dishonesty, stealing, cheating), nor should they misappropriate someone else's property, or take goods which others may have lost or forgotten. The *shila-vrata* is to control passions and to abstain from pre and extra-marital sex. The fifth vow *(parigraha-parimana)* limits a person's desire for material needs, acquisitions and possessions, and encourages Jains to be generous, philanthropic and to share ones fortunes. The ecological implications of these vows are worth noting. We are better able to limit the impact on the environment, and to live in harmony with our surroundings if we are not continually trying to cut it down, dig it out, or shape it into something to meet our 'supposed needs'.

The Reinforcing Vows *(gunavratas)*

The three *gunavratas* are designed to reinforce one's resolve to strengthen and discipline the mind. These are *dig-vrata, desavakastika-vrata*, and *anartha-danda-vrata.* The *dig-vrata* (directions-restraint) places voluntary spatial restraints on one's sphere of action. Essentially, these vows are self-imposed limits on travel. The intention here is to check the unimpeded spread of desire, to save oneself from situations in which unfamiliar surroundings may compel one to undertake un-virtuous activities, and to guard against the loss of tranquility and inner peace. Historically, strict observance of this vow by ascetics has limited their reach and influence beyond their immediate surroundings, which may include just their village, district, state, etc. To a great extent this particular vow has impeded the spread of Jainism. Serious aspirants to ascetic life take this vow, but most laypersons only try to observe the spirit of the vows.

The *desavakasika-vrata* (time-restraint) encourages us to restrict our servitude to our habits by limiting the time we spend engaged in those habits. It suggests that we try, for example to refrain from eating one day a week, or give up a favorite food (like chocolate) for a certain period. The vow is obviously designed to curb weaknesses and gain self-discipline.

Finally, the *anartha-danda-vrata* (harmful activity restraint) is designed to ensure that Jains do not pursue livelihoods or activities, which are harmful to others. Thus, Jains must refrain from engaging in the manufacturing or supplying of weapons, or in violence-based professions like butchering. It should come as little surprise to readers then that one would not find a Jain leather tanner, shoemaker, or a chicken or potato farmer. This vow goes further, however, and includes refraining from boasting or talking and thinking ill of others.

The importance of practicing these vows to gain self-restraint, and remain focused on the goal of liberation, is self-evident. The majority of Jains do not take these vows formally (in the presence of a monk) but manage to live by them. They have sought occupations such as teachers, professors, doctors, engineers, lawyers, or traders. They build healthy, balanced diets of lentils, vegetables, rice, and fruit, and follow a specific lifestyle prescribed for physical and mental health. Although the introductory vows are designed to lead an aspirant towards the life of an ascetic, a very small minority of Jains goes on to become ascetics.

The Spiritual Exercises *(shiksha-vratas)*

A *sravaka (or sravika* - a female layperson*)* who has gone through the first eight simpler introductory-vows, may now want to get a glimpse of the next phase of the rather austere, self-disciplined life of monkshood. This is possible through the next set of four *shiksha vratas*, which in actuality are spiritual exercises. These are: (i) *samayika* - daily meditation and attainment of equanimity; (ii) *posadhopavasa* living the life of a monk or a nun for a given period, (iii) *bhogopabhoga-parimana* - putting limits on consumption of non-essentials and (iv) *atithi-samvibhaga* - taking food only after having served someone needy or hungry.

The mastery of all the 12 vows takes a *sravaka or sravika* from the fourth *gunasthana* (*avirati*) through the fifth (*desa-virati*) to the sixth (*sarva-virati*) *gunasthana*. This two-stage spiritual progress requires climbing the 11 rungs (*pratimas**) of the progress

* Eleven *Pratimas* (steps or rungs of a ladder) are not to be confused with the 14 *gunasthana* (stages of spiritual progress.) Having awakened at the 4th *gunasthana* (stage), we begin our journey towards the 14th. However, we have to climb 11 *pratimas* (steps) between the 4th and the 6th *gunasthana* (stage). See Chapter 4, page 34.

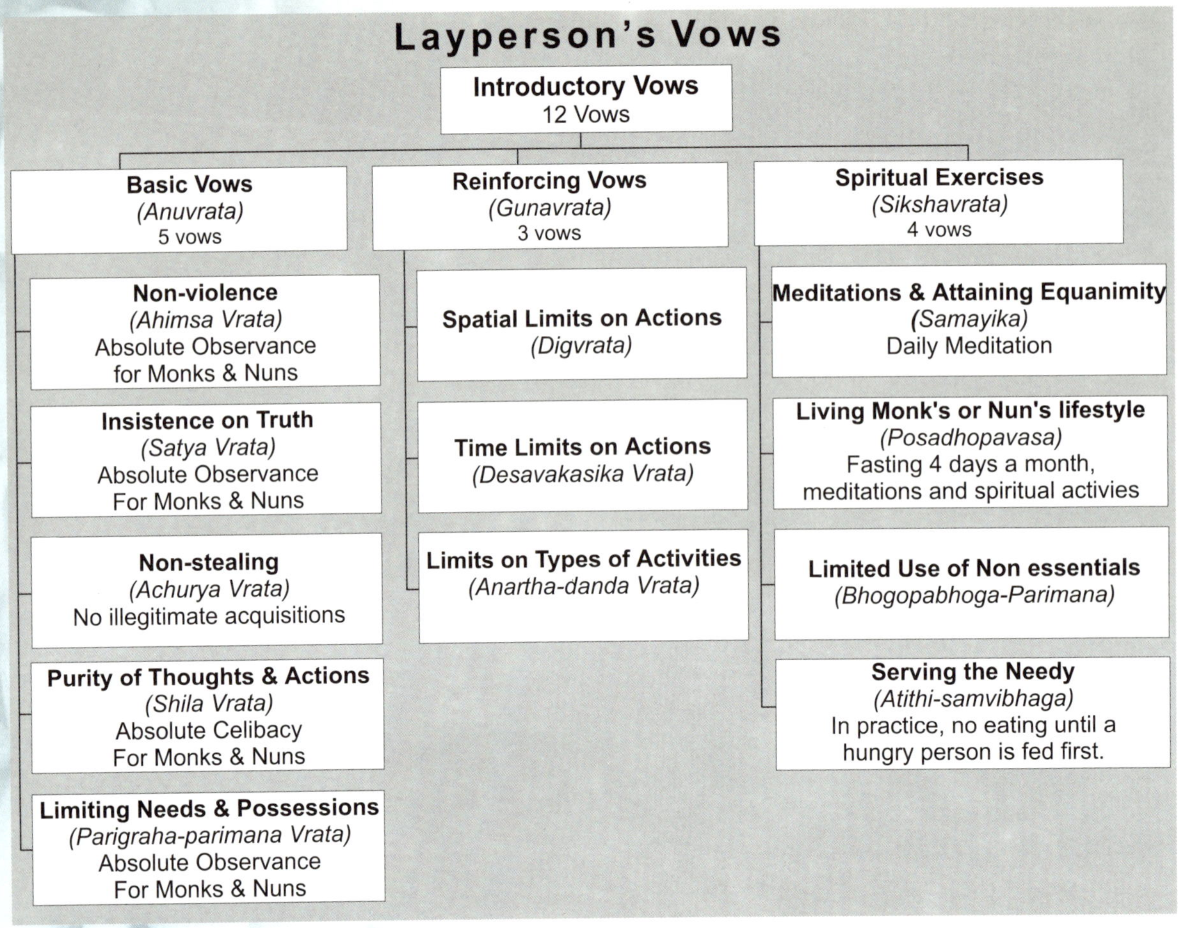

ladder. At the last of the eleven rungs of gradual progression, he/she is virtually a recluse, with sufficient self-control on emotions and senses, and necessary detachment. She is now ready to take the next step. Ready and prepared, she may now request an *acharya* (a guru) to ordain her into the ascetic order on her journey to the fourteenth stage required for liberation.

Newly ordained men or women join their order simply as a *sadhu* (monk) or *sadhvi* (nun). Jain ascetics cannot marry and must remain celibate. They live a simple life in temples or wandering the countryside, and survive off the generous offerings of Jain followers. They spend much of their time in meditation, the study of scripture, and provide spiritual guidance to their followers. Both monks and nuns can expect to progress through the ranks and can become the head (*acharya*) of the order. Mahavira, the last *Tirthankara* has specifically authorized *acharyas* to

issue official interpretation of the scriptures. Acharya Chandanaji, the head of an order of nuns in Bihar, India, has officially interpreted parts of the scriptures as a call for Jains - ascetics as well as laity - to get involved in social consciousness issues, and runs a 200 bed hospital that is free to its clients, and several schools, including one opened recently to serve the poor in the earth-quake stricken area of Gujarat.

On the gradual climb to *moksha*, one reaches *sayoga-kevlin*, the thirteenth stage, where the soul is freed forever from the last vestiges of earthly influence. It reaches the state of omniscience called *arhat.* From here to the fourteenth stage of total liberation (*moksha*), the climb is almost automatic. An *arhat* may continue to live because of the residual non-destructive *karma*, but attracts no more new *karma*; therefore the possibility of slipping back to the lower stages does not exist anymore. The residual non-destructive *karma* also fall-off, at death the soul attains *moksha* and reaches *siddhaloka*. No more rebirth and pain!

The path to *moksha* is indeed a long one, and the practice of vows is only a humble beginning. Realization of the long path to *moksha* cultivates humility in a *sravaka*, just as the recognition of ones place in the cosmos can. Few Jains formally follow the actual path to liberation, but many embrace the spirit of the vows allowing them to lead simpler, more peaceful lives. They recognize that while *moksha* may not be their tangible reward, at the very least, a life free from the stresses of material desires and passions can be.

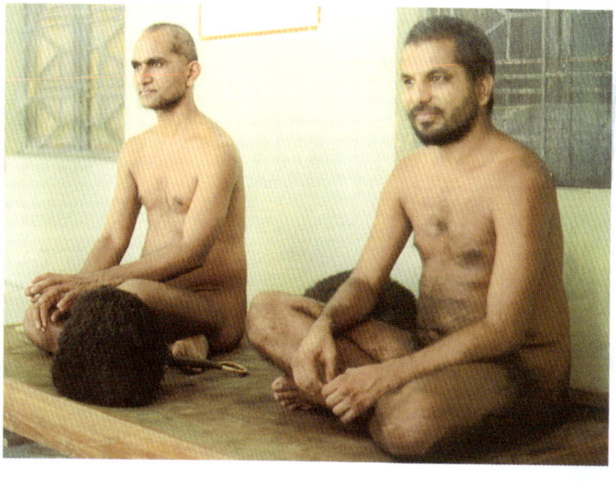

4

4. The Jain Path

Hopefully by now, you have begun to understand the spirit of Jainism and its path from awakening to liberation. As I have stated previously, the 'awakening' of a person occurs at the fourth spiritual stage (*gunasthana*), a stage of becoming aware of the reality and the path that lies ahead for the purification of the soul. Now that the *sravika* has become aware of the true nature of soul (*jiva*) and of its ultimate goal of liberation (*moksha*), her journey begins with the beginner's vows and daily practice of spiritual exercises.

The 'first steps' are always difficult in every project. The twelve vows are particularly difficult because they involve training and disciplining a very crafty candidate - our mind. The novice may need years of practice just to gain a reasonable control over her own mind; however, the very fact that she is willing to take the vows is, in itself, an indication of the strength of her awakening. Depending upon the degree of her success with these vows, the least she may achieve is some self-discipline, equanimity, and a bit of relief from the stress of daily living, but for now, she is still at the fourth *gunasthana* and at the bottom of the eleven-step *pratima* ladder. This ladder will take her to the sixth stage. After reaching the sixth *gunasthana*, perhaps she may remain motivated to continue and enter the ascetic life to achieve the ultimate goal of moksha.

Although her goal is to reach the Himalayan heights of *moksha,* her journey is only about to begin. She has identified the goal, reviewed the path, and has mentally and physically conditioned herself to undertake the expedition. As she observes and practices her daily vows, she begins her climb on the rungs (*pratima*) of an eleven-step ladder to reach the sixth spiritual stage (*gunasthana*).

The Ladder

Let us review the eleven rungs of the ladder that will take her to the first base camp - the sixth *gunasthana*. These rungs are designed to instill more rigors in her practice. The lowest rung at the bottom is the:

1. ***Darsana pratima*** the stage of awakening *(samyak-drsti)* to the reality. Life was full of ignorance and delusion before the awakening. Nevertheless, the awakening has made her aware of the existence of her soul and its ultimate goal. This has set her off to the next stage:

2. ***Vrata-pratima*** Here she took her vows to practice the basics of the code, and gain some self-control and equanimity. She practiced restraint through four 'spiritual exercises', described in the previous chapter. These exercises are undertaken with more frequency and rigor during the next two rungs.

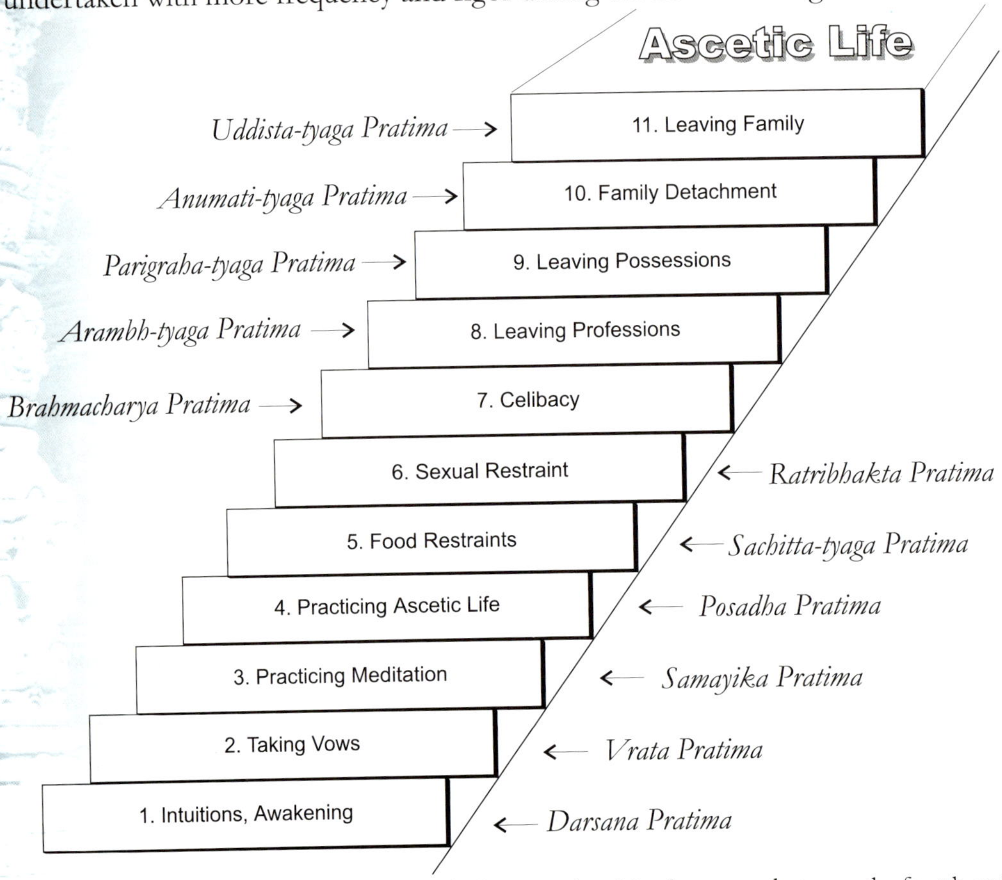

FIGURE 4.1: Eleven steps (*pratimas*) of a layperson's spiritual progress between the fourth and the sixth spiritual stages (*gunasthana*).

3. ***Samayika Pratima*** - Having taken the vows at the second rung, it is now a matter of practicing the vows. One of these is to practice daily meditation (*samayika*). Samayika is a religious activity integrating deep meditation and yoga. It is both a method of attaining peace of mind through self-restraint, and a spiritual path aimed at searching for the true self. In effect, the daily practice of *samayika* produces progressive detachment of one's consciousness from all external objects. Jain scriptures repeatedly commend this ritual as the highest form of spiritual discipline. At the third rung she resolves to practice *samayika* three times a day (as required for the monks and nuns) and perform morning *puja* (worship). The Jain *puja* includes singing a hymn in praise of the *tirthankara*, chanting a passage from the scripture and often also anointing the idol with a paste made of saffron and sandalwood.*

4. ***Posadha Pratima*** The next step is to practice living like a monk or a nun at least on certain days of the month. This involves virtually abandoning all social, business, or domestic activities normally required of a layperson, and fasting on those days.

5. ***Sachitta-tyaga-pratima*** This is the fifth rung of the ladder. Now her focus is on both the quantity and the quality of the food she consumes. Jain reverence for *all life* implies that vegetarianism alone is not enough. We must eat to survive, but this step challenges her to do so with a minimum of violence to or destruction of other life including plants.

As mentioned earlier, the Jain diet avoids root-vegetables such as potatoes, carrots, and onions because their consumption requires uprooting, and thus killing, the entire plant. Jains believe also that a root vegetable, being under the soil, is both a living space for many microbes and insects, as well as a source of new life for the plant. A devout Jain would rather survive on non-root vegetables, fruits, and grains harvested when ripe without killing or hurting the plant. Furthermore, certain foods and drinks can affect body chemistry and likely cause a loss of self-control. Therefore, Jains avoid mind-affecting drugs and alcohol. Even foods such as onions act as mild stimulants.

Gaining control over one's mind and emotions is a slow, difficult, and gradual process. Rungs six and seven are therefore designed to help her achieve gradual control over the most basic of biological urges.

---

* For details, see Chapter 6.

6. *Ratribhakta-pratima* encourages self-restraint or control over sexual urges during the daytime.

7. ***Brahmacharya-pratima*** encourages celibacy or total self-restraint in sexual activities.

8. *Arambh-tyaga-pratima.* Now, is the time for her to prepare for entering monastic life. Indeed a very emotional and difficult step ! She has now to decide if she has the strength to cut all the family ties and be a nun. She must ask, "Is her spiritual calling strong enough?" Once a nun, she has to give up all her past, her family, her neighborhoods, even her name. *Arambh* means 'the beginning', and *tyaga* means to 'sacrifice'. The self-sacrifice now begins ! Until now, she has experienced the ascetic life only periodically and without any commitment, but now, if because of her strong spiritual calling she decides to be a nun, she begins to withdraw from her job, business, or other commitments. Her time is now devoted mostly to the study of the scriptures and spiritual activities.

9. *Parigraha-tyaga-pratima.* At this stage she becomes emotionally detached from all her possessions and family. It is also the time for physical detachment as she prepares her family for her departure. The close family members are already aware of her calling and are expecting her decision to leave home and enter the monastic life. Nevertheless, they all have to endure the trauma of her formal announcement. In fact, Jains take pride in having someone in the family become a monk or nun. Therefore, her formal announcement, like that of a girl getting married, is greeted with mixed emotions. This is evident from the fact that the actual ordaining ceremony, like a wedding, is often celebrated with great pomp and fanfare.

Once the decision to be a nun is formally announced, it is time for her to give away all her wealth and possessions. She may still play a role in household decisions, but having given away all her possessions and ready to leave the home, for a monastery, she tends to stop participating in the family decision-making process. Family too must get used to life without her ! Once she enters this phase of the ascetic life, she is ready to climb the next rung of the ladder.

10. *Anumati-tyaga-pratima* At this rung, she is almost completely detached from the family ties, and the family has fully accepted her decision. The idea here is to avoid even emotional involvement in the family affairs. No longer does she participate even as an advisor in the family matters !

11. *Uddista-tyaga-pratima* - This final rung in her life is to cut-off all connections with the family by leaving the family residence, and she begins living in a monastery as an apprentice nun. The rest of her life will now be devoted to only spiritual activities. These eleven rungs have brought her to the first base camp of her expedition. For those wanting to become monks or nuns, the real journey is yet to begin. So far her participation as a layperson has been like that of an amateur member of a mountaineering team. To reach the summit of *moksha* she needs to now take the five great vows (*mahavrata*) of the ascetic, which will allow her to scale to even loftier heights.

Most *acharyas* (heads of the orders of monks and nuns) advise the aspirants to climb as many rungs of the *pratima* ladder as possible before asking to be initiated into the order. In fact, good acharyas insist that an aspirant climb all the eleven steps before being ordained. Heads of some orders, however, do initiate even children into their order. Those who are initiated without completing that climb are made to undertake rigorous self-disciplinary training and study scriptures.

The life of a Jain monk or nun is demanding but exciting. It is full of the anticipation of achieving that life long goal of *moksha* and ultimate bliss; however, the novice must be warned that even anticipation itself means an attachment to emotion. As we will see later, emotional attachment may block liberation! Therefore, and paradoxically, Jain monks or nuns must learn to stop craving for *moksha* itself!

5

5. The Jain Lifestyle and Contemporary Life

We may rightfully conclude that the Jain code (*samyak-charitra*) described in the previous two chapters, and the entire regimen of vows (*vrata*), rungs (*pratimas*) and stages of spiritual progress (*gunasthana*) are really designed to turn an individual into a monk or nun seeking liberation. However, how many of us really want to become, or are capable of entering a monastic life?

The lifestyle of *eat, drink and be merry now,* or the street philosophy of *don't worry about tomorrow,* may be an ignorant (*mithya*) extreme of reckless living. At the other extreme is the rational (*samyak*) and enlightened lifestyle of a recluse who has given up everything and has a singular focus on *moksha*. Both these extremes may appear to be impractical for most laypersons. While the Jain path can lead some ultimately to the highest goal of *moksha*, in the short term it provides the average Jain with a guide to living a moral, healthy, and satisfying life in contemporary society. It is a peaceful alternative to the hectic, stressful, and violent living choices of the 21st century.

The Jain lifestyle is a blend of the principles and the practice of the Jain code of conduct that can help one live a much better life. One who follows the code strictly, takes the vows, and undertakes the path to *moksha* may reach the goal in this lifetime, or will increase his/her chances for *moksha* in the next life. However, most Jains believe that they are at the fourth stage (*gunasthana*) of their spiritual progress (by virtue of their *karma* in previous lives), and will remain at the fourth or the fifth stage. Family responsibilities often preclude laypersons from taking even the introductory vows because they are afraid that these vows may force them to abdicate their obligations to their loved ones. Short of taking these vows (either out of their sense of responsibilities or because of perceived lack of self-confidence) many laypersons simply decide to follow Jain principles and practices to the best of their ability.

Such ambivalent attitude towards vows has given rise to an interesting rite known as *pratyakhyana* or *pachchhakhana* in which laypersons take limited, time-bound vows renouncing certain activities for a fixed period of time. For example, one may publicly or privately vow that she or he will fast for a fixed number of days, or will meditate for a fixed period each day for a finite number of days, etc. This way one can attempt to balance one's domestic role with a desire to live a more devout life.

By following the introductory vows or the simple *pratyakhyana*, one is certain to be rewarded by a well-organized, self-disciplined lifestyle full of peace and tranquility. The rewards of *moksha* are certainly worth the attempts, although a lifestyle that gives us a healthy, stress-free, peaceful life is no less an achievement on a personal level. Further, at the community level, Jains have produced a culture, which is rich in arts, literature, and scholarship - a type of culture, which flourishes only during peaceful periods. Therefore, on a global level, the wider adoption of a peaceable Jain lifestyle could bring harmony and serenity to our contemporary world filled with its wars, violence, and environmental degradation.

As we have seen Jain lifestyle is rooted in three central codes of conduct:

The reverence for all forms of life (a*himsa*),
Respect for differing and varying opinions (a*nekantavada*),
Emphasis on minimizing one's wants and possessions (a*parigraha*)

Since the Indian words for these three phrases start with the letter 'A', let us call them the "Triple 'A's of Jain Conduct. Jain rituals and daily practice incorporate these triple 'A's. To these, add ethics such as non-stealing, truthfulness, and sexual restraint, and we get a good picture of the Jain lifestyle. Whether Jains take formal vows or not, these in reality are their daily exercises for healthy body and healthy mind.

Healthy Body

The Jain emphasis on self-control has resulted in health practices such as:

Vegetarianism *(Shakahara)*:

Vegetarianism is among the most important of Jain practices. Jain reverence for life has produced a compassionate, non-violent life style. As a result, meat, poultry, fish, and eggs, (the food obtained by destroying or hurting animal life) are considered unacceptable. (In response to the cruelty to cattle in today's dairy industry, some modern Jains are abandoning milk and milk products also. The term "vegan" means vegetarians who do not eat, drink or use any animal products, including dairy products and eggs.) Jains obtain their protein from lentils and legumes. The benefits of vegetarianism have long been apparent.

Periodic Fasting *(Upavasa)*:

Many Jains choose to fast for 2-4 days a month in an effort to control their desire for food. While this may be an effective exercise in the Jain pursuit of mind-control, the body also benefits from periodic fasting by allowing the digestive system to cleanse itself. As well, the liver is stimulated to release toxins, which then travel through the bloodstream, and migrate south to exit the body.

Light Eating *(Unodarika):*

At every meal, Jains are expected to stop eating before they are full, and snacking in between the meals is prohibited. While this practice helps us gain self-control, it also promotes good health by enabling us to maintain a comfortable body weight, and reduces lethargy commonly experienced after heavy meals.

Boiled Water

Many Jains drink water only if it is pre-boiled. This practice renders drinking water safe by eliminating bacteria, and heat-sensitive chemicals. This seems like a paradox since their code of nonviolence forbids active destruction of any life form. A plausible explanation for this practice is that it originated in hot humid climate of India where most homes have to store potable water for at least twenty-four hours. Jains believe that a bacteria population will grow exponentially in un-boiled, stored water. Consuming un-boiled water, therefore, will be in the end more harmful both in terms of ones health and in terms of number of bacteria killed.

Eating Before Sunset *(Chouvihar)*

Jains normally do not eat after sunset. This practice aids digestion and contributes to a more satisfying sleep and healthy body weight.

Healthy Mind

Strengthening the influence of mind over healthy body has always been the cornerstone of Jain practice and rituals. In a recent study, Dr. Herbert Benson of Harvard University's Mind/Body Medical Institute reported[10] that sixty to ninety percent of illnesses presented to doctors do not respond to medical intervention as they are related to stress and mind-body effects. Metabolism rates in twelve to seventeen percent of his subjects decreased through the simple act of meditation. Within three to five minutes of beginning meditation, their brain waves altered significantly, blood pressure lowered and respiratory heart rates decreased.

Similar changes occur in people who are in a deep sleep and fully relaxed. The ancient philosopher-monks designed Jain daily rituals with similar observations. Their daily rituals integrate four essential elements of well being namely, physical, spiritual, psychological, and social. Where as the rites described above look after the physical health of the individual, those described below integrate both spiritual and psychological health. These rituals are performed regularly in many Jain households to develop a healthy mind through self-control.

Prayers and Worship *(Deva- and Guru-vandana)*

As a part of their daily activity, Jains visit their temples or a shrine in their own home, and pray. (Many Jain homes have pictures and small statues of the *Tirthankaras* or simply a dedicated place in their home for quiet meditation or contemplation.) These prayers are spiritual acts, simply to appreciate the tranquil qualities of *Tirthankaras* and to draw inspiration for the spiritual progress.

Asking for Forgiveness *(Ksama-yachana*)*

Christians say grace to thank their God for the food they are about to eat. However, many Jain families begin their meals by asking for forgiveness. This step recognizes the destruction of other life forms during food preparation, and human transgression towards earth and Mother Nature. Therefore, they ask for forgiveness from all beings that are hurt or killed during the production of the food they are about to consume. *Ksama-yachana* reminds them of their duty

[10] Benson, Herbert: *Timeless Healing Power and Biology of Belief*, Fireside Originals, 1997

* Khammami savva jivanam, savve jiva khamamtu me
Mitti me savva bhudesu, vairam majjham na kena vi
I forgive all living beings and may all living beings forgive me (for all my transgressions).
I cherish friendship towards all and harbor enmity towards none.

towards the well being of the entire universe. This can be viewed as the daily practice in humility and environmental awareness.

TERMS TO REMEMBER	
Chouvihar	Eating before sunset
Ksama-yachana	Asking for forgiveness
Pratikramana	Confession
Shakahara	Vegetarianism
Samayika	Meditation
Unodarika	Light eating, Semi-fasting
Upavasa	Fasting for 36 hours or more

Meditation *(Samayika)*

The Jain daily routine requires at least one session of *samayika*. Each such session is supposed to last for 48 minutes. Typically, a Jain would have a *samayika* session at dawn or dusk, sitting alone in a lotus position in a dark, quiet corner of the house to avoid any disturbance. The word '*sama*' means 'balanced' or 'equanimous' state of mind free from attachment or hate, '*aaya*' means 'on the path of liberation' and '*ika*' means aspiration. '*Samayika*' therefore means 'aspiring for liberation through equanimity. It is a religious activity integrating deep meditation and yoga. It is both a method of attaining peace of mind through self-restraint, and a spiritual path aimed at searching for the true self. In effect, the daily practice of *samayika* produces progressive detachment of one's consciousness from all external objects. Jain scriptures repeatedly commend this ritual as the highest form of spiritual discipline.

Confession *(Pratikramana)*

The word '*prati*' means 'towards', and '*kraman*' means 'to go' or 'revisit'. A daily, personal session of *pratikramana* is designed for introspection, while acknowledging and making ourselves aware of the offenses we commit during our day-to-day activity. These offenses may have been the direct or indirect result of our actions, or may result only from our thinking or uttering ill of others. Unlike other religious traditions, confession need not involve a priest, but must result in (i) repentance for transgressions, (ii) renunciation of evil thoughts or actions, and (iii) a resolve to gain strength to prevent such offenses in the future. *Pratikramana* serves to exercise control over one's mind by prodding it to overcome its weaknesses and encouraging it to strive for forgiveness, humility, and strength. This may also include *samayika* or meditation mentioned earlier

These rituals form part of the Jain lifestyle. All Jains are not necessarily on the active path to monkshood and *moksha*, but most do follow some, if not all, of these rituals. To the extent that they do, they experience serenity and calmness in their lives. The self-discipline and the principles they demonstrate through these rituals nurture an attitude of generosity, respect for others and non-aggressiveness. Collectively, such an attitude contributes to community peace, mutual help, and philanthropy, a point to which we return at greater length in Section IV. The worldview that generated such peaceful and healthy practices and the philosophical basis of the Jain lifestyle is discussed in the next section.

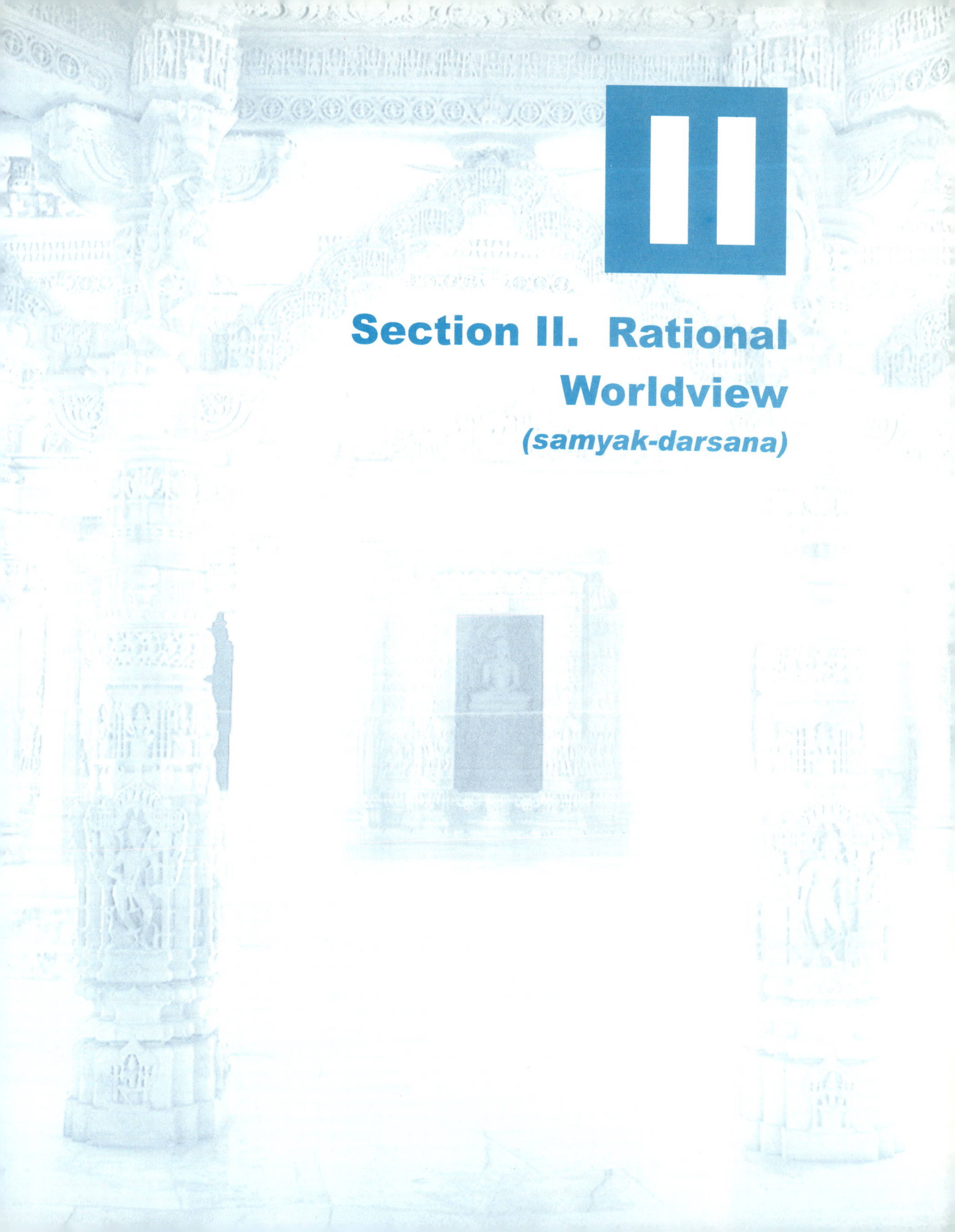

II

Section II. Rational Worldview

(samyak-darsana)

SECTION PREVIEW

In section 1, we learned that the Jain lifestyle is simple, austere, respectful of all living beings, and non-confrontational. It is a lifestyle governed by the "Triple 'A's" of ahimsa, aparigraha and anekantavada, known collectively as rational conduct.

The lifestyles of individuals really depend upon their set of beliefs, their worldview, and their confidence in accepting such beliefs. Therefore, in this section we will examine the Jain worldview (Jain darsana: the intuition of their philosopher founders) and the logic behind such a worldview. After all, conduct can be called 'rational' only if it is backed by a rational worldview. In this section we will examine the rationality of the Jain worldview.

In Chapter 6 we examine the Jain worldview. The Jain understanding of 'Reality' is that the universe itself is eternal and self-governing. There is no need to believe that God exists, or that He created the universe and somehow operates it in an inexplicable, mystical way. We examine in Chapter 7, the logical arguments in support of the Jain worldview of reality. Chapter 8 deals with the nine operating principles, which Jains use to explain how the universe governs itself. Contained within these principles is the Jain Theory of Karma. This is explained in Chapter 9.

6

6. Reality

When I first started reading about Jainism in an encyclopedia, the statement that grabbed my attention the most was the cryptic and rather crude entry that said that the Jains are atheists, and do not believe in God.

"There must be something wrong here", I thought, "scientists believe that the God does not exist, but this is religion ! How could there be a religion without God?" That encyclopedia made me re-examine my own decades-old religious practice. "Just what was I doing every time I went into a Jain temple to pray? Whom was I praying to?" I certainly didn't consider myself an atheist, and did believe that the idols in those temples represented God. Nevertheless, I decided to investigate by going to the source the Jain scriptures.

Jainism has structured much of its worldview on the scientific methodology of observations, insight, experience, and analytical conclusions.

Soon it became apparent to me that Jainism, though a religious system, has structured much of its world-view on the scientific methodology of observations, insight, experience and analytical conclusions. While the founders of this 8,500*year-old religion did not have the tools and technology of modern science, their intuition and reasoning ability must have been very sharp. These were the people in search of ultimate happiness. Their hunch that the key to happiness is not up in the heavens but in their own minds and hearts was based upon their experience and observations. Like a scientist, they had to confirm their idea. "If our mind is the source of all happiness and misery, what would happen if we managed to control our mind? Would we be able to control our misery and fate?" they wondered. They then practiced rigorous self-discipline and spiritual

* According to Jain lore, Jainism is millions of years old. While this is not the place to justify or deny that claim, recent archeological evidence, ancient Hindu scriptures and Jain lore allows us to suggest that Rikhava's period may be 6500 BCE or earlier. See Chapter 18.

purification to get full control over their minds. It is believed that these practices led to a deep spirituality and to a new understanding of reality - an ultimate truth.

Jain Understanding of Reality

What then is the Jain understanding of reality? The Jain philosophers found it hard to accept that a mystical force sits beyond the far reaches of human senses, beyond imagination, beyond the limits of all logic, and is the source of joy, misery, wars, destruction, quakes, floods, life and death. Rational thinking convinced them that these phenomena were natural, and could be explained based on the functioning and the interactions of the fundamental constituents of the universe. Furthermore, they reasoned that the concept of a supreme being is illogical, full of contradictions, unverifiable, and unnecessary to explaining the workings of the universe. Instead of assuming that an imaginary external power has created this universe, they postulated that our universe is itself real and eternal. The Jain philosophers, in their search for reality, concluded that there are only six fundamental elements (*dravya*)* in the universe. Nothing else exists. These six have existed forever and are eternal. No one has created them nor can anyone destroy them. This is reality. These elements, according to the philosophers, can be organized into two groups namely, (1) soul or animate elements *(jiva)*, and (2) non-soul or inanimate elements *(ajiva)*.

This Jain worldview reconciles well even with the modern big bang theory. "The six elements do interact and transform themselves. The big bang is just an event marking the sudden transformation of these eternal elements. In fact", Jains would argue, "the suggestion that God *created* all this out of nothing is illogical and difficult to reconcile with the big-bang theory of the scientists". If called upon to prove the existence of the soul, Jains simply draw attention to our own experience of self-awareness. "Who am I?" they will ask and proceed to answer, "Am I this body? Will this body still have self-awareness if the "I" in it leaves and the dead heap of matter is left behind?" Jains view the answers to these questions as providing an adequate, even self-evident, spiritual proof of the existence of souls in living beings.

---

* The word *'dravya*" is generally translated as "substance" or "object". However, these English words imply that we are describing a tangible *material* thing. This confuses the reader because, the term 'dravya' includes both tangible matter as well as non-tangible Time, Space, etc. We use the word "Elements" to convey a more accurate meaning of the word *dravya*".

The Animate Elements *(jiva)*

According to Jainism, there is no single universal soul or *jiva*.* Instead, there are an infinite number of distinct and independent *jivas* in the universe. Every living being is made up of *jiva* and matter (which is *ajiva*). Absolutely pure *jiva* has four intrinsic characteristics, namely, (i) infinite perception, (ii) infinite knowledge [together (i) and (ii) constitute infinite consciousness]♦, (iii) infinite energy and, (iv) infinite bliss. All *jivas* are equal in their potentialities, and intrinsic Characteristics. Every living being is a single *jiva* entrapped in a material body. *Jivas* interact with fine material particles and thus become polluted.** The individual *jivas* have always existed in a polluted state from time immemorial, but can be purified through human effort. It is this process of purification that leads one to an understanding of reality and eventually to eternal bliss. No external intervention or divine grace is needed for this.

Pure Soul
Infinite Bliss
Infinite Energy
Infinite Perception
Infinite Knowledge

Each *jiva* is eternal. *Jiva* of any living being has limited consciousness, bliss, and energy because it is in the polluted and bonded state. A soul can fully realize it's potential only if it manages to completely dissociate itself from matter and become pure. A pure soul will never again be defiled but until then it will continually be reborn, though not necessarily in human form.

The rebirth may not necessarily be on this earth. An impure soul may be destined by its *karma* to assume any one of four forms (*gati*), namely, (i) celestial being (*deva*), (ii) human being (*manushya*), (iii) plant, animal or microbe (*tiryancha*), or, (iv) hell♦♦ being (*naraki*). A swastika with a crescent with three dots illustrates this concept. The four squares represent four '*gatis*', and the crescent represents the abode for the pure liberated souls.# During each life cycle, a soul may rid itself of some associated material particles but may also attract and associate itself with

* The Western or even Hindu concept of the Soul is not the same as *Jiva*. *Jiva* is not a part of a divine force that re-merges with the whole. Each *jiva* is an eternal entity with its own unique qualities and characteristics. Consciousness is one of its main characteristics. There are infinite numbers of *Jivas*, each retaining its identity, both in the liberated as well as in the non-liberated states. For the convenience of the reader, however, we will continue to use the words Soul and *Jiva* interchangeably.

♦ 19th century German philosopher G.W.F. Hegel introduced similar concept in the Western world. "Spirit is none other than self-consciousness of one's own being. It involves an appreciation of its own nature, and also an energy enabling it to realize itself; to make itself actually that which it is potentially." Hegel, G.W.F., *The Philosophy of History*, trs. J. Sibree, Dover, New York 1956, pp 17-18.

** Details in Chapter 9

♦♦ Jain cosmology has concepts similar to heaven and hell. They are, 'deva-loka' and 'narak' respectively. These are not permanent abodes. Souls take birth here, but when the karma responsible for their birth in these abodes come to fruition, souls leave here to be reborn in one of the other three '*gatis*'.

In the 20th century, Adolph Hitler adopted a corrupted version of the ancient swatika to symbolize his misguided power and vanity.

new ones. In this almost endless cycle of birth and death, the human form is thought to be the only one when we can knowingly and purposefully work towards the total purification of our soul and thus liberate it. Various terms such as *'moksha' 'nirvana'* or liberation are used to describe this liberated state.

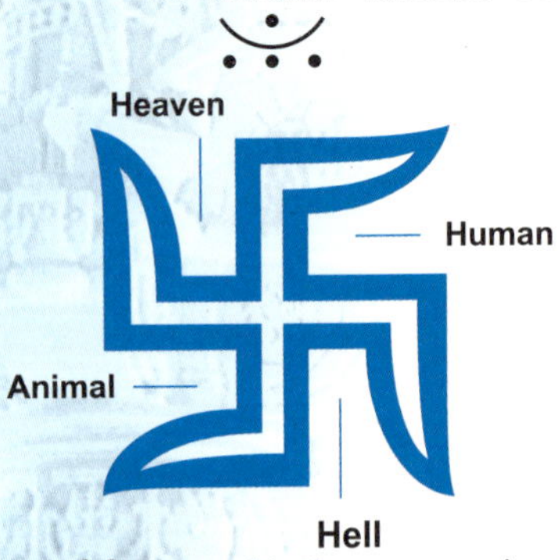

Figure 6.1: A graphical representation of four destinations for rebirth.

What about the other forms? Could they not also work towards the liberation of their souls? We will have to understand the *karma* theory to appreciate the answers to these questions. For now, let us accept the statement that only humans (not even celestial beings) are capable of purposefully working towards liberation.

This comprehensive concept of innumerable souls, their purity, the cycle of birth and rebirth, and human initiative to purify soul by a path laid down by the *Tirthankaras* (Jain spiritual masters) is central to the Jain world-view.

The Inanimate Elements *(ajiva)*

Jain philosophers have classified all inanimate elements (*ajivas*) into five types - each with its unique characteristic. Intrinsic and common to all of them however, is their inability to achieve consciousness. These five elements are:

1. Matter (*pudgal-astikaya*) - {*astikaya means collection of spaces*}
2. Space (*akas-astikaya*),
3. The principle of motion (*dharm-astikaya*),
4. The principle of rest (*adharm-astikaya*), and
5. Time (*kala*)

Thus, together with *Jiva*, we now have six fundamental elements (*dravya*). These six comprise the 'Reality' in Jainism. All these 'exist', and are real, eternal, and logically acceptable. They have their unique intrinsic qualities, and are subject to perceptions and understanding. None are destructible, nor can they be created. Mutual interactions of these may change their forms but one element cannot be transformed into another.

Matter

Like soul, there are an infinite number of small units of matter also. The smallest indivisible unit of matter is called *anu.* These material particles exist in clusters or as single, non-continuous units. They occupy space (they have size and form), co-exist, and possess qualities such as touch, taste, smell, and color depending upon their combined form. The matter that we conventionally see, feel, or touch is an aggregate of these small units, their different combinations producing different substances. The word *anu* is commonly translated as atom; however, in the Jain concept *anu* is the smallest, indivisible, sub-sub-atomic particle of matter. Unlike atoms, all *anu* particles are identical.

Space

Space is an entity that holds other *dravyas* or elements. The specific characteristic of space is to accommodate other elements. Space too is made of infinite number of space units (*pradesa*), but unlike the units of *jiva* and matter, space units are in a continuum, and are inseparable from one another. Space is divided into cosmic space (*lokakasa*) and trans-cosmic space (*alokakasa*). Units of all other elements are confined to cosmic space. Although, nothing exists in trans-cosmic space other than its own infinite space units, expansion of cosmic space (*lokakasa*) into trans-cosmic space (*alokakasa*) is theoretically possible by virtue of the characteristic of the space units (*pradesa*) to accommodate other elements.

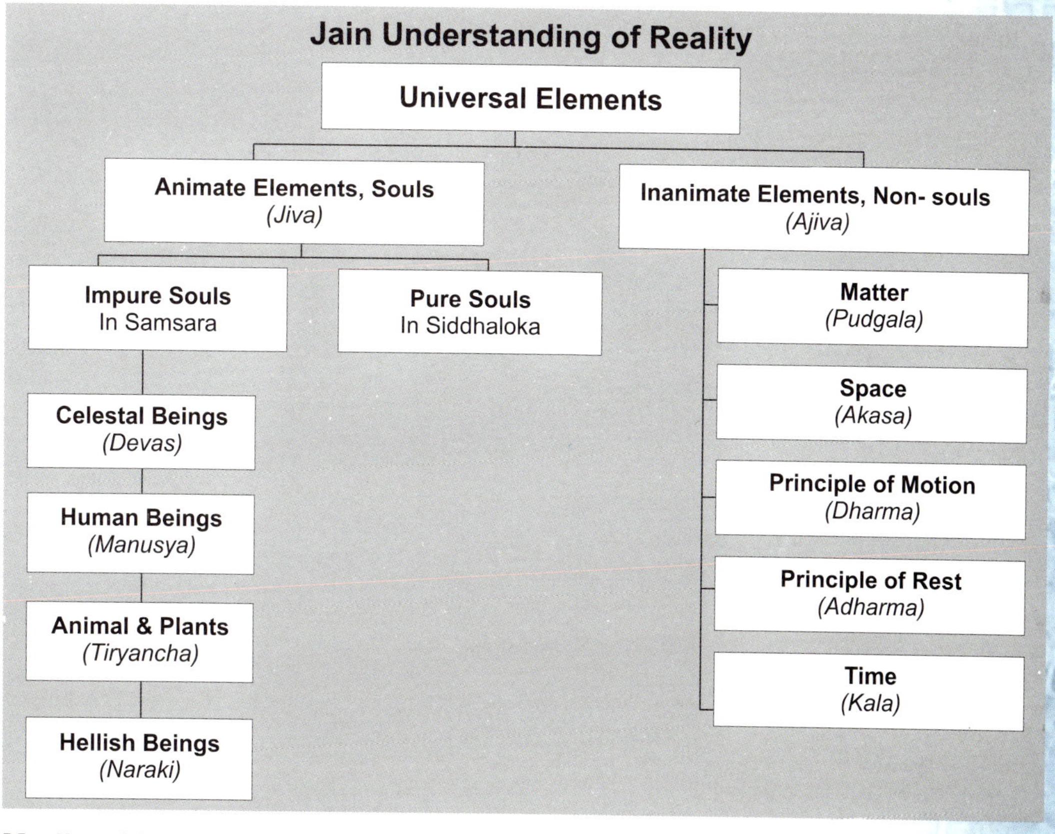

Media of Motion and Rest

The function of the Media of Motion and Rest is to act as the supporting causes for the movement or rest of the individual units or aggregates of matter and soul. Like space, these two media are also made of infinite number of units, all of which are in a continuum and occupy the entire cosmic space.

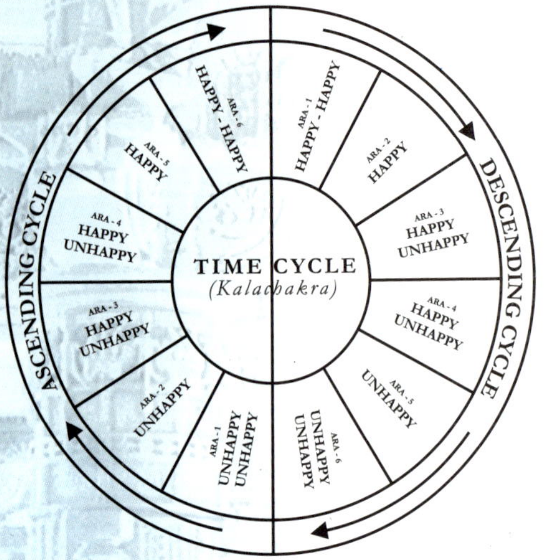

Figure 6.2: The Time Circle *(kalachakra)*

Time

Time is instrumental for the changes in other substances. Real time is made of infinite number of units, which are non-continuous (unlike space and the media which exist in a continuum). Units of time such as seconds, minutes, hours, days, etc. are simply the forms of conventional (not real) time. Unlike the Western belief, which stresses the linear progression of time, the Jain concept of time is cyclical.According to this concept, there is neither a beginning nor an end to time. It is eternal. The universe undergoes the natural process of creation and destruction through endless cycles of time. A full cycle of time consists of two halves. One of these semi-circles* is a period of ascent (*utsarpini*), and the other half marks a period of descent (*avasarpini*). During the ascent period, everything in the entire universe - happiness, knowledge, human, and animal nature, life spans, etc. - gradually improves. When the pinnacle is reached, the other half of the cycle begins and the conditions begin to gradually deteriorate until the period of ascent begins again.

Each period has six divisions (*ara*). The general level of happiness, prosperity, health, life span, etc. changes from division to division. For example, the first division of the descending period is the most prosperous and paradisiacal time (happy-happy time). This happiness decreases through each successive division until we reach the sixth one, which is the most miserable period (unhappy-unhappy times), and then the ascending period begins. Prosperity, longevity, and happiness now improve through each of the six divisions in the ascending period until we reach the paradisiacal times. The cycle thus continues eternally.

The fourth division (unhappy-happy time), of either period, is supposed to be the

* In most texts time is traditionally pictured as a circle with two halves one representing the ascent period and the other representing the decent. This author feels that such a picture implies that things come back to the same point eventually, that is, that there is no real progress in the universe. A more accurate representation of the cyclical nature of time might be the waveform, with the crest representing the peak of the ascending period and the trough representing the end of the descending period, the waveform itself being eternal - without a beginning or an end.

best for the development of human civilization and culture. These times produce a number of great personalities including *Tirthankaras* who achieve *moksha* and show their path.

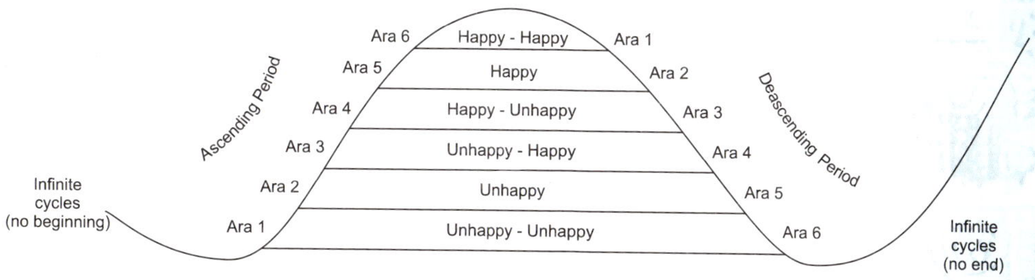

Figure 6.3: Time as a cyclical waveform with ascending and descending periods and aras

This cyclical concept of time is important for Jains because linearity would imply that there is a beginning and an end of time. It also implies that everything must end or be destroyed at the end, and be created at the beginning. This could not be so because the six elements of the universe including time are eternal and indestructible. We, our civilization, our planet, are just current modes of the elements and can be altered in form (see below). The Jain scriptures describe the functions of time as:

> *Bringing about incessant, minute, imperceptible change; perceptible transformation, activity, anteriority and posteriority are the functions of time* [11]

Thus, without Time, change would not occur, the soul could never be purified.

The Apparent Contradiction

Jains talk of the permanence of the six elements while maintaining that through mutual interactions they change their form. Doesn't the change destroy the original object? "Not so", would be the Jain response. "In fact, these six elements are both 'permanent' or eternal (*nitya*) as well as 'impermanent' or changeable (*anitya*)". "Double-speak?" you might respond. "How could something be both 'permanent' as well as 'impermanent'?"

Here comes a philosopher's peculiarly commonsensical view. According to the Jain view, the fundamental identity of an object is based on two factors, namely:

(1) its inherent qualities (*gunas*), and,
(2) its modes or forms (*paryayas*).

[11] Umaswati: *Tattvartha Sutra. A 2nd century text* V.22

Whereas the quality distinguishes one object from another, mode describes the different transformations of the same object. Both quality and mode are always in association with one another and no object is devoid of one or the other.

Our minds are conditioned to believe that everything originates, exists for a period, and then is destroyed. Jain philosophers suggest that this is not so. Generally, what we see are the different modes of the elements. The interactions between the elements may give us the impression that a specific element has changed, but in reality, only its mode has undergone change and its inherent qualities have not. A *dravya* or an element maintains its permanence by not losing its inherent qualities. The modes of an entity, on the other hand, are continuously changing. We may, therefore, perceive that a new object is created, has remained permanent for a while, and has been destroyed. In other words, the *six fundamental elements*, though permanent in terms of their intrinsic characteristics, are nevertheless impermanent in our perception in terms of their modes.

An example given to illustrate this point is that of a gold coin. When a goldsmith changes the coin into a necklace, the coin is destroyed and the necklace is originated. Later, the necklace is changed into rings. Therefore, even though the coin and the necklace are destroyed, gold remains the same (albeit in different modes) with its unique qualities in all modes, and hence is permanent. Similarly, the six *dravyas* of the Jain Reality are both permanent as well as impermanent depending upon our perspective and upon whether we focus on their intrinsic characteristics or on their modes.

The Gods, Monks and Temples

TERMS TO REMEMBER

Adharma	Medium of stability or rest.
Akasa	Universe, space
Aloka-akasa	Space that is not inhabited
Anu	Indivisible sub-atomic particle
Dharma	Medium of motion
Dravya	The six 'Real Elements'
Kala	Time
Loka-akasa	Space inhabited by the elements
Pudgala	Matter
Samsara	Cycle of birth and death

Our earlier statement that Jains have no Creator God gives the impression that Jains are atheists. Yet, Jains have built an extraordinary number of magnificent temples in India. They are continuing to build these places of worship outside India, in Britain, and North America as well. In these temples they have installed hundreds of idols. Made mostly of granite or marble, these images look almost alike - seated or standing erect, with their arms and hands held tightly at the side, and in deep meditation. Jains pray and worship these idols. If Jains do not believe in God, why do they build these temples?

Whose idols are these? What do they pray for? Whom do they worship?

God, for Jains, is not an abstract supernatural entity controlling this universe. To them, god is an ideal. Since, liberation of the soul is the goal of every practicing Jain, those human beings who are believed to have achieved this goal are their ideals. Furthermore, after having achieved omniscience, those who taught and demonstrated the path to liberation are their super-ideals. These are the twenty-four *Tirthankaras* - the Peaceful Liberators. It is to these *Tirthankaras* that Jains have built the temples and the monuments. The images in the temples are those of them. Jain prayers and worships are directed towards these teachers who are believed to have built a ford across this vast ocean of *'samsara,'* or cycle of rebirth and death, and thus have shown the world a path to ultimate bliss.

TERMS TO REMEMBER	
Anitya	Non-eternal, impermanent, transitory
Guna	Quality, attribute, property
Naya	Viewpoint, standpoint
Nitya	Eternal, permanent, constant
Paryaya	Mode, modification, format
Pramana	Instrument of valid cognition,
Sapta-bhangi	Seven-fold predication
Syad	"In a certain sense, or viewpoint"
Syat	Same as Syad, also "relatively"
Syadvada	Doctrine of qualified assertions.

Through their prayers and meditation, Jains seek inspiration to progress on the path to liberation. Who else but these Peaceful Liberators can provide such inspiration? In their prayers Jains do not ask for mercy or relief from their bad *karma*, because Jains know that they, and they alone, have to work out their *karma*. A Jain prayer is more a time for reflection, where a devotee desires the ability to

model him/her self after the examples set by these great teachers. They do not seek the divine intervention of these *Tirthankaras* or of a God. In fact, *Tirthankaras*, being fully liberated souls, cannot interfere and help a worshiper (except to inspire) to overcome his problems. In actual practice the intention of a layperson in offering a prayer may differ from that of a monk or a Jain scholar. Influenced by the surroundings, and sometimes overcome by the challenges of mere survival, a person's desire for miraculous intervention is understandable. Having recognized these human weaknesses, Jains later created a pantheon or set of celestial beings - most have been drawn from among the Hindu pantheon - to satisfy this lay desire.

Some of these are deemed helpful and protective. For example, numerous *Indras* and *Indrayanis* are not only routinely worshipped, but their role as celestial attendants of *Tirthankaras*, is also played out in the form of a drama during Jain ceremonies. Jain mythology speaks of the 'guardian' deities (*sasana devatas*) who supposedly attended to, protected, and helped potential *Tirthankaras* during their difficult journey to moksha. Some of the prominent ones are: Chakeshwari, Padmavati, Dharnendra and Ganesha (also called Parsva-yaksha). Their images are often found in the less prominent parts of the Jain temples. Most laypersons visiting a temple are aware that they alone are responsible for their *karmic* plight and cannot expect relief or intervention from any deities - *Tirthankaras* or *sasana devatas* - and yet, hoping against hope, they seek relief by worshiping these idols.

A daily private visit to a nearby temple is routine for a lay, idol-worshiping Jain. There is no priest nor is there any sermon at this time. The visit simply involves sitting quietly in meditation in front of the idol, saying personal prayers and reminding oneself of the need to reduce *karmic* bondage, reach the ultimate goal, draw inspiration from the courage and determination of the *Tirthankaras* and to pledge continuation on the Path. Such visits often include veneration and singing a hymn in praise of the *Tirthankara*, chanting a passage from the scriptures, or anointing the idol with a paste made of saffron and sandalwood.

The most sacred Jain prayer - chanted repeatedly by Jain devotees - is called the *Namokara Mantra* in which the devotee simply pays her respects, not to any particular individual or *Tirthankara*, but to all spiritual leaders. In so doing she reminds herself that these are the souls, which inspire her to continue her progress toward total purification. The Mantra and its meaning is given below:

NAMO ARAHAMTANAM
(I bow and seek inspiration from those souls who having gained total victory over themselves and have shown us the path to moksha.)

NAMO SIDDHANAM
(I bow and seek inspiration from all the perfect, pure and liberated souls.)

NAMO AYARIYANAM
(I bow and seek inspiration from the heads of the religious orders)

NAMO UVAJJHAYANAM
(I bow and seek inspiration from the teachers of the scriptures)

NAMO LOE SAVVA SAHUNAM
(I bow and seek inspiration from all the ascetic monks and nuns in the world)

ESO PANCHA NAMOKKARO
SAVVA PAVA PANAASANO
MANGALANAM CHA SAVVESIM
PADHAMAM HAVAI MANGALAM
(Salutations to these five types of great souls will help diminish my inauspicious *karma*. These salutations are most auspicious - so auspicious as to bring everyone happiness and peace.)

The temples serve another important function - that of building the community and creating a sense of identity for Jains. The philosophy and the code of conduct of Jainism would suggest that the religion is very much a personal and private matter. Indeed so, Jainism preaches that each individual is responsible for his/her *karma* and can eliminate them through self-discipline and asceticism. This, of course, is the personal and private side of the religion. However, religions often institutionalize themselves to serve the spiritual and community needs of a particular society. A profusion of Jain temples, therefore, may be looked upon as a necessary facet of the community demands on this very personal religion. For example, temples serve as a site for drawing a community together. While individuals may offer daily *pujas* privately, collective worships are also frequently arranged at the temples. There are no sermons at the collective worship, and no monk or nun officiates. The occasion usually involves devotional singing, music, and even dancing. It is mostly a social function with spiritual overtones, often accompanied by some fund-raising for temple maintenance and social causes.

Examples of the community-building role of the temples can be seen in North America and U.K. where Jains have migrated relatively recently. These new immigrants probably would have remained socially and spiritually isolated and scattered but for the lead taken by a few individuals. Visionaries like, Shri Chitrabhanu - a former monk, and late Sushil Kumarji, a - reformist Jain monk who belonged to an order, which does not even believe in temple worship - traveled to North America in 1970s inspired Jains to build temples and to come together as a community. As a result, several temples and more than sixty Jain organizations have sprung up throughout the major cities in Canada and the United States. At conventions every two years, as many as 10,000 Jains get together under the auspices of an umbrella organization called JAINA (Federation of Jain Associations of North America).

TERMS TO REMEMBER

Arahant	Omniscient ones who show the path
Ayariya	Head of the order of monks or nuns
Bhattaraka	An administrator-cleric (who is not a monk)
Ghee-boli	A fund-raising technique for the temples
Namo	Reverent salutation
Namokara	A holy litany of reverent salutation
Puja	Worship
Pujari	A care-taker of idols in a temple
Sahu	Monk, nun, ascetic
Uvajjhaya	Ascetics who teach scriptures.

Jains are presumed to have borrowed the notion of temples, idols, and worships from Hinduism. However, textual evidence for the existence of an idol of a *Tirthankara* dates back to first century BCE inscriptions of Kharavela. Indeed rituals such as *'arati'* (waving a lamp in front of an idol), bathing and decorating idols, offering flowers and fruits to the idol and singing devotional songs are central to both religions. Most of these can be traced back to a eighth century Jain monk - Jinasena - who, having perceived the dangers inherent in interacting with the Hindu majority, co-opted some Hindu practices and rituals in order to appear less conspicuous. While these rituals are meant to inspire a devotee to retain his goal of liberation, many have become

popularly and mistakenly identified with the idea of buying merits. These merits, many believe, will speed one on one's path toward *moksha* or liberation of the soul.*

The temples, the rituals, and the ascetics all play an important role in community building. While monks and nuns do not offer sermons or officiate services, they do serve to deepen religious understanding in a community. Their *aparigraha* (non-possession) vow forbids them from staying at one place for any length of time. Except for the four rainy months in a year, when travel is difficult in India, these mendicants are constantly on the move. With bare feet, they walk miles between villages and cities where they are given temporary shelter, often in a hall adjoining the temple. During their short stay there, laypersons listen to their religious discourses and try to understand some philosophical intricacies of Jainism. The visit by a monk or a nun is often a great social occasion for the community. Laypersons revere these visitors and consider it a great honor if a monk or nun comes to their house and asks for food. This dependency of laypersons on wandering ascetics for spiritual guidance, and of ascetics on laity for sustenance, has enabled Jainism not only to survive for thousands of years but also to remain true to the basic teachings of the *Tirthankaras.*

Tirthankaras

Tirthankaras are the teachers who are believed to have reached the thirteenth *gunasthana* of *sayoga-kevalin* through rigorous ascetic practices, achieved omniscience, and preached their path before attaining *moksha.* Their images in Jain temples look all alike except for those of the seventh *Trithankakra* - Suparsva and the twenty-third - Parsva. These two are depicted with a canopy of hooded snakes above their heads, Parsva with seven hooded canopy and Suparsva with five or nine (but never seven). However, each image has an identifying emblem

* In Southern India, for example, Jain temples are managed by a special group of administrator-clerics known as *bhattarakas* who wield great power over the lay community and exercise their authority to raise funds for the temples. The temples in the Northwest are administered not by priests or monks but by management committees. Short of any authority and power over the community, these committees have developed a unique and quite successful technique for fund-raising. This, called *'ghee boli'*, enables them to auction off the rights to perform some of the above rituals to the highest bidders. The bidders are happy under the impression that they have earned some merits, and the temple is happy for the funds received!

carved on the pedestal. The names and identifying emblems for all the twenty-four *Tirthankaras* are given, in the order of their birth, in the following table.

	TIRTHANKARA	**EMBLEM**
1	Rikhava/Rishabha/Adi-natha	Bull
2	Ajita-natha	Elephant
3	Sambhava-natha	Horse
4	Abhinandana-natha	Ape
5	Sumati-natha	Bird - Partridge
6	Padmaprabhu	Lotus
7	Suparsva-natha	Swastika
8	Chandraprabhu	Moon
9	Suvidihi-natha/Pushpadanta	Crocodile/Dolphin
10	Sitala-natha	Four-cornered symbol
11	Sreyamsa-natha	Rhinoceros
12	Vasupujya-swami	Buffalo
13	Vimala-natha	Boar
14	Ananta-natha	Hawk or Bear
15	Dharma-natha	Thunderbolt
16	Shanti-natha	Deer
17	Kunthu-natha	Goat
18	Aranatha	Stylized Swastika
19	Malli-natha	Water Jar
20	Munisuvrata-swami	Tortoise
21	Nami-natha	Blue Lotus
22	Aristanemi-swami/Nemi-natha	Conch Shell
23	Parsava-natha	Cobra
24	Mahavira	Lion

7

7. The Roots of the Jain World-vision

Jains reject the concept of a creator God as unreal and illogical. To them, the universe with its six fundamental elements - soul, matter, time, space, and the principles of motion and rest -- is real, eternal, and logical. Anyone can actually experience it and logically accept it as real. These six elements govern the entire universe. In this chapter, we will look at how Jain philosophers developed their world-vision.

Jiva

Along with their theory of the 'Real Elements of the Universe', Jain philosophers deduced a whole set of logical doctrines to explain such basic questions as "Who am I? What is my purpose and goal in life? What makes my life happy or miserable?"

As the first doctrine goes, all living beings are made of matter and *jiva* in varying proportions. The logic of this argument is simple and can be expressed in the form of an equation:

Living Being = Body + Consciousness

At death our consciousness leaves and the body remains. Since the material body is without any consciousness, we can conclude that it is the consciousness (*jiva*, soul) that has left, and the matter has remained behind.

It is *jiva* that makes the material body live, creates consciousness in it, and makes it energetic and happy or miserable. If we accept the above conclusion, can we also assume that at death all the matter remains behind and pure *jiva* escapes? If so, isn't that the liberation of the soul? "Not so", says Jain metaphysics. What is left behind is only gross matter; what has departed is the *jiva* bonded with micro-matter, or what is described as *karmic* particles. The gross matter forms the 'body' of a being, but the micro, sub-atomic, material particles - called '*karma*' - actually bond with *jiva*. This bonding with *karmic* particles makes *Jiva* impure, obscures its intrinsic qualities, and is responsible for the entrapment of the soul in the cycle of birth and death.

There might be temporary pleasures in life but the entire process of living from birth to death for all living beings is full of suffering and limitations. The Jain philosophers reasoned that a *jiva* experiences all this pain and limitations because of its entrapment in the body, and these impediments will continue as long as *jiva* remains entrapped through its numerous births and deaths. A free soul, unencumbered by *karmic* particles would not experience any pain or limitations. In other words, "a free, liberated *jiva*", the Jain philosophers concluded, "must have infinite consciousness, infinite energy, and infinite happiness (bliss)". These, they decided, are some of the intrinsic characteristics of a liberated *jiva*.

Doctrine of *Karma*

The bonded *jiva* takes rebirth with all its baggage of *karma*, and enjoys (or suffers) the fruits of its *karma* - past and present. The bonded *jiva* goes through endless cycles of birth and death until it manages to free itself from all its *karmic* particles, and achieve liberation. Different living beings - men, women, animals, or plants - are simply different modes of souls bonded with *karmic* particles and trapped in gross matter (body). Their mundane existence may take different forms, depending upon the degree and type of bondage, but all these souls are potentially equal. All are impure, and all are caught in the cycle of birth and death; their limitless bliss, knowledge, and energy obscured. Furthermore, they all are at various stages of wanting to be liberated from the 'bonded' state.

Bonding with *karmic* particles makes *Jiva* impure, obscures its intrinsic qualities, and is responsible for the entrapment of the soul in the cycle of birth and death.

The greater the association of *jiva* with knowledge-obscuring *karmic* particles, the lesser is its ability to perceive the absolute truth. Since all living beings are made of *jiva* and matter, and since *jiva* alone has the ability to acquire enlightenment (true knowledge), it follows that living beings whose *jivas* are bonded with fewer knowledge obscuring *karmic* particles will have better perception and knowledge than those whose *jivas* are weighted down with more *karma*. Jain philosophers then went on to investigate how *jiva* is bonded with *karmic* particles and what are the ways to free it from this bondage. This is discussed in Chapter 8. Their

investigations of how different kind of bonding affects a living being are discussed in Chapter 9

Liberation *(moksha)*

If a *jiva* ever manages to purge itself of all its *karma*, it will become a liberated, enlightened, or non-bonded soul (a state of pure consciousness, which can be attained only through the processes and practices described in earlier chapters). According to Jains, this is *moksha* (salvation, liberation or *nirvana*). Such a non-bonded soul is in a state of permanent bliss. Every *jiva* longs for such a free state.

We can now examine how the Jain worldview of *jiva* and its corruption by *karmic* particles has given rise to three of the most important doctrines of the Jain code of conduct. In Section I, we saw that the three 'A's of the Jain code are *ahimsa* (doctrine of nonviolence), *anekantavada* (doctrine of manifold truth) and *aparigraha* (the doctrine of minimizing one's needs and possessions). In this chapter, we take a closer look at these doctrines, all of which are derived directly from the Jain view of the soul and its corruption.

Nonviolence *(Ahimsa)*

The Jain worldview that all life forms are bonded souls struggling to set themselves free, and that *karmic* particles are keeping them bonded, has made nonviolence perhaps the most important of all Jain doctrines. Jains maintain that all living beings - not just humans - have a soul, although impure to different degrees. The pure soul is the Jain ideal. Jains revere those who have attained that pure, liberated state. Jains maintain that even an impure soul must be revered because of its potential to be free someday. Hence, humans, animals, plants, all are similarly worthy of respect and reverence.

This Jain logic has generated a lifestyle of reverence for all living beings, and for the environment. If a person believes that his soul is potentially equal to that of another human being, he will not treat another human being - a person of another race, religion, nationality, or gender - with contempt and bigotry. Furthermore, Jains believe that harming another living being is, in fact, harming its sacred *jiva*. Such act only increases the *karmic* bonding of our own soul, and defiles it further. If we believe that ALL souls have the same potential, how could we carelessly destroy a plant or animal life? How could we dare to hurt or even think ill of another living being? How could we strive to be anything but non-violent? The Jain drive for minimizing hurting or killing another life form has evolved out of this view of the workings of the universe and has made Jains passinately vegetarian, non-aggressive, and stewards of the environment.

Jains do recognize that it is difficult to be completely non-violent. The air we breathe, the food we eat, our very acts of moving or walking, involve destroying many microbes and insects. Violence and harm to other living beings is thus inevitable. As a human, all we can really do is to examine our intent, inform ourselves, make intelligent choices based on that knowledge, and try to *minimize* harm to other living beings. Jains place great importance on the terms 'intelligent choice' and 'intent'. Later, when we study *karmic* theory, we will see how effects of *karma* depend upon our intent and passions. Jains believe that the world would be a better, more peaceful, more compassionate, and environmentally sustainable place if everyone embraced this concept of respect for all life.

Doctrine of Manifold Truth *(Anekantavada)*

One of the innate qualities of the soul is infinite perception. This quality enables the soul to perceive absolute truth. However, this characteristic is masked by the karmic particles bonded to the soul. Souls of all living beings are bonded and impure. Since impurities create impediments to full sensibility and experience, it follows that no living being has the ability to perceive or understand absolute truth. We are intrinsically incapable of understanding all facets of reality.

The realization that living beings cannot perceive absolute truth, has given rise to a uniquely Jain concept - *anekantavada* - or the Doctrine of Manifold Truth. This concept is now being accepted as a part of the post-modern thought. Jains contend that when it comes to absolute reality or absolute truth, we are faced with two basic difficulties. First of which, is the fact that we perceive truth through our faculties. Since our perceptions are subject to our own biases and conditioning, our very instruments of perception affect what we perceive, thus there can be no single truth. Everyone perceives truth differently. The famous Jain parable of "The Elephant and The Seven Blind Men" illustrates this point.

The second difficulty is with the very nature of 'reality' itself. Reality is identifiable both by its innate qualities (*gunas*) and by its modes of existence (*paryayas*) of the six basic elements (*dravyas*). Since a 'real' or basic element (*dravya*) has innumerable qualities, and can exist in innumerable transitory modes, it is impossible for an ordinary human being to comprehend a given reality in its entirety. All we can ever perceive is a facet of this reality. As we have seen earlier (Chapter 6), Jain philosophers describe the six elements of the universe, seemingly paradoxically, as being both eternal as well as impermanent. Soul, for example, from the point if its innate qualities (*gunas*) like infinite bliss, consciousness, and energy is permanent, but due to its interactions with other elements like matter and time, we perceive it in its ever-changing modes (*paryayas*). From our perspective, soul appears impermanent because we experience and perceive only its weak, sad, or ignorant modes some times and strong, joyful, and brilliant modes at other. We perceive only some modes or forms of a reality, and not the entire reality, only some facets of the truth, not the absolute truth. This is why, Jains maintain that it is wrong for any one to claim that he or she has the absolute truth. This commonsense philosophical argument, establishing the manifold aspects of reality and our inherent inability to comprehend absolute truth in its entirety, is called *anekantavada*.

The Elephant and Seven Blind People.

Once upon a time seven blind people, who had never been able to see, were taken near an elephant. One of them placed his hands on the elephant's ears, another on his legs, another on the tail of the elephant, and so on. When they were asked to describe the elephant, one person said: "Oh, to be sure, the elephant is a big flat fan-like animal". "No", said the other, "I touched the animal, and it is certainly like a thick round post all the way from the ground to as high as I could reach." The third person shouted, "You are both wrong. Let me tell you for sure. It is a long rope-like thing with lots of hair on it and it wiggles all the time. I tried to catch it but it always wiggled away. Each one claimed that he alone was right."

Finally, the owner of the elephant said, "all of you are correct in what you have described, but all are also wrong because each of you has touched only one side of the elephant. Had you been able to examine all the sides with all your senses, you would have realized that each of you is right from your individual viewpoint, but the truth is that the real elephant is something different altogether."

Doctrine of *Syadvada*
(Acknowledging Multiple Viewpoints)

With the realization that truth is multi-faceted, and people perceive different facets from their own perspective, came the realization that people's perspective could at once be right from their own perspective as well as wrong from the total perspective. Often, if people do not realize the manifold nature of truth, they erroneously start believing that they alone are right and other viewpoints are wrong. Conflicts arise out of such beliefs. The Jain philosophers have, therefore developed a method called *syadvada* for expressing the manifold nature of truth. The term *syadvada* is made up of two words, '*vada*' meaning a statement, and '*syad*' (or *syat*) meaning 'in a certain sense' or 'in some respects'. Whereas '*anekantavada*' is the recognition of manifold perspectives, '*syadvada*' is a practical technique of synthesizing the seemingly contradictory attributes of an entity in a coherent whole. For example, if we state that a given entity is permanent, we are in effect negating the impermanence of that entity. Our statement therefore is incomplete, wrong, or only partially true. *Syadvada* enables us to be more accurate.

The accuracy comes from the use of a qualifying clause in the statement such as, "from a particular viewpoint", or "in some respect". A statement such as - "the soul is permanent." - may be construed as incomplete because it implies only a one-sided view and negates the possibility of its impermanence. However, using the qualifying *syad* clause makes the statement "With respect to its intrinsic characteristics, the soul is permanent." - more accurate because now the possibility of the impermanent modes such as an impure, weak or unhappy soul is not denied. It is important to note here that the technique of *syadvada* is not a doctrine of doubt or uncertainty. On the contrary, it demonstrates the awareness and the wisdom of the speaker in explaining the perspective he/she has chosen.

Having recognized that reality is multi-faceted, and that we are unable to grasp reality in all its facets, Jain philosophers became obsessed with the nature and accuracy of any statement. A statement could be intrinsically correct or incorrect. Even a simple one like " I am your teacher" may be correct from the perspective of one's students but incorrect from the perspective of others for whom one is a son, a father, or a brother. Jains took their pursuit of precision a step further.

Syadvada would introduce the framework for that statement, however, to be more precise, Jain philosophers developed a system of seven-fold (*sapta-bhangi*) application of *'syat'*. Factors such as time, place, attitude of the observer, relative nature of the object observed, etc. would have bearing on the accuracy of this statement. They suggested that to be accurate, a statement must take into account a comprehensive, all-sided view. Such absolute statements are called *pramana* statements. However, such accuracy is for the philosophers who might be engaged in a debate over the finer points of reality. For most of us practical statements (*naya*) are sufficient. Jainism would suggest that such statements are only partially true. Given that these are only partial truths, we need to assimilate or organize or respond to the information we receive and communicate differently. A full understanding of *anekantavada, syadvada, sapta-bhangi, pramana, naya,* etc. is valuable particularly for those involved in events such as conflict resolutions, negotiations and inter-faith dialogue. Interesting philosophical details of these can be found in, *Studies in Jaina Philosophy*, by Nathmal Tatia.[12]

[12] Tatia, Nathmal, *Studies in Jaina Philosophy*, P.V. Research Institute, Hindu University, Varanasi, India 1951

Jainism teaches an appreciation of the doctrine of multiple perspectives, the possibility of there being multiple valid viewpoints, and the knowledge that in our development as humans we have a limited ability to fully comprehend absolute truth. This teaching helps to foster a fundamental underlying respect for those who espouse alternate beliefs and paths, and reduces the potential for dogmatism. This Jain doctrine of Manifold Truth (*anekantavada*) is ultimately a practical principle because it preaches respect for differing viewpoints and thus encourages us to avoid conflicts. Most conflicts in the world including religious wars have originated because of a lack of understanding, appreciation, and respect for differing viewpoints. Contemporary thinkers would agree (and hope) that the practice of *anekantavada* on a wider scale would have avoided (and could yet avoid) wars started in the name of righteousness. The doctrine of *anekantavada* and the practice of reconciling differing views through *syadvada* have enabled Jains to follow a non-aggressive lifestyle and survive many religious upheavals throughout their history.

Doctrine of Minimizing Needs and Possessions *(Aparigraha)*

Aparigraha - the doctrine of minimizing personal needs - is the third of the triple 'A' principles on which Jainism's code of conduct is based. Like the other two, *ahimsa* and *anekantavada*, the principle and practice of minimizing one's needs and possessions is an outcome of the Jain concept of the soul and its corruption.

Jains have developed a complex but logical theory to explain how karmic particles bond with or separate from the soul. Our emotions play a significant role in attracting and bonding karmic particles to the soul. The stronger the emotional attachment to an object, the stronger is the bond between the soul and the karmic particles attracted by such emotions. Obviously then, the more we possess, the greater is our involvement or attachment to them and, the greater is the defilement of our soul. If liberation by purifying our soul is our goal, we must become increasingly detached from such objects. In other words, giving up possessions and minimizing needs, so that greed and attachment do not govern our lives should be our goal. Living with few possessions, or *aparigraha*, should be our sought after lifestyle. Giving up possessions is not easy. The Jain path to liberation acknowledges this in recommending the *Pratima* ladder (Chapter 4) to achieve a gradual, stress-free spiritual progress and detachment.

The importance of this principle in our modern world is worth discussing here. The term"happiness" usually involves a response based on physical comforts.

More money, a bigger house, a luxurious car, and fancier clothes -- these are the images confronting us daily in this consumerist world. There is no doubt that these provide physical comforts and a (false) sense of security and happiness. One may even argue that a desire to acquire such comforts drives the engine of human ingenuity and economic, social, and scientific progress. However, such comfort-based happiness is:

- dependent on external objects - we become unhappy even with the mere thought of the possibility of losing such objects.
- transitory - no sooner do we acquire the much-desired object of comfort, we become unhappy with it and desire more, better or bigger comfort.
- destructive - an individual or a society rooted in comfort-based happiness can, and often does employ, directly or indirectly, violent and destructive means to acquire such objects of comfort. This is evident in the human history of wars to acquire land resources, riches and wealth, and in the depletion of resources and environmental degradation resulting from our ever-increasing desires for consumer goods.
- unfair - because of the exploitation involved in wealth accumulation, as evidenced in the unequal distribution of wealth both within and between nations. And,
- responsible for greater unhappiness because greed knows no limits.

By contrast, the principle of *aparigraha* generates a mindset which is genuinely satisfied with whatever we possess, unperturbed by the prospects of losing any of our possessions, and indifferent to the momentary joy or pain associated with any gain or loss. It is non-destructive, non-aggressive, fair, and gives everlasting happiness. This is the happiness most of us are seeking, and this is the bliss the Jain path to liberation promises us !

The Dilemma

We as ordinary householders and laypersons face a dilemma when confronted with the doctrine of *aparigraḥa*. *Aparigraha* makes sense particularly when it comes to the desire and love of material goods; but love and kindness are strong and meaningful emotions. Are we meant to be apathetic to other humans and living creatures? Marriage and family are simply more attachment -- should Jains avoid these responsibilities? These questions come to mind for anyone trying to understand

Jainism. The dilemma is real and there appears to be very little discussion on these issues in the Jain literature. I can only present a personal viewpoint.

As stated earlier, Jains focus on *moksha,* for which the basic requirement is an absolute commitment to the goal, and a total victory over oneself. Absolute victory over oneself means one must overcome passions such as desire and hatred. In earlier chapters, I've described a gradual process for achieving this victory, one possible only through years of rigorous practice of austerity. Such a practice would require giving up all possessions, eventually cutting all bonds with the surrounding world including family and friends, and finally dedicating oneself to the path of a mendicant where one's mind becomes indifferent to such passions. This indifference leads to the unbinding of karmic particles and to the total purification of the soul. Jains are unequivocal about this belief. So, what does it say for the rest of us - the lay persons- who enjoy our families and friends and are loath to give them up?

Mahavira, the 24th *Tirthankara*, recognized this dilemma and came up with a logical solution. He divided the community into four groups of people: monks (*sadhu*), nuns (*sadhvi*), laymen, (*sravakas*) and laywomen (*sravikas*). For the monks and nuns, the absolute goal is *moksha*, and the code of conduct they must adopt is the non-compromising, strict observance of all the vows they take at the initiation. The *sravakas* and *shravikas* need not strive for this final goal immediately. They are expected to work towards the purification of their soul in the best possible way while fulfilling their obligation to their community, their society, and to all other suffering souls.

While *moksha* is an ideal goal and monkshood is an ideal path, those who choose not to follow that path could make an intelligent choice to follow the Triple 'A' to the best of their ability and conscience, and thus fulfill their obligations to their world

'Fulfilling obligations' is a very broad term, which includes a reasonable indulgence in passions such as love and kindness, as well as accumulating wealth to ensure the well being of one's family and community. The fundamental message of Jainism to lay persons could thus be stated as: "While *moksha* is an ideal goal and monkshood is an ideal path, those who choose not to follow that path could make an intelligent choice to follow the Triple 'A' to the best of their ability and conscience, and thus fulfill their obligations to their world." In other words, while Jainism strongly recommends the path of the mendicants, it respects one's decision to pursue human attachments, and accepts these as 'normal' at a particular stage in human spiritual development. The guiding principle, however, is that a *sravaka* or *sravika*, even while accumulating possessions and wealth, must remain "emotionally detached" from these possessions and must always remember that the possessions are merely to fulfill their obligations.

This story is from *Nayadhammakahao*. Mahavira used it to illustrate the importance of seeking permanent bliss instead of trivial pleasures. Haribhadra - a 7th century Jain monk has given the following interpretation of this parable. In the table below, in the left column are the characters from the story, and the interpretation is in the right column. Re-read the story with the interpreted meanings for clear message.

The Story of The Man in the Well.

A man, seeking fortunes in other lands was passing through a thick jungle. Suddenly, a wild elephant with upraised trunk charged him fiercely. He tried to run fast, but his path was blocked by an evil demon. Surely, the only escape route now was to climb the huge, tall, banyan tree to the East. He ran and reached the tree but could not decide if he had the will and power to climb the mighty tree. Right below the mighty tree was a deep well, all covered with grass and reeds. "This well would save me", he thought, and jumped in it.

As he was falling through the grass and the reeds he looked below and was terrified. Right below him lay many terrible snakes enraged and hissing fearsomely. In addition, deep down below was a black and mighty python with angry red eyes. Afraid, he held on to a clump of reeds hanging from the top and clung on to it. He thought, "My life will only last as long as these reeds hold fast", and he looked up.

There he saw two large mice, one white and one black, their sharp teeth ever gnawing at the roots of the reed-clump. Up above, the wild elephant was charging, repeatedly, at the banyan tree. This disturbed the beehive hanging from a branch right above him. The angry bees swarmed down on him and his whole body was stung. Just then, as he was looking up and cursing himself for not climbing the tree, a drop of honey fell on his face and somehow reached his lips.

That was a moment of sweetness. He looked up again, forgot all the dangers around him and just craved and waited for more drops of honey to come down his way. In his excited craving for yet more drops of honey, he lost awareness of the reality the python, the snakes, the mice, the elephant, or the bees.

The Man	The Soul
His wanderings in the forest	Soul's rebirths in the four types of existence
The Wild Elephant	Death
The Demon	Old age
The banyan tree	Path to salvation. Fear (of elephant or demon) itself is conquered on this path.
Weakness to climb the tree	Lust for sensual and trivial pleasures
The well	Human life
The snakes	Passions (*kasaya*) which impede human judgment
The Python	The hell if fallen here, the soul suffers excruciating pain.
The tuft of reed	The man's pre-determined life-span
The Mice	The day and night the passage of time.
Bees	The diseases of life
The drops of Honey	Trivial pleasures. Lust for these spells the man's peril.

In this chapter, I've tried to outline some of the key Jain doctrines upon which the practice of Jainism is based. In the next chapter, we will discuss the operating principles, which the Jains believe, govern the universe.

8

8. The Operating Principles of the Universe

Having outlined their perspectives on 'Reality', Jain philosophers wanted to explain how the entire universe operates. We will now review the concepts discussed earlier and try to understand how the six elements interact with one another to create our universe and govern it by the nine universal operating principles. These principles are:

1. Existence of the Soul (*jiva*)
2. Existence of Non-Soul (*ajiva*)
3. Inflow of *Karmic* Matter (*asrava*)
4. Bondage of Soul (*bandha*)
5. Auspicious *Karmic* Bondage (*punya*)
6. Inauspicious *Karmic* Bondage (*papa*)
7. Stoppage of the Inflow of *Karma* (*samvara*)
8. Process of Partial Dissociation of *Karma* (*nirjara*),
9. Total Dissociation of *Karma*. (*moksha*).

Umaswati's *Tattvarth Sutra* (1.4) treats numbers 5 and 6, auspicious and inauspicious bonds (*papa* and *punya*), as the integral part of the *Principle of Bondage* (*bandh*). Accordingly, there are only seven operating principles. However, the idea of treating *papa* and *punya* as separate principles is popular perhaps because of the ease of explaining them. We will look at each of these principles in turn.

The Existence of the Soul *(Jiva)*

As seen earlier, Jainism recognizes the plurality of souls, both pure and impure, and believes that there are infinite individual souls. Soul exists in every living being. Impurities trap the soul in painful cycles. Depending upon the impurity, the corrupted soul becomes embodied in a celestial (*deva*), human (*manushya*), plant/

animal (*tiryancha*), or in a hellish (*naraki*) form. Escaping from this entrapment is the ultimate goal of all souls. The pure soul -- that which is liberated from karmic corruption -- is free from the cycle of birth and death.

According to Jainism, a soul can escape from this entrapment if it manages to purge itself of all impurities. A human being can purify his/her* soul and achieve freedom from rebirth by following a path to liberation. *Tirthankaras* are believed to have achieved their own freedom (*moksha*). They have also shown us the path. Many people have achieved *moksha* by following this path and even today, many are on this path.[13]

The Principle of Non-Soul *(Ajiva)*

Matter is one of the non-souls. Its tiniest sub-atomic particles are responsible for making the soul impure. These are called "karmic" particles. However, these particles by themselves do not pollute the soul. They are everywhere in the 'occupied' universe (*lokakasa*) and would not interfere with the souls had the souls not attracted them. All sub-atomic *karmic* particles are identical but their polluting effects on the soul vary depending upon the nature and mechanism of their attraction by the soul. We will learn more about this in the next chapter.

The Principle of Inflow of *Karmic* Matter *(Asrava)*

There are an infinite number of polluted souls in the universe. An infinite number of tiny, sub-atomic, karmic particles of matter are also floating around throughout the occupied universe. This being the case, how is it that some of these material particles are attracted towards some souls and pollute them? Jains theorize that the attraction and inflow of particles is the result of an individual's activities. Any activity

TERMS TO REMEMBER

Asrava	Inflow of *karmic* matter
Bandha	Bondage of soul with karmic matter
Papa	Inauspicious or unwholesome bondage
Punya	Auspicious or wholesome bondage
Navatattva	Nine operating principles of the universe
Nirjara	Dissociation or shedding of *karmic* matter
Samvara	The stoppage of *karmic* influx.

* Although a great majority of Jains believe that both men and women can achieve liberation in their life time, one group of Jains believes that females - not because their souls are any more inferior to those of men, but because of the limits on their ability to observe absolute non-possession - are not capable of reaching this goal. The logic behind this argument is that 'absolute *aparigraha*', which means giving up even clothing, is a non-compromising requirement for *moksha*. Since women, even if they become nuns, cannot move around naked, they cannot be considered as absolutely detached and hence cannot achieve *moksha*.

13 *Saman Suttam*, 529; *Uttaradhyana Sutra*, 9.35; *Anatagaddasao Suttam* - The entire book is full of the stories of monks who attained moksha by destroying their karma.

good or bad, intentional or unintentional, physical, mental or verbal, generates vibrations (aura) and triggers the inflow of the karmic particles towards that soul. What happens when the inflow begins? The inflow does not necessarily pollute the soul. In fact, the result depends on several factors including:

1. perverted world-view (*mithyattva*).
2. carelessness (*pramada*),
3. lack of self-discipline (*avirati*), and
4. passions (*kasaya*),
5. type of activity (*yoga*)

For example, every activity generates inflow. Karmic particles will be attracted even if the activity is devoid of passion, however, they will form weaker bonds with the soul, and will dissociate or 'fall off' after fruition. It is the passion involved in an activity that provides a powerful adhesive force and cause stronger bondage between the already polluted soul and the karmic particles.

The Principle of Bondage *(Bandha)*

A pure, formless soul does not and cannot attract polluting particles. Once liberated, the soul does not become re-polluted, and is never reborn. The impure soul, on the other hand, is weak because of the material impurities in it. As we will see later, this weakness causes the soul's embodiment, its activities, the inflow of karmic matter, and further bondage of the soul. Passion-prompted activities not only cause bondage but also determine how that bondage will take shape. Bondage is determined by four factors, which are:

1. The quantity of karmic particles bonded.
2. The strength or weakness of the bonds formed i.e., their intensity.
3. The predetermined duration for which the bondage remains, and
4. The nature of bondage i.e., the effect of the bondage on the soul.

The stronger the passions, the greater the number of particles bonded, and the stronger are the bonds that are formed. The intensity of the bondage, and its duration are, in turn, greater as well. For example, let us examine an activity, such as killing another living being, performed under three different circumstances.

In one case, the killing is unintentional, accidental, and the killer is even unaware of the destruction. In the second case, the killer had no choice but to kill (e.g., for food, self-defense, etc.) but tries to minimize the number of lives destroyed and

TERMS TO REMEMBER

Aviriti	Non-restraint
Deva	Heavenly beings
Kasaya	Passions
Manushya	Human beings
Mithyattva	Deluded viewpoint
Naraki	Hellish beings
Pramada	Carelessness, non-vigilance
Tiryancha	Animals and plants.

the pain he is causing. The killer is remorseful and repentant. In the third case, the killing is deliberate, driven by passions such as greed, anger, vengeance, and is performed cruelly without any regard for the pain and hurting caused.

Although the activity is the same, the three acts differ in the intensity of the passion involved. All three will involve karmic bonding but the last case will result in the strongest bonding with longer-lasting intense consequences for the killer.

The Principle of Auspicious and Inauspicious Bondage *(Punya and Papa)*

The Sanskrit word for activity is *karma*. Since activities inevitably cause bondage and result in good or bad consequences, good activities can be seen as 'auspicious' *karma* and bad can be deemed 'inauspicious' *karma*. Whereas inauspicious bondage takes a soul away from the goal of liberation, the auspicious ones takes the soul closer and into situations where the soul would have greater opportunities to shed its bondage. Thus, from the standpoint of making progress towards *moksha*, it is better to contribute several "good" acts during one's lifetime -- helping the poor, being charitable, educating the ignorant -- than to simply sit still and accumulate minimal karmic particles. In the absence of any activity, in other words, opportunities to shed *karma* will be minimized and the goal of *moksha* will never be attained. Jain philosophers have gone much deeper in analyzing and classifying the various effects of karmic bondage and have classified *karma* into eight primary groups. These are discussed later.

The Principle of the Stoppage of the Inflow *(Samvara)*

Activities are essential for the process of living. If every activity causes the inflow and bondage of karmic particles, and if it is better to have some activity, is there any way to stop - if not reverse - the process of bondage? Jainism teaches us that the answer lies in remembering the key role that passions play in creating bondage. The Jain Path (described in Section I) is designed to gain progressive control over our passions. The self-discipline thus achieved enables us to control the bonding factors, and then slow down and eventually stop the inflow.

The Principle of the Partial Dissociation of *Karma* (*Nirjara*)

While the inflow and the bondage of the karmic particles can be slowed down or completely stopped through self-discipline, how can the particles already bonded be purged? Fortunately, that too is possible. Earlier, we saw that the duration of bondage is already pre-determined at the time of bonding. All bonds, weak or strong, break off after the fruition of karma. The fruition may happen in one's own lifetime, or may even require several rebirths. However, once the consequences are enjoyed or suffered at the pre-determined time, the responsible particles fall off immediately. This is the principle of natural dissociation. In fact, in every living being, the processes of the natural dissociation of some particles and the bondage of new ones are ongoing.

Nine Operating Principles of the Universe *(Navatattva)*

Principle	**Operation**
Jiva Exists	Each soul has been in a polluted state forever. Impure souls are trapped in *Samsara*. Humans can purify their souls.
Ajiva Exists	Material particles pollute the soul. Time and space enable elements to change modes.
Asrava	Vibrations created by impure soul attract *karmic* particles
Bandha	Passion-based activities create bonds between the soul and the *karmic* particles
Punya	Bondage resulting from auspicious activities - produce good results.
Papa	Bondage resulting from inauspicious activities - produce bad results.
Samvara	Austerities and self-control enable us to control or eliminate passions and thus to stop new bondage.
Nirjara	(1) Bonded particles fall off naturally after fruition. (2) Bonded particles forced to fall off through austerities and penance.
Moksha	At higher levels of spiritual progress *asrava* becomes negligible and *nirjara* dominates resulting in total elimination of *karmic* particles.

If natural dissociation were the only way to eliminate karmic particles, a soul may never be totally free. Fortunately, through human effort, karmic matter can be made to dissociate from the soul even before it has yielded its fruit. The effort consists of making spiritual progress through the fourteen-stages (*gunasthana*) of the Jain path to liberation. The Jain path is designed not only to stop the inflow through self-discipline and control over passions, but also to remove the bonded *karma* through the practice of external and internal austerity. Daily activities like meditation, atonement, and renouncement of possessions, work towards this goal.

As we progresses along the path to liberation, the inflow of karmic particles slows down and the dissociation speeds up. The reduction of inflow and simultaneous increase in dissociation ultimately produces a karmic balance sheet with zero *karma* balance. The soul is now free of all bondage. This is liberation !

Liberation *(Moksha)*

A liberated soul is now free from the debilitating influences of the material impurities. A liberated soul regains its innate characteristics of infinite perception, infinite knowledge, infinite energy, and infinite bliss. The omniscience, omnipresence, and omnipotence are the Jain ideal. To Jains this is a godly state ! To achieve that state is the goal of every Jain. One who has achieved that state is their hero, and worthy of respect and worship !

9

9. Karma

We have seen that ancient Jain philosophers used experience, experimentation, observations, logic, reasoning and analysis, to formulate their theories. Today such an approach is called 'scientific methodology'. A 17th century French philosopher Rene Descartes is given credit for developing this methodology. "Doubt what isn't self-evident, and reduce every problem to its simplest component", was Descartes' advice to the would-be scientists.

It appears that Jain philosophers have used this method centuries earlier, not only in doubting and rejecting the existence of a creator God, but also in subjecting the complex problem of suffering and misery on our planet to its simpler components and logical analysis. Their quests lead them to the idea of the soul and its corruption, and to an analytical path to discover the mechanism of pollution and liberation of the soul. A proper path for purification of the soul could not be designed unless the causes of the soul's pollution were accurately analyzed.

As will be evident soon, Jain philosophers explained the complex idea of the pure and impure soul by first reducing the problems to a set of questions: " What is soul? What are its qualities? What happens when it becomes impure? What causes its defilement? What is the nature of the corrupting factors? Can the process of defilement be stopped? Can it be reversed? Is it possible to absolutely purify soul? If so, how?

Based on their everyday experiences they concluded that it is the soul inside a living being, which learns, perceives and knows. This led them to the next conclusion that a living being is the product of a dynamic interaction between the soul (which has the ability to perceive) and matter (which cannot perceive anything). If the soul is all consciousness, and, as we learned in Chapter 7, we humans are incapable of perceiving absolute truth, can we not conclude that the matter is obscuring our soul's full capacity to know and to perceive? If so, they mused, how does matter manage to obscure soul's innate qualities?

The answer, they determined, lay in the particulate nature of matter. Since matter is made up of very tiny sub-atomic particles, these particles must be somehow attaching themselves to the soul.* At the time of death, the soul must leave with these tiny (*sukshma*) particles, and only the gross (*jada*) matter or body must be left behind. Such were the logical conclusions of their investigations.

The souls themselves are responsible, through their actions, for the bondage and suffering they are in

Through reduction - the scientific technique of reducing a larger problem to relatively simpler ones and tackling them first - these philosophers were led deeper into their analysis. What are these tiny particles? What causes the soul to be bonded? The intrinsic characteristics of all matter are the same. Therefore, at the sub-atomic level all bonding particles must also be same. If so, how is it that the bondage of souls with identical particles results in the formation of different life forms and varying degrees of impure souls? Why are the results of bonding different in different beings? How and why do we experience pain and suffering?

Years of study, discussion and debate must have been undertaken before they arrived at the conclusion that the soul itself must somehow be responsible for its bonding. Human pain and suffering must result from the simple law of cause and effect. No effect is without a cause. Therefore, pain and suffering must be the effect of the acts committed by the bonded souls. In other words, the souls themselves must be somehow responsible, through their actions, for the bondage and suffering they are in. Such a conclusion may sometimes appear to be too harsh and difficult to accept. For example, it implies that a person, who is seriously ill with cancer, has brought this tragedy upon himself due to his/her bad acts or negative *karma* in a present or past life. Regardless of how harsh this may sound, such is nature's law of cause and effect, and no other logical explanation is possible. If actions cause bondage, then different actions must produce different results ranging from pain to enjoyment and love. Furthermore, if all the bonding

* This description of material particles somehow attaching themselves to the soul is merely for visualization. Since souls are formless and without any matter or mass, karmic particles cannot truly glue or attach to a soul. Ancient texts give various descriptions to help us understand the concept. Some such descriptions are: (i) matter defiles soul, just as pure water is muddied by tiny dust particles. OR (ii) the brilliance (limitless omniscience, energy, bliss, etc.) of soul is dulled by karmic particles just as clouds cover the brilliance of sun. Or (iii) as dust obscures the brilliance of a diamond. We will continue to use the "attachment" simile throughout our presentation with a warning that the concept itself is abstract.

particles are identical,* but the results of bonding are different, it is reasonable to assume that the difference must be in the mechanism of bondage.

The Cycle of Birth & Death *(samsara)*

The bondage of the soul with material particles has had no beginning. That is, the soul has always been impure (this is identical to what Christians believe, "we are born sinners"). A soul is likely to remain so almost indefinitely, unless purposeful human actions enable it to cut all bondage and liberate itself. A corrupted soul is trapped in the *samsara* (cycle of birth/death) in various states of embodiment. The very act of living is full of desires and passions (*kasayas*). Under the influence of these passions and activities (the vibrations of body - physical, vocal and mental), the soul attracts and causes more *karmic* particles* to bond with it. Since the bonding results from our actions (*karma*), the bonding particles are called '*karmic* particles'.

As more bondage happens, the soul is trapped deeper in the cycle of birth and death. Rebirth of the bonded souls is not confined to our planet only. The rebirth can occur anywhere in the universe. The four main destinies (*gatis*) of the bonded souls are:

1. celestial beings (*devas*) - bonded souls whose past *karma* merit a relatively happy, pain-free, enjoyable existence,
2. humans (*manusya*) - an existence which offers opportunities to purposefully cut *karmic* bonds and progress towards liberation,
3. hell-beings (*naraki*) - an existence in which souls are bonded heavily with pain producing *karma*, and are made to suffer the consequences of their evil actions, and,
4. Animals and plants (*tiryancha*) - an existence where souls passively enjoy or suffer the consequences of their past *karma*. They can neither perceive the idea of liberation nor can they work actively towards self-liberation to the same extent as humans.

Only humans, thanks to our suffering and our thinking capacities, can awake to the reality (*samyak drsti*), become aware of the goal, and purposefully act to control desire, cut bondage, and liberate the imprisoned soul. Animals and plants also suffer the consequences of their *karma*, but are unable to und erstand or follow

---

* Jains classify aggregates of material particles into various groups (*vargana*) such as *audarika-vargana* (gross -body forming), *vaikriya* (subtle-body forming), *mano-vargana* (mind forming), *karman-vargana* (*karma*-forming), etc. The karmic particles are from the *karman-vargana* group.

Any path out of their sufferings and hence cannot achieve *moksha*.* All they can do is to quietly suffer the fruits of their past *karma*, and, since *karma* fall-off after fruition, lighten their load of *karmic* bondage so that their soul may be born in human form in some future life cycle. Celestial beings are apparently happy, and neither worry about nor perform austerities for achieving *moksha*. Hell-beings on the other hand have no choice but to suffer their intense pain and agony. Their souls experience a quick shakedown cycle of their *karma* and emerge with a lighter *karmic* load to be reborn in other realms.

The Mechanism of Bondage *(bandha)*

The Jain philosophers believed that material particles, called *'anu'*, are floating freely in every part of occupied space. These particles are grouped into eight different categories. One such group is called *karman-vargan* because only these particles are involved in *karmic* bondage. Our actions are governed by the bonded soul within us. Such actions may be psychic (*mana*), vocal (*vachana*), or physical (*kaya*). They, in turn, produce vibrations, which attract *karmic* particles. Although the *karmic* particles attracted are all identical, the resultant *karma* effects may vary depending upon the nature of vibrations and the passions involved. Vibrations may draw the *karmic* particles towards the soul but the resultant bondage may be momentary unless passions are also involved in the process. The greater the intensity of the passions, the stronger is the bond, making it difficult for the soul to purge itself of the *karmic* particles.

The actual bonding process is interesting. The *karmic* particles already bonded to the soul initiate our activities. These activities, in turn, generate *karma*-causing vibrations. The vibrations are of two types. First there are simple vibrations generated by fairly neutral actions. The bondages caused by these vibrations are called *'dravya karma'*, and are only weak. However, because of this bondage, further vibrations arise. If or when one's actions are driven by psychic activity including passion, emotion, and intention (*bhava*), complex vibrations are created. The bondages caused by this more complex set of vibrations are stronger, and are called *'bhava karma'* (or intentions based *karma*).

The interesting point to note is that the already bonded particles generate activities and attract more particles to the soul. The new particles in turn generate

* However, Jain literature contains stories about how certain animals were able to achieve moksha. Invariably, this is attributed to the past lives of the said animal during which many activities had taken its soul almost (but not quite) near liberation. Some residual *karma* had to be worked out and hence the present birth in the animal form. During this lifetime however, the residual *karma* came to fruition (chance listening to *Tirthankara's* sermons helped) and dropped off, thus liberating the soul.

more vibrations and attract even more particles and the cycle continues. Fortunately, if no intentions or passions are involved in the activities, the weaker bonds formed by the newly attracted particles simply break off almost immediately, preventing more corruption of the soul. This explains why our action (such as killing an insect), if accompanied by passions harms our soul, whereas the same action without any intention does minimum damage. Thus, material *karma* and its spiritual counterpart are mutually related as cause and effect, each of the other. Alternatively, the *dravya* and *bhava karma* feed each other and the cycle continues until the soul in its human existence consciously and purposefully acts to extricate itself from this cycle.

Types of *Karma*

Jain philosophers have divided *bhava-karma* into eight primary classes (and 93 sub-classes). The root cause of both the influx and bondage of *karmic* particles is activity. Therefore, this division is based on the activity involved.

Eight Primary Classes of *Karma*

The eight types of primary *karma* are further grouped into two groups. The first four types listed below (numbered 1, 2, 3, 4) are harmful to the soul and are called 'Destructive' or *'Ghatiya' karma.* They obstruct the soul from achieving its full potential, and are mainly responsible for keeping soul entrapped in the *samsara.* Consequently, annihilation of *ghatiya karma* ensures liberation, thus enabling soul to achieve its full potential of infinite knowledge, perception, bliss, and energy. The set of next four types (numbered 5, 6, 7, 8) are non-consequential to the process of liberation, and are therefore called 'Non-destructive' or *'Aghatiya' karma.* The point to remember, however, is that this classification as '*Ghatiya*' or '*Aghatiya*' is based purely on the ability of the *karma* to obstruct liberation. *Aghatiya karma* may make us suffer in many ways during our worldly existence but are not considered destructive because they do not affect a soul's innate qualities.

1. Knowledge-Obstructing *(jnanavarniya)*

Activities such as neglecting or ridiculing learning or knowledge; insulting, disrespecting, harassing or hating the learned; remaining idle, obstructing others in scholarship activities, and spreading incorrect information can cause the soul to accrue knowledge-obstructing *karma.* These *karma* impair or obscure the soul's capacity for cognition, comprehension, and knowing. There are five sub classes of knowledge-obscuring *karma.*

2. Intuition-Obstructing *(darsanavarniya)*

If the above-mentioned activities are directed towards a visionary or his/her vision, the soul is bonded with intuition-obstructing *karma*. The soul so bonded lacks intuition and vision. There are nine sub-classes of this type of *karma*.

3. Energy-Obstructing *(antaraya)*

These obstruct the infinite energy of the soul, and our ability to obtain or enjoy wealth, power, and spiritual activities. Obstructing those who are engaged in social and spiritual activities, charitable giving, helping or serving the needy, and providing happiness to others, produce these *karma*. The soul so bonded lacks the ability to enjoy life, and resources; lacks capacity to make an effort, or to contribute and be generous with one's time, energy or money. One suffers a lack of recognition, respect and honor within one's community and society.

4. Deluding Karma *(mohaniya)*

Although these *karma* are further sub-divided into twenty-eight different classes, there are two basic types of deluding *karma* - world vision-deluding *karma* (*darsana mohaniya*) and character-deluding *karma* (*charitra mohaniya*). Believing in or propagating false ideas about absolute truth, advocating values disrespectful of difference and diversity, and neglecting the spiritual welfare of the soul, causes such bonding. Influenced by vision-deluding *karma*, a person lives a confused life, unable to realize true insight into his soul's nature. Such a person is:

- an extremist, and unable to even consider another viewpoint,
- a skeptic, lacking conviction about the validity of truths learned,
- ignorant, and unwilling to learn new concepts, ideas and truths, and
- deluded in the belief that all spiritual paths are the same.

Such a deluded person does not reach the 'awakening' stage (discussed in Chapter 2) and thus cannot even begin the journey on the path to liberation.

Character-deluding *karma* generate dangerous passions like greed, anger, deceit, pride and lust. Since passion-driven activities generate stronger karmic bonds, such person's soul keeps on sinking deeper into more bondage.

The four types of *karma* described so far obstruct, obscure, distort, pervert, hide, or prevent the full expression of the intrinsic qualities of the soul. Therefore, they are labeled as 'destructive'. The next four, on the other hand, merely affect the quality of life of a being but do not impede soul's ability to liberate itself. They are therefore labeled 'non-destructive (*aghatiya*)' *karma*.

5. Pleasure and Pain-Causing *(vedaniya)*

Straight and simple! Activity generates *karmic* bondage. If actions such as love, compassion, forgiveness, help, service, charitable giving, etc. bring pleasure and comfort to other living beings, you have generated pleasure-producing (*sata-vedaniya*) *karma*. On the other hand, killing, hurting, causing pain or sorrow, and destruction - caused to someone else - either directly or indirectly, either mental, verbal or physical - will generate pain-producing (*asata-vedaniya*) *karma*. The influence of such *karma* on you is clear. You shall pay or receive in kind, if not in this lifetime, then surely in the future. However, *vedaniya karma* will not obstruct a soul's liberation and are therefore not regarded as destructive.

Eight Primary Classes of Karma

KARMA

- **Destructive Karma** *(Ghatiya Karma)* 4 sub classes given below
  - **Knowledge Obstructing Karma** *(Jnanavarniya Karma)* 5 sub- classes
  - **Intuition Obstructing Karma** *(Darsanavarniya Karma)* 9 sub - classes
  - **Energy Obstructing Karma** *(Antaraya Karma)* 5 sub - classes
  - **Deluding Karma** *(Mohaniya karma)* *28 sub- classes*
- **Non - Destructive Karma** *(Aghatiya Karma)* 4 sub - classes given below
  - **Pleasure and Pain Producing Karma** *(Vedaniya Karma)* 2 sub - classes
  - **Life - span Determining Karma** *(Ayus Karma)* 4 sub - classes
  - **Physique Determining Karma** *(Nama Karma)* 93 sub - classes
  - **Status Determining Karma** *(Gotra Karma)* 2 sub - classes

6. Life-Span Determining *(ayus)*

The effects of this *karma* determine both the form (as celestial beings, human, animals and plants, and hell-beings) and the span of our next lives. It determines the form of our next life, and, correspondingly, the opportunities we might have to work towards the liberation of our soul. For example, a lifestyle, which is full of violence, cruelty, or unjustly gained wealth, generates intense karmic bondage. With little chance of the soul's liberation, the soul passes on to another form. In this case, it is reborn as a hell being. One may spend an infinite amount of time trapped in that form. At the same time, if we respect human and animals but wantonly destroy lower forms of life, such as insects, plants and microbes, we may be reborn as one of those lower forms and suffer a fate similar to that which we have just destroyed.

Just how long a soul will remain in any of the forms, and thus the life span in its next birth is determined by the intensity of the *karma* attached. The primacy of *ayus-karma* is because its bondage determines all the other factors governing our next embodiment. For example, determining that our next lifespan will be one of only a few moments may lead to our soul's rebirth as a simple microbe, a life span of a few years may mean an embodiment as a particular animal, between 70 and 100 years would suggest rebirth as a human, or even as a tree.

However, if we are living a simple, life under the influence of the triple 'A's (*ahimsa*, *aparigraha* and *anekantavada*), we may warrant another chance of rebirth as human beings to make progress on the path toward liberation. If we meticulously observe the triple 'A's, make a concerted effort to progress towards liberation and collect many non-destructive *karma*, we may be rewarded a celestial rebirth to enjoy the rewards of our earthly efforts, or take birth again as humans to complete our progress. At some point it is expected that these *karma* will come to fruition and purge from the soul, resulting in a rebirth in some other form

7. Physique Determining *(nama), karma*

These *karma* also account for various forms of embodied existence such as existence in hell, plant and animal world, human world, as well as celestial region. At the same time *nama karma* determine birth in the various classes of living organisms. For example, if rebirth is in plant or animal world, nama *karma* determines the actual species of that birth.

8. Status Determining *(gotra) Karma*

The rise of status-determining *karma* is responsible for high or low status of an individual.

Commentary

To the extent that all religious doctrines are words of the wise for the betterment of the society, the Jain doctrine of *karma* is a powerful and effective social document. Living beings, by their nature, can never be without activities - verbal, mental, and physical. The activities have consequences - good, bad, or indifferent. In the case of humans, these consequences affect the society in which they live. A simple, peaceful life, full of love, kindness, and respect for other living beings could have a positive social influence resulting in the formation of a similarly kind and caring society. Religious doctrines are usually formulated with this in mind; however, their true worth depends upon how effective they are in influencing the social behavior of their followers.

A self-righteous doctrine that refuses to acknowledge differing viewpoints, or urges its followers to push and spread its message as the 'only' truth, may influence a society to be aggressive, militant, and prone to conflicts and wars. A doctrine, that preaches that we have the right to kill, and destroy other living beings (even other human beings in the name of religion) may promote (however indirectly) arrogance, cruelty, ecological disaster, and eventually, the destruction of our planet. Even the cruelty of humans towards other humans will never end as long as we continue to believe that we have the right to kill or hurt other living beings.

The Jain doctrine of *karma* emphasizes the cause and effect principle of "as ye sow, therefore shall ye reap". In addition, by logical analysis and scientific reductionism, it makes the idea effective and intellectually acceptable to the modern thinker. Its dynamism preaches that an individual's destiny is in his/her own hands. It is up to the individual to understand the true source of happiness and to actively go after it. A well-trodden path is already shown by the *Tirthankaras*. All we need is the courage and commitment to undertake the journey. The effectiveness of this doctrine can be judged from the fact that Jainism has not found it necessary to establish a hierarchy to police and enforce the observance of its 'code of conduct'. The Jain code is left entirely to the logical freethinking conscience of its followers. Jainism is a philosophy that advocates ultimate freedom of the soul and has seen it fit to leave the human spirit free to act on its own.

Pascal's Wager

Philosophies that try to explain 'reality' can be classified into two broad groups: (1) a group of systems that posits God as a supernatural power controlling the universe and (2) others that do not accept that our fortunes are governed by a supernatural being. Jainism, Buddhism, Humanism, and modern science come under this later group. Given the centuries-old debate between the two camps, a modern mind wonders about the choice it may have between the paths advocated by the two camps.Unable to come up with any tangible proof of God's existence, the advocates of the first camp often resort to the *reasons of the heart* theory. "Ours is the path of absolute faith and surrender" they preach, "Believe in Him. Surrender your life to Him. Lead a good life in His shadow", they promise, "and you will be granted an eternity of happiness and bliss in heaven. This line of reasoning asks the individual to suspend usual logical thinking patterns, and take a leap of faith. It plays on beliefs and fears of 'missing out' on salvation or heaven.

The advocates of the second group, on the other hand, claim that their path promises happiness and bliss too. Modern science promises physical ecstasy in this life (companies and scientists have often talked about 'better living through chemistry'), Buddhists promise transcendental bliss in *nirvana*. Jains downplay the physical pleasures but promise internal peace in this life and absolute bliss in after life. Which claim is right? Which path should one follow?

The Jain path may be slow and difficult but at the least it is rationally plausible, allows for here-and-now peace of mind and happiness, and hence less risky.

To convince the confused, the advocates of the first group use a gambler's wager to help sway the skeptics. Years ago, a French philosopher Blaise Pascal came up with a suggestion as to how to proceed in the face of uncertainty. "If you have to choose between two uncertain proposals, place your bets on the less risky one." This is known as Pascal's Wager. Invoking this wager they invite us to choose their camp and Live a good life. "The consequence of not making that choice is bringing eternal doom. Therefore, why take risk?" they ask, "Even if God doesn't exist, what have you got to lose by living a good life? All your camp offers is rebirth and possible liberation sometimes in the future". The argument sounds convincing - at least on the surface.

Jains certainly do not have any argument against living a clean, good life and their *anekantavada* doctrine would encourage them to examine, if not accept, the validity of this wager. Their focus, however, would be on two phrases, namely "the good life", and "risk". For them, "the good life" is a lifestyle in which our happiness is controlled by our own mind and not by some external objects. "Good life that depends on external objects like wealth, fame, etc. is only 'temporary comfort', and not true happiness. Take away these objects and our good life is gone. True happiness is in being at peace with oneself", they would say. "So, we have no argument with at least part of your philosophy if you agree that good life is the austere lifestyle in which our mind is always on guard to take charge of our happiness". The second phrase in the wager is "risk". Jains would argue that, "If less risk is our real concern, should we not be choosing the logical and intellectual path of Jainism? After all, if the very existence of God cannot be rationally supported, where is the safety in accepting an irrational uncertainty?" "The Jain path", they would claim, "may be slow and difficult but at the least it is rationally plausible, allows for here-and-now peace of mind and happiness, and hence less risky".

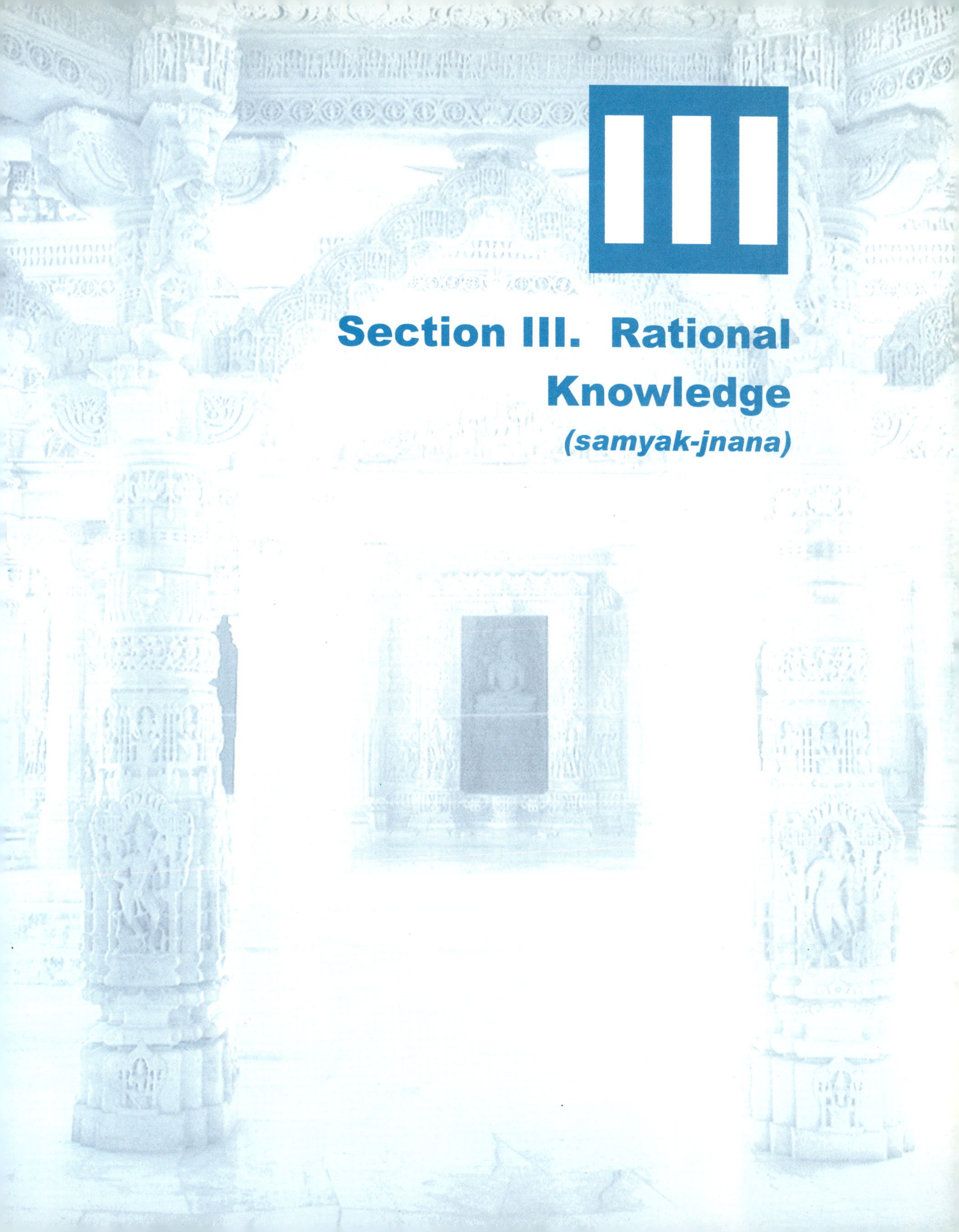

III

Section III. Rational Knowledge

(samyak-jnana)

SECTION PREVIEW

Jainism's insistence on rationality and intelligent choice has an appeal with the contemporary mind. Jains call their way of life as "Rational Living" (Samyak-charitra), and their worldview as Rational Worldview (Samyak-darsana). What makes their world-view 'rational'?

That begs another question. What makes a faith 'blind', an idea simply 'hunch', and an action merely a reckless 'gamble'? The obvious answer is "lack of knowledge and analysis"! Knowledge gives rational support to a faith without which it is simply 'blind', 'hunch' or gamble. Knowledge is thus an all-important criterion of rationality and has been a subject of great interest and study for Jain philosophers.

In the next two chapters we explore the results of this study. Ancient Jain scriptures give minute details of the very phenomenon of "gaining knowledge". It is a fascinating study, both for its details as well as for the methodology used. For the Jain philosophers, an understanding of knowledge was of supreme importance because their entire claims to rationality rests on it. In the final analysis, the validity of Jain lifestyle and worldview rests on the teachings of Tirthankaras who, they claim, gained absolute knowledge - omniscience - and then showed us their path to omniscience and liberation. After reading scriptural account of the theory of knowledge, Tirthankara's claim to omniscience is easy to appreciate and accept.

Next two chapters give a very brief outline of the Jain theory of knowledge. It is a fascinating reading - even if just to gain an understanding of the detailed analytical process used.

10

10. Rational Knowledge

You may have encountered, as I often do, people who say, "God exists." If you ask them, "How do you know?" they would simply say, "My heart tells me so." They may even cite some mysterious event in their life, which they would say is the proof enough for them. Such a response is based on emotions, not knowledge. Nevertheless, that happens to be their belief system. They are ready to base their faith in it and are not prepared to analyze it any further. For the 21st Century modern mind it is a response without any rational support, hence difficult to accept.

The conduct or the lifestyle of an individual is really governed by the set of beliefs and the worldview of that individual. These beliefs, in turn, are shaped by the factors such as the culture, the religion, the upbringing, and the surroundings, in which the individual finds him/her self. Powerful individuals - the prophets, the sages, and the political, social, religious, leaders - strongly influence these factors from time to time. They can thus help build a culture of peace and understanding, or can even turn their followers into suicidal terrorists. Their messages, ideas and concepts, as interpreted by those who bring them to the masses, become the cultural, political, and religious foundations of a people. What is the foundation of Jain thought and conduct?

An important message to Jains from their *Tirthankaras* is that the path to liberation is a three-fold path requiring rational conduct, rational belief, and rational knowledge. This is interesting because the message does not emphasize just the right conduct and belief, but stresses that the conduct and belief must be backed by knowledge to make the path to liberation truly rational.

Devotion and faith are no doubt important ingredients of religious conduct. If there is no faith or belief in the goal, and in the efficacy of the path to be followed, progress along the spiritual path is difficult. However, as noted earlier, mere blind faith may produce only dogmatism and orthodoxy. Real progress on a spiritual path needs rational faith. A path as rigorous and difficult as the one prescribed by the *Tirthankaras* will not even be tried, unless there is a rational understanding of the goal and of the means to achieve it. Thus rational understanding or true knowledge of the Jain view of Reality became a cornerstone of Jainism.

Knowledge thus became an important field of enquiry for the Jain philosophers. The Jain thinkers have defined knowledge as the essence of soul. "There can be no knowledge without soul and no soul without knowledge".[14] The soul has other intrinsic characteristics also, but the Jain philosophers always emphasized knowledge as the main characteristic possessed by the soul. Consciousness is intrinsically natural to each soul but our souls being defiled by material *karmic* particles, cannot perceive the real knowledge. Only the soul that has reached the stage of omniscience or perfection-*kevala* (13th *gunasthana*) can cognize the real nature of all things; and can accept everything relatively and conditionally in the remaining step of their salvation. Jains claim their worldview and path to be rational because it is based on the preaching of those who did reach the omniscience and thus have perceived, experienced, and lived reality. Moreover, they had no attachments, hatred or other motivations to preach anything but truth. Is omniscience of *Tirthankaras* a myth - an article of blind faith? Our exploration of the Theory of Knowledge, which the *Tirthankaras* preached thousands of years ago, may be one of the convincing proofs. Here is what they have preached about the knowledge itself !

The Detailed & The General Knowledge

First, intuition itself is knowledge. According to Jainism, our soul has infinite perception and knowledge but our perception is obscured by the *karmic* particles. Thus, the phenomenon of 'receiving knowledge' is really the 'falling off of the perception-deluding and knowledge-obscuring *karmic* particles'. Some events may trigger the removal of these *karma* and give us the understanding or knowledge of an object, event, etc. This understanding could be 'just general', or 'in detail'. It could either be limited to just being aware of the object in its existential generality, or we may fully comprehend the object with all its individual characteristics. Jain philosophers have classified knowledge based on whether it is limited or complete. The limited understanding is called the undifferentiated knowledge, the indistinct understanding, the indeterminate cognition, perception, or just intuition (*darsana*).

[14] Umaswati: *Tattvartha Sutra,* 2.8

The complete knowledge is, on the other hand, called the differentiated or detailed knowledge, the distinct understanding, the determinate cognition, or comprehension *(jnana)*.]

The difference between the two terms is really in the details. The perception or intuition (*darsana*) is the knowledge without the understanding of the details, while in comprehension (*jnana*) the details are perceived. Jain philosophers emphasize both *samyak-darsana* as well as *samyak-jnana* because unless one becomes aware or perceives reality (*darsana*) one may not even be motivated to seek comprehensive knowledge of that reality (*jnana*). Therefore, *samyak-darsana* is the start-up part of the process of getting detailed knowledge. When *darsana* (perception) is critically analyzed and backed up by rational knowledge, it truly becomes *samyak-darsana.* Faith in a *darsana* without this rational support could be mere blind faith.

Perceptive Knowledge (*darsana*)

Perception is a preliminary stage, i.e. the first stage of knowledge where we have only a general awareness of the object. When we become just aware of the existence of an object, we often enter the next stage almost automatically. We begin in our mind, the process of establishing its identity by comparing the new information with the one in our memory. We may 'know' a number of things, that is, we may be aware of those things, but if we do not critically analyze our new knowledge, and do not understand its relationship with the characteristics of the objects we already know, our new knowledge will remain at the sensation or perception level only. However, critical analysis of the new data, its comparison and classification with the already existing data provides the needed rational support and makes the same new data, i.e. the perceptive knowledge, the comprehensive knowledge.

There is a subtle difference between the Jain and Buddhist understanding of comprehensive knowledge. Buddhists maintain that the perceptive knowledge is so indeterminate that the mind does not at all notice any qualifications, e.g. generality, quality, substantiality, type, etc. at that stage. According to them, all these qualifications of the object are the forms of thought which is always determinate.

Jains view perception as 'becoming aware' of the mere existence of an object. Accordingly, perception includes only that qualification which defines the existence of the object. Without this qualification, they argue, the mind will not become aware of the existence of the object and will not proceed to the comprehension stage. Other qualifications, which provide distinction and determination of the object, are not noticed at this stage. Receiving those qualifications and processing that information to identify, classify, or determine the nature of the object belongs to the comprehension or determinate stage.

Jain scholars are not unanimous in their views on perception. Scholars like Virasena[15] and Brahmadeva[16] believed that the above position of perception as the knowledge of the general and comprehension as the cognition of the particular, was taken by early Jain philosophers merely to accommodate the contemporary non-Jain philosophers. It is not in keeping with the Jain scriptural teachings on: 'consciousness as the inherent characteristic of soul', and 'bonding or shedding of knowledge-obstructing *karma*'.

The same faculty of cognition is called perception when it senses the self and comprehension when it knows external objects.

In keeping with the scriptural teaching, they define perception as the cognition of one's own self, consisting in the striving for the origination of comprehension. The comprehension then is the subsequent cognition of external object. In other words, according to the scriptures, that which cognizes the nature of both generic and specific qualities of an external object is comprehension (*jnana*), and the introspection of the self of the same nature is perception (*darsana*). Thus, the same faculty of cognition is called perception when it senses the self and comprehension when it knows external objects.[17] This definition explains why scriptures emphasize both: *samyak-darsana* or rational intuition or rational perception at the awakening stage, and *samyak-jnana* or rational knowledge during the progression on the path to liberation.

The important point made in these debates between different schools is that for cognition - indeterminate or determinate - the object must have its unique characteristics or qualifications. An entirely unqualified object never enters into our cognition, since discrimination between qualities is the most fundamental character of consciousness.

Comprehensive Knowledge (*Jnana*)

Comprehensive knowledge is definite and determinate but may or may not be total, absolute and perfect. Except in case of those who have reached the stage of omniscience (perfect-*kevala)*, any comprehension by any one of us is not absolute but relative because of two factors. This is so, firstly because of the

---

15 Jain, Hiralal, *Satkhandagama* of Puspadanta and Bhutabali with Virsena's *Dhaval -tika*, 1.1. Hindi translation, Jaina Sahityoddharaka Fund Publication, Amaravati, 1939-1959.

16 *Tarkabhiprayena Sattavalokanadarsanam*, 44, by Brahmadeva.

17 M.L. Mehta, Jaina Theory of Knowledge, Gujarat Vidyapith, Ahmedabad, 1995 p. 15

objective condition of each real 'element'. As seen earlier (Chapter 6), each fundamental element is both permanent and impermanent depending upon our perspective and focus on its inherent qualities (*gunas*) or its modes (*paryayas*), and the modes of an element are continuously changing. Secondly, our comprehension of the reality is also relative to us - the knower - who cannot perceive all facets of the reality, because of the association of our soul with the knowledge obstructing *karma.*

According to the Jain philosophers, cognition can be secured through any one or all three means namely, physical senses, mind, and directly by means of soul. In other words, comprehension could be sensory, i.e. conditioned by the senses and mind, or extra-sensory, i.e. derived from the sources of consciousness (soul itself) without any assistance of the senses and mind.

Comprehension of an object begins with its perception either through object awareness or contact-awareness. Object-awareness is really a start of the relation between the sense organ and the object in the form of sense-specific data supplied by the object. It is momentary and always confined to the mere occurrence of cognition, which is indistinct and indeterminate. Hence, it does not lead to comprehension, which is distinct and definite.

The contact-awareness, on the other hand, is an awakening of consciousness by the direct contact between the object and the senses. Only four (excluding sight) sense organs are capable of establishing a close contact with their object. These four-types of contact-awareness are longer lasting and could lead to comprehensive (but not absolute) understanding of the object.

The cognition follows next in the wake of perception, and the sensory comprehension could be either non-verbal (*mati-jnana*) or verbal (*sruta-jnana*). The perceptive knowledge, which is initiated by contact awareness of the non-verbal type, could lead our mind through the following seven steps:

1. enquiry to acquire more facts;
2. speculation to advance towards a distinct awareness by examining specific features of the object;
3. increased perception to ascertain the specific features of an object by excluding the non-existent qualities and ascertaining the right;
4. retention which is the final determination of the object, retention of the cognition, and recognition of the object in the future;

5. recollection which stimulates the emergence of our past experience to the surface of consciousness;
6. recognition which helps us to make a judgment by combining perception (i.e. the freshly received data about the existence of an object) and recollection, which is a latent mental trace of the data previously received about the same or similar object;
7. and reasoning which is the mental process of comparing possibilities and finalizing the judgment about the identity of the object.

The above steps together with all other avenues of cognition are discussed in the next chapter.

11

11. The Avenues of Knowledge

Jains give so much importance to knowledge that a much revered second century Jain scripture *Tattvartha Sutra* - states in its very first sentence:

Rational world-view, knowledge and conduct are the three elements essential for liberation.

The first chapter in this text is devoted, almost entirely, to the Jain theory of knowledge. The Jain theory of knowledge begins with a simple assumption that the 'knowledge', the 'knower', and the 'known' are the three essential elements of knowing. A simple statement like "the grass is green" involves:

the **knower** - the person who learnt
the **known** - the grass, about which the information is obtained, and
the **knowledge** that it is green.

The Knower

We just stated that the person who learnt is the knower. According to Jainism this is an inaccurate statement. To be accurate, the soul, not the person himself, is the knower. A person is a combination of his material body - which, by itself, has no ability to 'know" - and his *Jiva* the soul. The soul is the consciousness (*chetana*), the one with the ability to know.

Consciousness is such an intrinsic, inherent, inseparable and inalienable attribute of the soul that the soul cannot exist without it. Thus, more precisely, "soul and consciousness being inseparable, soul itself must be omniscient, i.e. it is all-knowing and all-perceiving. In other words the knowledge and the knower are the same".

The Jain epistemology maintains that a living being already possess all the knowledge by virtue of him having a potentially omniscient soul. Knowledge does not come from outside, it is already with the soul. This fact is not always obvious because of the individual's *karma*.

A soul, unless it is liberated, is always associated with its *karma*. The soul-contaminating *karmic* particles, which are material in nature, manage to cloud up a soul's inherent qualities. Qualities such as infinite perception and knowledge are obscured by destructive *(ghatiya)* *karmic* particles - specifically the perception-obscuring (*darsanavarniya*) and knowledge-obscuring (*jnanavarniya*) *karmic* particles. Removal, shedding or annihilation of these particles (when 13th stage of spiritual development - *gunasthana* - is reached) enables the soul to manifest itself and reveal its true characteristic its omniscience. This idea is similar to that of polishing off layers of dirt from the surface of a diamond to release its brilliance.

The Known

According to the Jain world-view, the cosmos is made of only six fundamental elements, viz. soul, matter, space, time, and mediums of motion and rest. These six are, therefore, the only objects of knowledge (i.e. the 'known'). Note that soul is both the 'knower' as well as the 'known'. No other object has consciousness and cannot be a 'knower'. When a soul knows itself, the knowledge is subjective; knowledge about every thing else is objective.

The Knowledge

The scientific or the analytical genius of early Jain philosophers becomes evident when we examine their analysis of this whole process of so called 'gaining knowledge'. How does one get knowledge? What happens when we 'gain knowledge'? What interactions take place between the knower and the known?

Since knowledge and the 'knower' are the same, the process of 'gaining' knowledge does not really involve any 'flow' of information from the 'known' to the 'knower'. The whole process is therefore that of consciousness - the 'knower' becoming conscious of the 'known'.

How does that happen? How does knower become conscious of the known? Remember the '*karmic* particles' that bond and obscure consciousness? There are several kinds of *karmic* bondage and becoming conscious of something (i.e. gaining knowledge of something) is merely the removal or shedding of the *karmic* particles that were obscuring that particular knowledge. This shedding may happen either naturally (because of the predetermined duration of bonding) or through one's initiative and concerted efforts (self-discipline, and penance.) The more one manages to shed off one's knowledge-obscuring *karma*, the more enlightened one becomes.

Avenues of Consciousness

For the purpose of simplicity, we shall now use the terms 'consciousness' and 'gaining knowledge' interchangeably. In the last chapter we saw that knowledge was classified as apprehensive and comprehensive knowledge. This classification was based on the degree of consciousness achieved by the knower. Jains have used 'avenues of gaining knowledge' as one more criterion for classifying knowledge. The Jain theory states that there are five main avenues of gaining knowledge as follows, and have classified knowledge accordingly.

1. Empirical knowledge (sensuous cognition - *mati-jnana)*
2. Articulate knowledge (conceptualized through languages - *shruti-jnana)*
3. Clairvoyant knowledge (extra-sensory perception - *avadhi-jnana*)
4. Mind-reading knowledge - *mana-paryay jnana*, and
5. Omniscience - *kevali-jnana*.

Of these, the first two involve our senses. A combination of shedding appropriate knowledge-obscuring *karma* and stimulation of our senses by external sources (the object of study) results in our becoming conscious of the object (the known). Such knowledge, gained through the medium of senses, is called, ***indirect*** or ***acquired*** knowledge. This knowledge could easily be corrupted or distorted by several factors such as our senses, the state of the object, and the state of the knower (soul) itself. On the other hand, knowledge through the last three avenues, being extra-sensory, is ***innate*** and is likely to be less distorted, or perfect as in the case of omniscience.

Since the acquired knowledge could easily be distorted, Jain philosophers have devoted considerable energy to analyzing the avenues of Empirical and Articulate knowledge. In fact, they have classified empirical knowledge in to as many as 336 different sub-categories based on the sources of distortion.

Empirical Knowledge

Empirical knowledge is based on sensual perception and the analytical capacity of the intermediary - mind. The five senses, viz., sight, hearing, touch, smell and taste are organ based (*indriya*) whereas some regard mind - the intermediary - as a non-organ based (*anendriya*) quasi-sense. Space limitations do not permit full discussion of each of the 336 sub-categories of empirical knowledge, but the following illustration gives an idea of the logical and scientific framework used by the Jain thinkers.

For example, let us consider the knowledge obtained through just one sense - hearing. Let us imagine that you just heard a faint sound in a very dark room. With it your perception of the event goes through a four-stage process:

1. **'Initial perception'** - sensing the existential characteristics of the object
2. **'Specific inquiry'** - conclusions derived from data received in stage 1
3. **'Cognitive comprehension'** - cognition or definite identification,
4. **'Imprint'** - retention of knowledge as memory.

The 'initial perception' is the very first step of sensing the general characteristics of an object without knowing any details about it. (The faint, indistinct sound makes you aware of the existence the object that made the sound.) The initial perception is immediately followed by the subsequent stages of 'specific inquiry' and 'cognitive comprehension'.

During the stage of 'specific inquiry' the mind analyzes the sound in terms of some similarities and differences. ("It sounds like footsteps, or whispering, or scratching".) This is followed by a determination of the existent qualities in the object to the exclusion of the non-existent ones ("It is a human voice, definitely not that of walking".) The initial perception is now transformed into identification and conclusion (e.g., "it is a whispering sound, therefore, another person is in the room"). Comprehension of the object is now almost complete.

TERMS TO REMEMBER

Anendriya	Non-sensuous
Avadhi	Clairvoyant knowledge
Indriya	Senses
Kevali	Omniscience
Mana-paryaya	Mind-reading
Mati	Empirical
Sruti	Articulate

In the final stage, an imprint, or the retention of the knowledge in the memory of the knower for a length of time follows the articulate comprehension. This retained knowledge is the empirical knowledge and is variously called as intelligence, remembrance, reasoning power, recognition, etc.

Empirical knowledge gained through any other senses also follows the same four stages. At any stage the senses, the state of the knower, the condition of the known, and the medium of learning may distort it. In other words the acquisition of empirical knowledge is affected by both the object to be studied as well as by the mental ability of the learner. This in turn, is the effect of the learner's *karma*. The same data received by two different learners will be cognized and interpreted differently depending upon the *karmic* influences on the learner's soul. The *karma* that obscure or impede a soul's manifestation of the empirical knowledge are known as 'empirical knowledge-obscuring' *karma*.

The knowledge thus gained acquires opposing duality (e.g., it may be either true or false), subject to the state of the knower. Scriptures describe six pairs of such opposing dualities. Thus, the empirical knowledge, at each of its four stages of acquisition, through each of the senses, passes through each of these six opposing pairs, i.e. twelve types of comprehensions on its way to imprinting, intelligence, memory, etc. This gives rise to 228 (**6** senses X **4** stages X **12** comprehensions = **228**) sub-categories of empirical knowledge. This number increases to 336 because of other considerations, which we cannot discuss here.

The Articulate Knowledge

The articulate knowledge is received through reading, listening, and by interpreting signs. This knowledge also is subject to errors and distortions at several stages. Firstly, unless the original preceptor or receiver is omniscient, he/she may have initially received it empirically (through senses) in the distorted form (due to the receiver's knowledge-obscuring *karma*). Then there is a possibility of second stage of distortions and errors when this receiver attempts to put it in an imperfect medium of words or pictures. Obviously, the reader or the listener could be

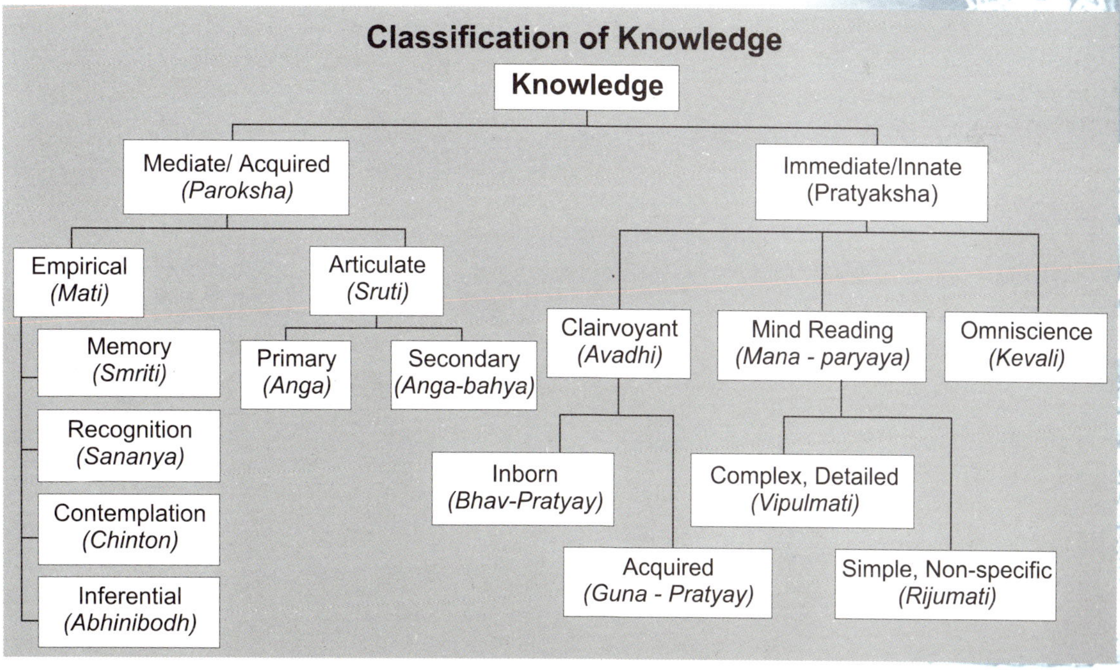

receiving a doubly distorted version of the original knowledge. Having recognized the distortion inherent in the articulate knowledge, Jain philosophers have warned against accepting any word, written or spoken, be it from the scholars, priests or pundits, mullahs or rabbis, as ***absolute*** truth. Absolute knowledge/truth is really beyond our reach until we manage to shed all our destructive *karmic* particles, become omniscient and can perceive the absolute truth. If all articulate knowledge is distorted, what about the scriptures? Do they not state the absolute truth?

Regardless of the religion the scriptures are written by the mortal beings. That mortal being may claim his works to be directly from an incarnation of God, son-of-God, a prophet, an *acharya*, a scholar, or a priest. The truth he/she professes may even be claimed as the 'revealed truth'. However, all such works are likely to be distorted unless the souls of the original receiver (the knower), as well as of the one who scripted that knowledge, have eliminated all their destructive *karma* and become omniscient. Otherwise, the knowledge-obscuring *karma* play their role.

Furthermore, farther the author is from the original revelation, more distorted is likely to be the version of the scripture. Obviously, those who cite their scriptures as "absolute truth" need to understand that the so-called truth is really the reflection of their own understanding of the written statement, which itself might be distorted by the author's understanding of the original message.

The Jain scriptures (the *Agamas)* are not the 'revelations from above'. They stem from the liberated souls of the *Tirthankaras* - the omniscient ones. Omniscience being their source, the knowledge in the *agamas* could be <u>almost</u> absolute if not the absolute. A small degree of uncertainty theoretically arises because the disciples who may themselves not be omniscient may have recorded the knowledge of the omniscient ones. Jains do recognize this possibility and have therefore grouped their sacred literature into (1) *Anga*-Agamas (Primary or Main texts based on the knowledge received by the omniscient - *kevali* - direct disciples of Mahavira,) and (2) *Anga-bahya* Agama (Subsidiary texts written by the learned ascetics who were not the direct disciples). (See Chapter 20)

The Clairvoyant Knowledge

The next three categories of knowledge are "innate" or "direct" type, i.e. they are independent of our senses but are direct knowledge from the soul itself. Such knowledge is therefore not subject to sensual distortion and limitation. Awareness of this knowledge, which is already within us, comes with the elimination of specific knowledge-obscuring *karma*. Clairvoyance enables a person to know an object without being in direct contact with it. This knowledge is not subject to the limitations of time, space, senses or mind. Clairvoyance could be innate (inborn) or acquired. Souls born in heaven or hell (celestial and hellish beings) are born in those realms with innate clairvoyance. For us humans, clairvoyance is acquired by the destruction of 'clairvoyance-obscuring *karma*' through meditation, penance, and self-control. Depending upon the extent of annihilation of such *karma*, one can know of things, persons and events of the past and future, and of those happening at far-off places.

The Mind-reading Knowledge

This may sound spooky, but we can, through self-discipline and austerities, mange to shed our *karma*, which obscure 'mind-reading' ability. We can then read the mind, the ideas and the thoughts of other persons without the help of any medium or outside agency. Mind-reading knowledge could be simple or complex. It is non-specific, fallible, shallow, and rather limited in scope. In comparison, complex-mind-readers read many different complex modes of mind, and penetrate more deeply into the minds of others. The complex mind-reading ability lasts until one attains omniscience. Simple mind reading relates only to the thoughts about object or action, whereas those capable of complex mind reading can penetrate deeper and can read motivations and beliefs that lie behind a person's thoughts.

Persons with this faculty are rare because this stage, being only steps removed from omniscience, is reached only after annihilation of almost all knowledge-obscuring *karma*. Only those who carry a light *karmic* bundle from the past lives, and follow a strict, self-disciplined ascetic path, can hope to reach this stage.

Omniscience

This stage is reached when the soul manages to purge itself of the four 'destructive' (*ghatiya*) *karma*. This is the stage when a person is free from all passions, all the causes of bondage of new *karma* have disappeared, and no new bondage is possible. The remaining non-destructive (*aghatiya*) *karma* can break off by the natural process. An individual achieves omniscience as soon as the *ghatiya karma* are purged. The individual may continue to live thereafter (because of the continued bondage with the 'life-span' - *ayus karma*) but will not bond new *karma*, and will achieve liberation upon death.

Only the omniscient ones could access distortion-free, unlimited knowledge because they are free from all destructive *karmic* particles including the knowledge

- obstructing *karma*. Only they can grasp all the facets of the manifold reality. Theirs is the pure, absolute, complete, and total knowledge. Jain *Siddhas*, *Arihantas* and *Tirthankaras* have reached this supreme stage. *Tirthankaras* are believed to have reached omniscience by shedding their *'ghatiya' karma*. Their *'aghatiya' karma* however allowed them to continue to live to give us their knowledge of reality and to show us the path to liberation.

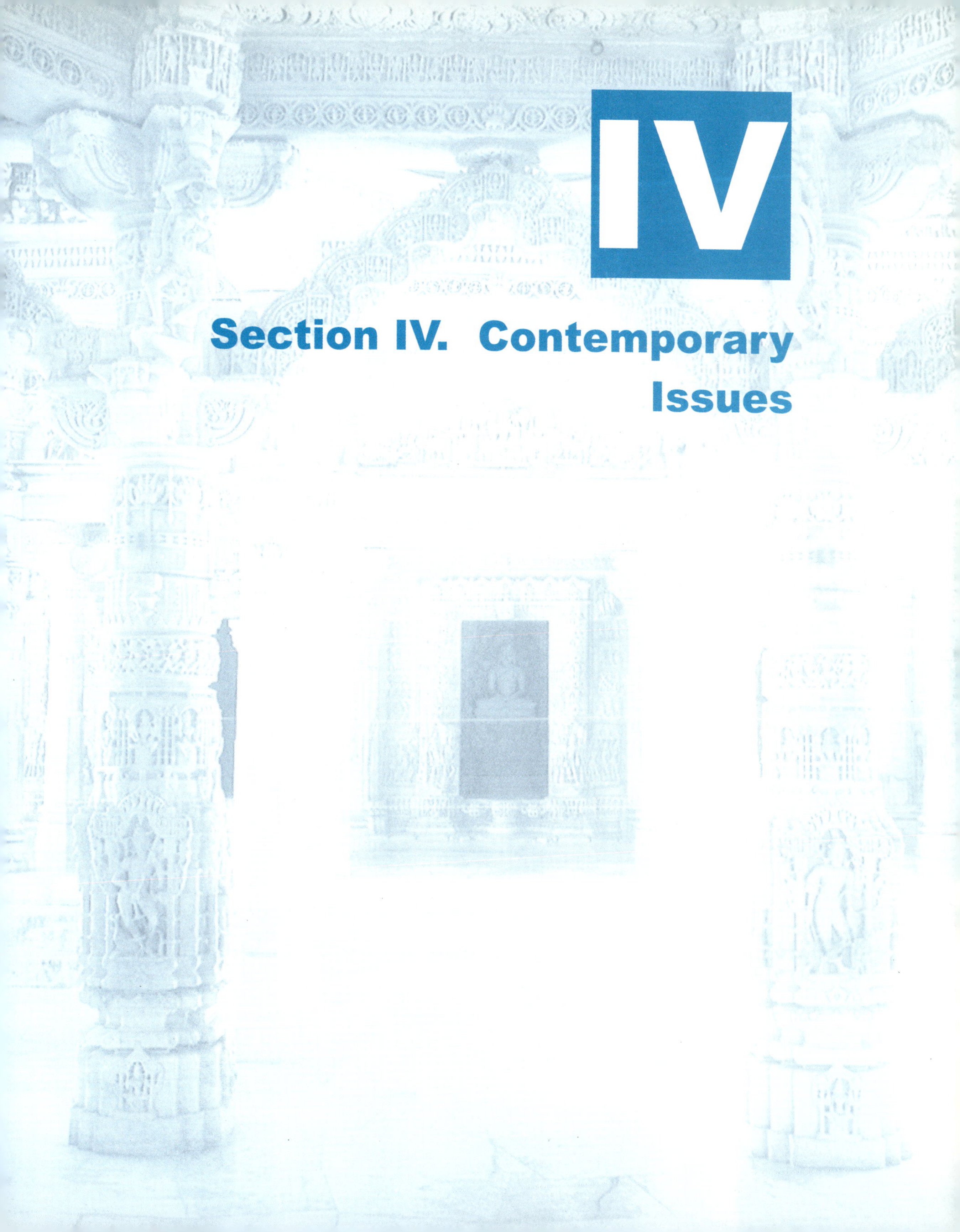

IV

Section IV. Contemporary Issues

SECTION PREVIEW

Issues such as eroding spiritual values, wars, poverty, cruelty to animals, environmental degradation, fundamentalism, and terrorism are becoming increasingly worrisome for our civilization. Finding rational solutions to these varied problems is a major concern for the contemporary thinker. This concern is reflected in the continuously evolving spiritual values. In fact, the new spirituality can now be defined as one "that promotes faith without restricting rationality and freedom of human thought, recognizes the rights of all living beings, acknowledges universe as a self-sustaining entity whose magnificence must be preserved, and prepares a mindset for personal and global peace."

The Jain lifestyle (samyak-charitra), which is governed by the doctrines of ahimsa, anekantavada, and aparigraha, could ease some of these problems. Jains have a long history of philanthropy, kindness to all living beings, environmental concerns, and non-confrontational, non-threatening, multi-faith dialogue. Contemporary Jains are therefore invited to use their experience in the use of these doctrines and expertise in multi-faith dialogue to become "the catalysts and leaders in a global dialogue on nonviolent stewardship of this endangered planet." They could actively participate in the process of resolving issues surrounding global peace, human and animal's rights, social and economic justice, religious conflicts, etc., and thereby demonstrate that this ancient religion is perfectly in tune with the demands of the new spirituality. Their active participation could help Jainism regain its vitality and glory.

12

12. The Contemporary Thinker

The Contemporary World

Preference for rational thinking, and concern for the future of our civilization are the two important attributes that define a modern, 21st century thinker. Both these attributes can be traced back to the phenomenal success modern science has achieved in the past four hundred years. The unprecedented physical comfort we enjoy today is an eloquent proof of the effectiveness of free and rational thinking of science. Ironically, our unprecedented ability to produce weapons of mass destruction, to dominate nature, and to destroy our ecology is also a graphic proof of the success of science. There is a danger that, if left unchecked, our preoccupation with science and technology might permanently damage our planet and doom our future.

We cannot deny that science is now as much of a force in our life as religion once was. How can this incredible scientific force be controlled and channeled? Can governments control science? Can religions guide galloping advances of science? I believe that any attempt to 'control' science - be it by governments, religions, or other agencies - is bound to fail. Human history is a witness to this observation. Imposed controls - whether on individuals, societies, or institutions - have never worked. Such attempts fail miserably particularly when those imposed upon are on a winning streak. Moreover, modern science, for now, is on such a course !

The Science-Religion Dichotomy

Once upon a time, religions had reined supreme over the affairs of human beings. Religious authorities had managed to establish absolute control over its flock by proclaiming 'laws to live by,' and devising elaborate systems to police and punish the lawbreakers. Control over the state, favoritism, and the promise of heaven and the fear of hell were some of the tools used by religious authorities to keep humans subdued. As a result, liberty, rights, and free will of human beings had become secondary to that of the church. The religious authorities even tried often to assert their authority by punishing or condemning to death those who favored logic or rationality over faith. However, about four hundred years ago in Europe, as science and technology began delivering physical comforts, financial freedom to satisfy human needs, and direct access to printed bible, humans felt empowered. Some emerging scientists even challenged faith and authority - the two main pillars of the church - and advocated use of logic, experience, and experimentation. With this, a dichotomy between the church and science began to develop in Europe.

This was the beginning of the end of the church's tight grip on the society. Kings and queens - the 'state' waiting in the wings to re-establish its authority - were the first to emerge from under the church control. Soon, the scientific advances empowered the masses and highlighted the importance of free and logical thinking. The Church's message of "absolute, unquestioned faith in God for a ticket to heaven after death" became secondary to that of sciences, "absolute, unquestioned mastery over nature for a ticket to better and comfortable living right now". The unfortunate outcome of this development, however, was that the spiritual values advocated by the church also eroded simultaneously, and base instincts such as greed, power, and materialism gripped the humanity. This dichotomy polarized Western society into two extreme camps - one remaining focused on an afterlife and blaming science for the woes of modern society, and the other seeking instant gratification today, and blaming religion for suppressing human free will. Neither camp seems to be much concerned about the tomorrow on this planet earth.

This mutual blaming has only aided in increasing human misery and has further burdened our planet with contemporary issues such as a deteriorating ecosystem, increased crime, racial and religious hatred, threats of nuclear war, and economic exploitation. Today co-operation, not confrontation is needed. Unfortunately, in the Western world, attempts to reconcile the 'scientific' with the 'spiritual,' and encouraging them to co-operate has been a struggle. Zealots on either side are not yet ready to be forgiving and generous to the other side.

"On the one hand, scientific materialism denies or ignores the existence of soul in its scientific exploration of reality, while on the other, religious fervor can turn too sharply toward the spiritual varieties and disregard the physical ones. This leads to an oscillating world-view in which we become unable to conceive of spiritual and material reality at once, and as a whole."

Nathmal Tatia in That Which Is - Tattvartha Sutra, Harper Collins Publishers, San Francisco, 1994

Religion concerns itself mostly with the afterlife, and science deals with material needs and life today. However, the very survival of our planet crucially depends upon our ability to blend the spiritual values of religion with the intellectual and logical philosophy of science. The Church's attempt to regain contol by blaming science for all the woes of the planet, or science's attempt to demonstrate absolute control over material nature without any regard for the ethical cautions, are both doomed to failure and the consequences for us could be devastating !

Contemporary Issues

The contemporary world has some contemporary problems. Some are global, some locality-specific and some intensly personal. Some problems have been with us for a long time, but even these have been exacerbated in recent years. There are no easy solutions and certainly no Jain panaceas. However, Jainism is uniquely equipped to deal with many of them because of its rich philosophy, long history and experience. Contemporary Jains, and those concerned with these issues, could draw much from these historical lessons and make a difference. Let us have a quick review of the problems facing us in the 21st century.

Spiritual Values: A universal complaint - be it from priests, pundits, rabbi, mullahs or monks - is: "Society today has no interest in the spiritual matters. Kids don't want to attend Sunday school, *pathshala* or *madarassa* and the parents don't care." Religious establishments are facing a severe decline in public confidence and allegiance.* This may be a matter of grave consequences for the priests and pundits, but should a modern man care about whether or not anyone attends churches, temples, mosques, etc. and whether the children attend Sunday school? Is this a problem for the contemporary thinker? Does it matter? Is this the spirituality and should we worry about its loss? (See next Chapter.)

Wars: Not that we humans did not wage wars and kill each other before ! In fact we were good at it even then. With our crude weapons like axes, spears and swords we fought crusades, invaded continents, and managed to wipe out civilizations. In the 20th century, thanks to our technological prowess, we invented efficient killing machines - machine guns and bombs ! The 20th century even managed to produce the personification of megalomania, bigotary, greed and

* Inevitably the sudden breakdown of the rigid attitudes of the past ages and greed generated by modern science and technology are producing chaotic and negative reactions. Many see the old power structures collapsing and have no vision of the structure of the future; they take refuge in various forms of rage, escapism, fantasy, terrorism, and fundamentalism. Some organized religions have even launched aggressive campaigns to pull the masses back into their fold. Perhaps, this explains the current paradoxical rise in attendance at the churches, mosques, etc., and also the rise in fundamentalist terrorism. Nevertheless, out of this turmoil and confusion a wonderful pattern - that of new spirituality and human rights - is emerging. See Chapter 13.

in the form of Hitler. Had this man access to the weapon stockpiles we have available today, he could have blown our planet to pieces. Let us not be complacent, there is no guarantee that the 21st century will not produce its own version of Hitler. As this book is being written, there are no less than thirty major conflicts and wars being played out in different parts (the U.S. army refers to these war zones as 'theaters of engagement') of the world, and of course, there were the events that lead to the tragic bombing of the World Trade Centre in New York and the Pentagon on September 11, 2001.

Poverty: Science and technology has given us the ability and means to produce an abundance of wealth. More food, more goods and more wealth are being produced now than ever before. Human ingenuity has produced a lifestyle which is supposed to be more comfortable than ever. But, can we tell this to the starving children and their anguished mothers in Africa, Asia and South America? Can we talk about it to the street people in the wealthiest nations and dazzeling cities like New York, Toronto, London, Sydney and Honk Kong? Their misery continues in spite of our scientific achievements. Why?

Environmental Degradation: In the contemporary world the wealthiest nations are worried about global warming and about the hole in the ozone layer, and the newly industrializing nations are worried about the lack of potable water and breathable air. The poorest nations are worried about their quickly depleting natural resources.

Fundamentalism - Religious, Political, Ideological: As contemporary thinkers turn to secular thought in increasing numbers, the 'old-guards' of the traditional religions are resorting to fundamentalist violence. Coincidently, as the previous sentence was being typed, the following news flashed on my computer.

Mulla Mohammad Omar has issued a decree to destroy every statue in Afghanistan including two giant statues of Buddha hewn into cliff and more than 16 centuries old. The order was given based on Islamic law, said the Taliban, the fundamentalist Moslem group that currently controls 90 per cent of Afghan territory.

- CBC News Online Staff

Cruelty to Animals: This issue is rapidly coming on the radar screens of contemporary thinkers. In many parts of the world, hunting a starteled wild animal with a high-powered gun from a helicopter is euphemestically called 'sports', rasing millions of cows and chickens in conditions where these animals are confined to tiny little cages for all of their stressful short life is called 'farming,' and catching thousands of fish by the sweep of a giant dragnet or clubbing to death thousands of seal-pups as they emerge from the sea within a few days of their birth is called 'harvesting'. Anyone who visits these 'sports-grounds' and 'farms' would not fail to notice the cruelty hidden behind these euphemestic terms. Witness how thousands of chicks - just two days old - are tossed alive into a meat grinder to produce animal feed, or how beaks of fifteen-day old chicks are chopped off so that they will not peck each other during the rest of their frustrated lives in a fourteen inch by fourteen inch cage. You would no longer wonder about the cruelty involved.

Globalization: This is a two-pronged issue. On the one hand, globalization implies migration and exchange of people between nations and continents. With the modern means of communications and travel this is happening with ever increasing frequency. In this context, the world has truly become a global village. Globalization as we know it today is a relatively recent development. In its present form globalization could be good (except for some associated problems). Problems associated with migration are mostly related to the majority/minority issues largely governed by fear, racism, bigotry, etc. New immigrants endure untold hardships due to such attitudes. However, with education, cultural exchange, and changes in attitudes these problems could be resolved. On the other hand, globalization means rapid spread of multinational corporations to exploit the natural and human resources of poor countries in the name of 'fair-trade practices.' The problem of exploitation by multinational corporations is a complex one and results in permanent damage to a nation or group of people. Tribalism as a reaction to globalization forces could also have negative effects.

Family Breakdown: Although this problem is becoming a serious issue in the Western countries, Eastern cultures are no longer immune to it. Furthermore, Jains themselves are migrating to countries in Europe, North America and Australia where the local stresses are straining their families also. The consequences of the gradual shift from 'joint-family' to 'nuclear family,' to 'no family' has become a subject of detailed study and research by social scientists.

Ethical Issues: Every now and then societies find themselves face-to-face with new ethical issues. Some religions believe that these issues are exclusively under their domain, and often rush to come up with new edicts, encyclicals and *fatwas*. Often these new directives are sheepishly or grudgingly accepted by the congregation, but sometimes these cause an emotional crisis that force dissenters to leave the congregation. Some of the issues confronting the contemporary thinker are gender equality, same-sex marraiges, gay/lesbian rights, euthanasia, capital punishment, the use of animals in medical research, genetic modification, cloning, nuclear weapons, the dominance of religion in the affairs of the state, etc.

Furthermore, young people today are confronting the issues that are intensly of personal nature. They are pulled in opposite directions by peer pressures and their parent's culture on issues such as drugs and drinking, pre-marital sex, abortion, etc. The intensity of theses issues may vary by place and by culture, but sooner or later all areas and all cultures will have to confront these issues squarely. Could religious authorities deal with these issues by issuing directives? Does Jainism have any special technique to handle such problems of personal nature?

Analysis

The foregoing is only a partial list of the issues facing our civilization. The issues may all look different, but an analysis will reveal that passion is the common thread connecting them. Passionate forces of anger, pride, deceit and greed (Jains call these the four *kasayas*) drive these issues. Greed for power or wealth feeds diverse issues such as wars, economic dominace, poverty, animal cruelty, and environmental degradation. False pride in religion, political views, race, culture, colour of the skin, etc. either excites our anxiety or encourages us to look down upon some thing different than that which is familiar. Consequently, we tend to react with fear, rage, or anger. Even the ethical issues, in the final analysis, are governed by these passions. Theoretically at least, if we can transform our strong emotions into wisdom, and manage to keep our passions under control, instead of letting passions control our mind, we should be able to resolve most of these issues. Do Jains have special insights in these matters? How would Jains handle, and how do they handle these issues? Can Jainism offer any help?

Activism

Many individuals and organizations around the world are trying to tackle contemporary global issues in their own way. Their actions take different forms such as: issue-based publications, conferences, rallies, demonstration on the streets, and some times even violent tactics to vent their frustration. Such efforts are often labeled as 'activism'. Those with vested interest in maintaining the *status quo* often paint a negative picture of activists as young, radical, violent and undisciplined anarchists. It is easy to understand why. People express their anger and unhappiness at the state of their world. Often, they feel disenfranchised. Their activism is then limited by their incapacity to do anything but kick down fences, burn effigies, buses and flags…symbols of authority. Well-meaning efforts of many have thus resulted in unfortunate confrontations and frustrations. Nevertheless, their concerns are genuine and the issues facing our civilizations are real. We cannot deny the fact that our planet is in grave danger unless we *proactively do something about these issues.*

Let us first understand what we mean by the term 'do something.' Techniques such as protests, rallies and street demonstrations produce both the positive as well as negative effects. On the one hand such techniques bring the issues into focus, widen awareness, and, unless turned violent and ugly, they attract more and more people to the cause. This is the positive side of activism. However, these techniques do very little for the cause because they send a negative message and create a sense of guilt among those whose immediate interests lie in the *status quo*. Their instant response then would be to neglect the long-term 'common good' solution, and instead to concentrate on building a protective mask to hide the guilt, and launch a counter attack. Often, as is the case with arms industry (peace movement), meat industry (vegetarianism movement), economic superpowers (poverty irradication movement), or major religions (multi-faith movements), the opponents of the change wield great power with which they can frustrate (if not crush) the activist movements.

The success of any activist movement would thus depend upon the ability of its leaders to shift their strategy from a negative 'shaming or making others feel guilty' to a positive, 'can-do together' approach. Mahatma Gandhi employed this 'gear-shifting' technique very successfully. His was the freedom movement and his adversary was the powerful British Raj with its vested interest in economic exploitation of India. Every now and then the Mahatma would encourage his followers to take to the streets and organize peaceful marches, protest rallies and so on. Each such event served to awaken Indians to the cause and attracted more and more people to the movement. Each such rally embarrassed the rulers who countered with the use of force, and the people's movement would turn ugly. Much to the frustration of his followers Gandhi would then abruptly issue a call to stop all street action, stage appeals to the decent-minded Britons, and invite the Raj to engage in a dialogue. Modern-day activists who want to 'do something' could achive results much faster by learning from Gandhi.

The Multifaith Movement

As an example, let us take one of the issues namely - religious intolerence and Fundamentalism. This issue has been a source of many conflicts and wars in the human history. A number of current conflicts around the globe, including the terrorist attack on the World Trade Centre towers in New York or the Parliament building in New Delhi, have this issue at their roots. In recent decades, the migration of people from the Orient into Western Christiandom has brought different religions in each other's neighborhoods, and to some extent, excited anxiety leding to hostility among conservative Christians in the Western world.

In the Judaeo-Christian traditions, the process of accepting a different belief system as a valid religion had begun several centuries ago, but has seen very little advance until recently. Traditionally, Christianity with its claim of universality has proclaimed itself to be the only true religion for all mankind, and Judaism, claiming exclusivity, was not open to anyone who was not an ethnic Jew. Consequently, both these traditions were not open for respectful dialogue with anyone outside their own faiths. For centuries, the main mission of the Christian church, therefore, was to convert those of all other faiths to the 'true faith' and to excommunicate or exterminate by death those already aquainted with true faith, but had come to challenge the Church's teaching (as authoritatively demanded by St. Thomas Aquinas).

This hardline attitude of Christianity began to ease a little during the European Reformation period at the Peace of Ausburg in 1555 (*cuius regio, eius religio* - in a prince's country, a prince's religion) when a prince's subjects were allowed to follow his faith (either Catholic or Lutheran). Although other Christian sects (e.g., Calvinists, Hutterites) continued to be persecuted, and even enlightened philosophers like John Locke advocated total intolerance towards atheists, the hardline attitude continued to steadily errode (e.g. Britain's William and Mary legislation, 1689). While Europe was slow in recognising religious plurality, the fact that most early immigrants to the United States were the refugees from religious persecutions in Europe should have made the recognition process somewhat faster in America. However, when confornted with Native Peoples - whom they called 'savages' (sometimes 'noble savages') - the new immigrants began to systematically persecute, and approptiate native lands (this continued right up to 1960s). In short, they too committed mass genocide in the name of Christianity.

The third major religion of the Middle East origin - Islam - is also undergoing this transformation after centuries of religious conflicts. However, its progress is very slow. Hardliner *mullhas* are still engaged in armed conflicts in many parts of the world. Although enlightened Moslems are participating increasingly in multifaith dialogues, the effects of colonialism are still contributing to Moslem conservatism and communal attrocities in a number of countries in North Africa, and in such countries as Afghanistan, Pakistan, etc. A historically interesting note, however, is that all three major religions of the Middle East, viz. Christianity, Islam and Judaism, that each claim to be the "true religion", have a long history of religious conflicts. It is strange that the Middle East should turn out to be a cradle of violence and continues to be engaged in violence even today.

The Indian subcontinent, cradle of three other great religions - Buddhism, Hinduism and Jainism has seen relatively much less religious violence. The conflict between the *Brahmanic* (Hinduism) and S*ramanic* (Buddhism and Jainism) has occasionally turned violent during the last 3500 years (since the birth of the *Brahmanic* religion), but often the conflict has taken the shape of religious dialogue and philosophical debates between the scholars of the various schools. In the relatively recent past, the advances of Islam in the subcontinent has given rise to violent conflicts and India's long-established tradition of the multifaith dialogue has suffered some serious setbacks.

By now, most of the world has come to terms with religious pluralism and is seeking an open dialogue not only with other sects but also with other religious traditions. All modern urban centers from New Delhi to New York, Tokyo to Toronto and London to Los Angeles are fast becoming religiously pluralistic in a significant proportion. Different communities in these centers are discovering that instead of an excuse for hostility and irrational hatred, religious differences can be celebrated as opportunities for intimate dialogue, increased appreciation of one's own spiritual heritage and awarenes of the global diversity.

This transition from violent religious conflicts to peaceful dialogue has already boosted the cause of 'common good.' For those who want to 'do something,' the effectiveness of shifting gears from violence to dialogue, or from shaming others to respecting their view points should be self-evident. Our understanding of the root cause of contemporary issues as 'passions' (*kasayas*), and appreciation of the effectiveness of shifting from violent conflicts to peaceful dialogue, enables us to suggest that Jains could play an important role in the global effort to resolve the contemporary issues. Thanks to Jainism's continued commitment to the Triple 'A's (*ahimsa*, *anekantavada* and *aparigraha*), the Jain tradition of nonviolence and recognition of multiplicity of viewpoints has endowed them with the skills in nonconfrontational multifaceted dialogue. Jains have now an opportunity and obligation to provide valuable insights to the newly emerging worldwide multifaith movement.

13

13. The New Spirituality

In the previous chapter we mentioned that the loss of traditional 'spiritual values' is one of the problems confronting our modern society, and we questioned if contemporary thinkers should worry at all about this loss. Such a rhetorical question cannot be answered unless we understand the term spirituality, how it has changed over the years, how present generation views this term, and how the term is likely to continue evolving further.

Spirituality

The concept of spirituality has been changing throughout the human history, and will continue to do so in the future. Many religious ideas originated with some exceptional individuals who were seeking sources of happiness and self-identity. These individuals designed many ethical 'codes of conduct' to help fellow humans achieve their happiness and full potential through good social behavior. Such codes, designed for the full development of human personality, represented true spirituality. Observance of such codes for the benefit of human beings, largely defined their spiritual behavior. People seeking happiness grouped around these exceptional individuals and organized themselves into different religions.

Soon a new class of people sprang up to help ordinary men observe the codes of behavior and lead a spiritual life. This was the class of holy men, the priests, the monks, the *mullahs*, and the rabbis - the new leaders of society,. It was now their responsibility to lead the flock on the path of spirituality and thus to keep the society happy. Unfortunately, ordinary people sometimes did not follow the codes laid down by their leaders, and at times, even challenged their authority. Such a challenge was, of course, unacceptable to the leaders who then reacted by issuing a series of pronouncements. The so-called 'codes of conduct' thus gradually

changed into the 'laws of behavior.' These laws were often full of contradictions, containing insights which pointed to the full human development, but also controlling human behavior according to class, caste, function, sex and so on. The 'laws' needed to be enforced. Therefore, enforcement mechanisms and grim sanctions such as excommunication, physical punishment, torture, and execution, and of course, the threat of eternal hell, soon followed. Spirituality now took on a new meaning - 'observance of the religious laws and their authority.' The net effect of this gradual change from code to law was to restrict the full development of human personality. Rights of human beings, and even those of the state, thereby became secondary to those of religious authority.

Human Rights

In the West, religious authorities continued to enjoy this power until about four hundred years ago when science and technology began challenging their 'absolute and revealed authority.' These challenges helped redefine spirituality. With science's push for logical freethinking, and with the printing presses making Bible readily accessible to the masses, the faith-based religious authority gradually weakened. The term spirituality started regaining its original meaning namely, 'acts to help humans to achieve their fullest potential.' The state was the first beneficiary of this weakening, and managed to free itself from the control of the church. By the 20th century, the term 'modern state' was being defined as the one that is completely free of any interference from religious authority. As we enter the new millennium, the long-established controlling mechanism of religions has eroded - either weakened or declared illegal - human spirit has become freer and assertive, and the threat of 'eternal hell' is being lifted from the human heart.

The modern trend is towards personal responsibility to formulate and live according to one's own ethical principles and individual conscience. Human beings are becoming aware of their rights and are wresting control from their community, their religions, and their governments. Human rights are gaining primacy. Spirituality is once again being defined in the terms of human rights. There is a general recognition now that human beings have a right to follow the religion of their choice, act according to their own conscience, and worship according to their own beliefs. A government which tries to compel, coerce, or insist that its citizens must follow an official faith or else be punished, is itself ostracized by the rest of the world. Spirituality has now become secular, and full realization of human potential has again become respectable and widely endorsed goal with this reformed spirituality. The signs of this change - the emerging global spirituality of human rights - are everywhere:

The peoples of the United Nations have in the Charter reaffirmed their faith in fundamental human rights, in the dignity and worth of the human person, and in the equal rights of men and women.

Preamble to Universal Declaration of Human Rights.
United Nations General Assembly
December 10, 1948.

- Various international bodies including United Nations, The Council of Europe and as declared in the Helsinki Accord, the right of all human beings to freedom of religion has been proclaimed, and governments are charged not only to abandon any formal policies of religious persecution, but also to act proactively to protect human rights.

- Societies and governments are becoming secular but the religious fundamentalists are turning to desperate terrorist acts. Recent series of publications by the Southern Baptist Church in the United States, denigrating non-Christian faiths such as Hinduism, the blowing up of sixteenth century Buddhist statues by the members of Taliban in Afghanistan, and the attacks on World Trade Center towers and Indian Parliament by Moslem fundamentalists must be viewed as desperate acts.

- There is a growing dialogue between the religions and interfaith movement, and it appears to be gaining momentum.

- Buddhist, Christian, Hindu, Islamic, Jain, Jewish, Shinto, Taoist - all scriptures are now translated and made available through electronic media. Different religious groups are exploring each other's scriptures.

- Religious leaders are getting worldwide audiences. For example, the convening of Parliaments of Religions in 1893, and 1993 in Chicago, and "*Sarva-Dharma-Sammelan*" held in Banglore, India, in August 1993. At the 1893 Chicago parliament each of other speakers had spoken of his God and his sect. However, Vivekananda the Hindu representative spoke of "all their Gods and embraced them all in the Universal Being,"[18] and Virchand Gandhi - the Jain representative - spoke of each one in the audience as a sacred soul capable of liberation to the godly state.[19]

---

18 Romain Rolland, The Life of Vivekananda and the Universal Gospel, Advita Ashram, 1965, pp. 36-8.

19 Gandhi V.R., Religion and Philosophy of the Jains, edited by Nagin Shah, Jain International, Ahmedabad, 1993.

- During the 2nd Vatican Council of 1962-65, the Catholic Church finally withdrew their charge of 'deicide' - killing of God - against the Jews. (However, the 'Doctrine of Papal Infallibility" - 1st Vatican, 1870 - was not revoked, and in the year 2000 Vatican seems to have reversed some of the progressive gains made in the 2nd Vatican Council.)

- All scriptures are increasingly coming under scientific scrutiny. Even the Catholic Church, which was opposed to such scrutiny of the 'Divine Revelation,' finally authorized it in 1943. Reformed schools of Judaism are similarly scrutinizing Jewish canon. Islamic theologians are still holding back, either asserting that all the ideas of modernity are embedded in the Koran, or else rejecting modernity as Western decadence. Buddhists, Hindus, and Jains have never claimed divine revelation for their canon. These being the works of their 'enlightened teachers' have always been open to scrutiny. Scrutiny makes religious claims to 'divine revelation' increasingly indefensible.

In the early 20th century a Jesuit priest, Teilhard de Chadrin (1881 - 1953), and a Hindu mystic, Sri Aurobindo (1872 - 1950) both suggested that general level of human consciousness changes from time to time, and therefore, celestial forms emanate from God in the form of prophets and *avatars* to take care of human beings. Krishna, believed to be an *avatar* of Lord Vishnu says:

To protect men of virtue and to destroy men who do evil, to set the standard of sacred duty, I appear on this earth, in age after age. - *(Bhagavad-Gita 4:8)*

Tielhard and Aurobindo's concept is too anthrocentric and implies that God does not care for the plight of his other creations. It ignores even the rights of survival for other living forms e.g. animals and plants. Furthermore, this concept still allows human lapses in responsibility, to be passed on to God, and leaves religious authority in control of human spirit. Nevertheless, though not a full recognition of a reformed spirituality, Aurobindo and Teilhard's concept is a step away from the religious claims to absolute truth, and towards human rights.

New Spirituality

Restoration of human rights is only one facet of the new spirituality. The emerging global spirituality is multidimensional. It encompasses the care and well being of our immediate universe and recognizes the interdependence of humans and their surroundings. Human interests cannot be served without caring for all living beings, our ecosystem, and our planet. An ethic of personal responsibility, concern for social justice, personal fulfillment, and human empowerment has now become the important dimensions of human spirit. The modern thinkers want major social institutions like religions and governments to recognize these aspects of the human spirit. Neither do they want to return to the dark ages of unquestioned obedience, nor do they ask total freedom to pursue unconscionable instant gratification. They feel that the traditional religious focus on 'afterlife' only, as well as science and technology's focus on living 'life for today and now,' are both unacceptable extremes. Instead, they want a balanced blend of concerns for life on earth here and now, as well as for the afterlife. The spirituality that draws forth their reserves of reverence and awe, promotes faith without restricting rationality and freedom of human mind. It recognizes the rights of all living beings, acknowledges universe as a self-sustaining entity, appreciates efforts to preserve the magnificence of our immediate as well as distant universe, and prepares a mindset for personal and global peace. These dimensions define new spirituality.

Coming back to the complaint about the loss of spirituality and whether or not a contemporary thinker should worry about it, we can now respond to the complainant by asking, "Which spirituality are you talking about?" I believe that the spirituality is well and alive. It is, in fact, thriving and in focus for contemporary thinkers and youth around the world. Those who complain about the falling attendance at the churches, mosques, and temples need to realize that the spirituality no longer resides in these buildings. The high priests of the new spirituality are busy working with the poor and homeless, with the ecologists who want to preserve our forests and ecosystems, with the peace activists who are trying to save our planet, and with those who are putting their lives on line to save the lives of all other beings.

The saints of the 21st century generation are the nuns who tend to the dying in the streets of Kolkata (Calcutta), to the blind and sick in Rajgir, and the earthquake afflicted in India. 'Doctors Without Borders' who rush from crisis to crisis to bring relief to disaster stricken individuals around the globe; the hundreds of martyrs who sacrificed their lives in the Tiannanman Square in China; volunteers who put their lives on line to save the street children in Brazil; and those who face the teargas and plastic bullets so that millions of dispossessed and disfranchised around the globe can be spared from the ravages of corrupt politicians and greedy multinationals - these are the high priests of the

The new spirituality draws forth reserves of reverence and awe from the contemporary thinker, promotes faith without restricting rationality and freedom of human thought, recognizes the rights of all living beings, acknowledges universe as a self-sustaining entity, appreciates efforts to preserve the magnificence of our planet, and prepares a mindset for personal and global peace.

new spirituality. We may or may not approve their methods, but their spirituality is dynamic, well, and alive ! The 21st century thinkers have not only gone back to the original roots of spirituality but are also expanding its scope to include all other living beings, our ecosystem and our planet. The new kind of spiritual action demands a commitment to emulate Buddha, Christ, Mahavira, or Mohamed, who cared so deeply for the poor and the afflicted. Just believing in them and seeking personal liberation is not enough.

Major religions have already started responding to this new spirituality by de-emphasizing doctrines concerning God, creation, sin, incarnation, redemption, or damnation, and by laying greater stress on concerns of humanity. For example, since the late nineteenth and early twentieth century, Christianity (and to some extent Islam) has started offering humanitarian services such as chaplaincy services in hospitals and prisons, marriage and family guidance, drug and alcohol addiction rehabilitation, sexual abuse counseling, and ecumenism and interfaith affairs, etc. (Although in the 1980s, the Worker-Priest Movement and Liberation Theology Movement were condemned by Pope John Paul II and the leading Vatican theologians, perhaps for political reasons.)

Jain Spirituality

Right from its inception, and certainly since its revival in 600 BCE. by Mahavira, Jainism has championed an all-inclusive spirituality. Development of human potential has no doubt been its main concern, but the welfare and happiness of all living forms has been equally important. Like other religions, Jains too established a code of conduct, but they never allowed it to be changed to 'laws' of comportment. Consequently, Jains never found it necessary to institute any debilitating enforcement mechanism for its code of conduct (*samyak-charitra*). Mahavira's code of conduct still defines Jain spirituality. While Jainism certainly teaches ethical values, the individual is left considerable freedom in his moral comportment, and is subject to neither the moral censure nor the threats with which morality is reinforced in other religions. Taking vows and observing the code without the fear of external sanctions is Jain spirituality. Enabling human spirit to become free and blissful is Jain spirituality. To critically examine the core principles of conduct viz.: *ahimsa*, *aparigraha*, and *anekantavada*, and then to act according to your own free will and conscience is Jain spirituality.

The Jain spirituality blends an experience-based worldview of the universe as a reality, a rational cause and effect based theory of karma, a soul based spirituality, a code of conduct that reveres all life, and a lifestyle that preserves our ecosystems, respects differing viewpoints and thus promotes personal and global peace.

In practical terms these Triple 'A's are the highest criteria for judging relationships between living beings and for reconciling extreme alternatives. They are the parameters of universal peace, which shaped Mahavira's movement. The observance of these parameters is left entirely to the conscience of the individual. The Jain spirituality blends an experience-based worldview of the universe as a reality, a rational cause and effect based theory of *karma*, a soul based spirituality, a code of conduct that reveres all life, and a lifestyle that preserves our ecosystems, respects differing viewpoints and thus promotes personal and global peace. The 8,500-year-old* concept of Jain philosophy thus meets all the spiritual demands of the modern mind.

Ahimsa in the Jain tradition is much more sophisticated and intellectual than the ordinary term 'nonviolence' or 'non-killing' would imply. The term is spiritual in the sense that it concerns the sanctity and liberation of souls. Since all living beings have souls that are potentially equal according to Jainism, hurting or killing any living being is damaging, not only to the lives we hurt but also spiritually to us who commit violence. This is so because the spiritual sanctity of our soul has been violated and we the offenders have thereby reduced our chances for the liberation of our own soul. This kind of reasoning is used by the *Tirthankaras* for their advice that we must refrain from not only the physical act of killing or hurting, but also from verbal and mental act of talking ill or even thinking ill of any other living being. The Jain focus on *ahimsa* is really a focus on the soul, and is thus spiritual. In modern terminology, it defines spirituality not only as human rights, but also as the rights of all living beings, including plants and animals, and recommends profound care of our environment and universe.

The Jain focus on ahimsa is really a focus on the soul, and thus spiritual. In modern terminology, it defines spirituality not only as human rights, but also as the rights of all living beings, including plants and animals

With the current multi-faith movement, a non-confrontational interfaith dialogue has become important because it acknowledges the right of another human being to express his spiritual beliefs. The doctrine of *anekantavada* is a Jain tool for interfaith dialogue and debate. Jains have used it for centuries to promote peace and harmony between different ideologies. It has been hailed by some commentators as demonstrating a very tolerant intellectual orientation. Another related tool - *syadvada* (the doctrine of qualified assertion) - is for tolerant practical orientation. Jains use this in interfaith dialogues to demonstrate that they have understood the opposing ideology, have critically examined it, and could accept it as valid 'from a certain perspective' of

* See Chapter 18: Jainism Before Mahavira.

their rivals. Such non-confrontational, qualified assertion of the opponent's ideas avoids conflicts and promotes further dialogue. *Ahimsa*, *anekantavada,* and *syadvada* are thus three of the many Jain doctrines that meet the critical demand of the new spirituality.

The modern concept of spirituality will continue to evolve. It took nearly four hundred years for human rights to emerge from under the old authority structure. Now as we enter the new millennium the increased interfaith dialogue would help define the new spirituality to include not only human rights, and the right to life for plants and animals, but also all the other dimensions mentioned above. The fast growing global movements such as animal rights, environmental, peace, etc., are the welcome indicators of this evolving concept of spirituality.

The New Spirituality and Contemporary Jains

Jains are justifiably proud of their doctrines of *ahimsa*, *anekantavada*, *syadvada*, etc. and are quick to point out that the new spirituality is the vindication of these doctrines, which form the basis of Jain spirituality. At a time when other religions are bemoaning the loss of traditional spirituality and struggling to respond to the demands of the modern thinkers, Jain intellectuals may take comfort in their own philosophical heritage. They could, rather smugly, claim that theirs is a philosophy, which has stood firmly for everyone's rights, for ecology, for social justice, for peace and happiness. However, regardless of how beautiful the philosophy may be, its effectiveness can be judged only by evaluating how contemporary Jains have responded to the changing demands and have put it into practice for the betterment of humanity.

There is a tendency among some Jains - lay as well as ascetics - to interpret *karma* theory and the ascetic's vows as an invitation to passivity with regards to the social justice issues. Jainism, they argue, is a world-renouncing religion, and Jain monks or nuns have renounced the world in favor of personal liberation, and therefore, must abandon worldly concerns such as wars, poverty, human rights and environmental degradation. Getting involved with service to humanity, physical and material well being of fellow human beings, etc. would only increase, they claim, their 'attachment' to worldly things. Attachment being one of the major causes of karmic bondage, passive detachment from such issues is what they prefer. Such a convoluted logic and justification of apathy not only makes a mockery of Jain principles but is also an outright insult to the very *Tirthankaras* whose teachings they are supposed to be following. After all, the *Tirthankaras*, instead of withdrawing after achieving their personal omniscience, spent the lifetime preaching their path and the message for the benefit of fellow human beings. Furthermore, even the *karma* theory promotes social justice by introducing the concept of auspicious (*punya*) and inauspicious (*papa*) *karma*. Contemporary Jains would do well by questioning the convoluted understanding of their co-religionists.

Falling attendance at temples is a Jain phenomenon too ! Jains who complain about it should ask themselves whether they, their *Societies*, their ascetics, and their temples are in tune with the new spirituality. Theirs is a beautiful philosophy whose focus is on the human mind. The new spirituality requires self-discipline to bring about a shift in human mindset - a shift to non-dogmatism and to non-materialism. The entire Jain lifestyle is designed to train the mind in self-discipline. *Anekantavada* and *ahimsa* are useful tools for conflict resolution. Jainism encourages rational thinking and rejects blind faith. Its rational cause and effect philosophy is in keeping with the contemporay thought. Co-operation, not confrontation has been a major part of the Jain tradition.

However, could such a tradition provide any inspiration to the contemporary rational mindset? Jains have a rich endowment and responsibility to be at the forefront of the new spirituality. Are contemporary Jains aware of the enormous power of social change they have inherited in *ahimsa, anekantavada* and *aparigraha*? Several internal debates on these issues could help bring their insights to the attention of the modern scientific world and help the community regain their lost glory. We will now examine how Jains have handled social issues, and could become effective in contributing to the solution of the issues related to the new spirituality.

14

14. The Science

The Debate

This is how it all begins ! Someone at a party casually claims: "Jainism is the most scientific religion."

"Poppycock," responds an antagonist, "just look at your model of the universe - a man standing with his hands on his hips ! - Universe really looks like that? Ha !"

"Ya...," another critic jumps in, "and you guys claim that your *Tirthankaras* had *keval-jnana* - they knew absolutely every thing !" How could they have even dreamt up something like that?

Such arguments sometime turn into a heated debate, both sides often skirting the real issue ! Let us take another look at the debate. The claim is: "*Jainism is the most scientific religion.*" There are two key terms in this statement, 'science,' and 'religion.' Let us first understand these two terms.

The bulk of knowledge that we humans have accumulated over the millennia is acquired essentially through two faculties, namely, Reason and Vision.

Science: The Faculty of Reason

The Faculty of Reason is based on observations, rational thinking, deductive logic, repeatable experimentation and verifiable facts. Modern science gives primacy to the faculty of reason. In the scientific methodology, vision alone is of a secondary significance because an imaginative vision may or may not reveal truth. The so-called 'scientific fact' must meet all the criteria listed above.

The process of arriving at a scientific truth usually goes through Descartes' reduction steps (page 79) of experience, experimentation, observation, logic, reasoning and analysis. Each of the conclusions arrived at also goes through a three-step process hypothesis, theory, and principle (scientific truth). At each step, it has to meet all the criteria of the faculty of reason. And, even after its acceptance as a truth, if ever any new observation challenges the validity of that truth, the scientific community immediately downgrades it to a mere hypothesis, and goes after a new theory. Science does not accept any statement as ultimate truth, no matter how distinguished an authority its author may be. Science accepts neither faith nor authority.

Religion: The Faculty of Vision

The faculty of vision is based on personal experience, imagination, intuition, revelation, mysticism, etc. Faith and authority have been the primary sources of knowledge in traditional civilizations. Someone would make a claim to a vision, a revelation, or a direct link to God. He would then ask the listeners to have faith in him, and would set up an effective organization to promote his vision or claim. Periodically, in an attempt to augment this vision, the faculty of reason will be brought in the form of a miracle or two. Such miracles would be then promoted as 'reason enough' to convince the masses that the performer is blessed with some super-natural power.

Most religions started that way. Once the message of the visionary is claimed to be a revelation, challenging that vision would amount to questioning the authority of God, and would be immediately labeled as blaspheme ! Unquestioned faith and allegiance become the cornerstones of almost every religion. Soon, religions frame codes of behavior for the followers, these codes then turn into 'rules,' and grim sanctions such as excommunication, physical punishment, torture, flogging, and even execution are instituted to enforce these rules. History of many religions is replete with clashes between logical free thinkers and religious authorities demanding blind faith. Such power struggles have resulted in many religious trials, inquisitions, and terrorist attacks or wars against the 'infidels !'

Jainism and Science

By contrast, Jainism started and evolved along an entirely different route. The first Jain *Tirthankara* - Rikhava - began his quest for human happiness, and quickly concluded that our own mind, not some external power, is the root cause of all misery and happiness. "How can I bring this mind (and thus this misery) under control?" he must have wondered. Like a modern day scientist he then began experimenting. Years of experimentation helped him develop a technique of self-control through rigorous discipline, meditation and ascetic practices. Like a modern day scientist, he then publicized his findings through his sermons, and asked people to experiment with his new technique for achieving personal happiness and peace. Thus began Jainism - the science of personal happiness and peace. Over the years it evolved, and was refined by twenty-three other scientists of peace and happiness - the other twenty-three *Tirthankaras* - who never performed any miracles, claimed divine revelation, or demanded blind allegiance. Some 2,600 years ago Mahavira, the last *Tirthankara*, reformed and preached this wealth of knowledge to his disciples, who then organized it into the *Agamas*, the Jain canon - the spiritual and scientific literature of Jainism.

Since the technique shown by the *Tirthankaras* required personal experimentation through ascetic practices, those wanting to explore the technique became monks and nuns. Their curiosity led these ascetics to explore many other fields of human knowledge, and over the years they accumulated a wealth of data in such diverse fields as astronomy, biology, medicine, psychology, ecology, sociology, and even particle science. Although judged as "scientific" because of their use of free-enquiry, logic and rationality, unlike science, the driving force for these explorations was spiritual - not material well being. It was the spiritual bliss they were after - not the physical comforts. They encouraged logical freethinking and experimentation, instead of unquestioned faith and loyalty to the religious authority. Instead of being hostile to the scientific methodology, they developed Jain philosophy in the true scientific spirit of free enquiry, which is akin to the modern scientific investigative technique of reductionism.

Obsession with logic has enabled Jain monks to develop ideas and concepts, which are comparable to those evolved much later by the modern science. Admittedly, without the experimental tools of the modern science, some of their conclusions may lack the required details or may be judged as 'inaccurate' by the modern scientific standards. However, the validity of Jain claims to 'being the most scientific religion,' must be judged not on the basis of the accuracy of its model of the universe, but on the basis of the fact that no other religion has tolerated, let alone accepted, the most important principles of science. These are: the openness to new ideas that stand or fall on the basis of validity and evidence rather than dogmatism. In fact, Rene Descarttes' 17th century 'reductionism technique', which forms the very basis of modern scientific methodology, has been employed by Jain ascetics to formulate their understanding of reality since Mahavir's time some 2600 years ago, if not earlier !

In many cases Jain monks and nuns have moved close to or beyond the frontiers of contemporary human knowledge, not unlike the modern scientists pushing the limits of knowledge. They made gains in spiritual areas such as soul, life, bliss and suffering, areas which are still beyond the scope of conventional science. *Tirthankaras* articulated properties, qualities, and inter-relationships of animate and inanimate substances, which make up the cosmos. It is surprising that very little in this ancient Jain science and philosophy is incompatible with the theories of 21st century science. Jain theories of cognition, perception and the nature of the cosmos are quite accurate in the context of the modern scientific criteria. Jain dimensions of the universe are comparable to those theorized by Einstein. Ancient Jain works include ideas and details such as:[20]

atomic make up of matter;
nature of elementary particles;
cause and effect concept;
existence of microorganisms;
plants too have life;
existence of extra-terristrial life;
link between mental and physical health;
meditation and mental peace;
dimensions of universe being comparable with those theorized by Einstein;
biological classification of plants and animals;
ecological principles for the preservation of nature;
theories of complex mathematics.

---

[20] Several works based on ancient Jain scientific treatises have recently appeared:
(1) Padmavathamma, "The Mathematics of Nemichandra Siddhanat Chakravarti", in *Jinamanjari*, Vol. 14, No. 2, pp. 68-76, Brahmi Society Publication, Toronto 1997
(2) Hayashi, Takao, "Geometric Formulas in Dhavala of Virasena", in *Jinamanjari,* Vol. 14, No. 2, pp 53-76, Brahmi Society Publication, Toronto 1966
(3) Bhattacharya, H.S., *Reals in the Jain Metaphysics*, S.S.K. Trust, Bombay, 1950
(4) Divyakirti Muni, *Visva Vijnana: Prachin Ane Navin* (Universal Science: Old and New) Ch. 5 of Tattvarthsutra (Gujarati), Sanmarg Prakashan Ahmedabad 1994
(5) Jain, B.C., *Jaina Logic*, University of Madras Press, 1992
(6) Jain, N.L., *Scientific Contents in Prakrit Canons*, Parsvanath Vidyalaya, Varanasi 1996
(7) Jain, N. L., *Biology in Jaina Treatise on Reals*, (translation of *Tattvatika Rajvartika* by Akalanka), P.V. Institue, Varanasi 1999
(8) Lal, R.B., *Religion in the Light of Reason and Science*, *Bharatiya Vidya Bhavan*, Bombay 1978
(9) Mehta, Mohalal, *Jaina Psychology*, Sohanlal Jaindharma Pracharak Samiti, Amritsar 1955
(10) Mardia, K.V., *The Scientific Foundations of Jainism*, Motilal Banarasidas, Delhi 1990
(11)Zavari, J.S., *Microcosmology: Atom in Jain Philosophy and Modern Science*, Jain Viswabharati University, Ladnum, 2nd edition 1991

We think of these as modern ideas, yet Jains have taught these for millennia. In fact, Jain scientific literature could inspire even more discoveries in modern science. Ecology, psychology, mathematics and medicine could gain considerably from research and understanding of Jain literature. Jain practices such as yoga, vegetarianism, meditation, fasting, and treating nature with reverence, are already gaining approval by modern scientists. However, Jain scientific achievements, in contrast to the modern science, are not based on a desire to conquer and dominate nature. The theater of its search for happiness is human mind - not the exploitation of Mother Nature.

Scientific explorations into space and the deep sea, and its promises of long, healthy life, and its offer of material comfort are exciting. However, the world bemoans the moral degradation, the pollution, the crime, the violence, and the urge to dominate and destroy. The Jain focus is on understanding, instead of dominating nature to promote self-discipline. Modern thinker rejects science's materialism, but he is also unwilling to return to the absolute obedience and faith demanded by the spirituality of the dark ages. In rejecting both these extremes, he is looking for - a spiritually scientific or a scientifically spiritual philosophy. The history of the development of Jain philosophy offers him a hope.

The Jain Promise

Imagine a world where science and religion work hand in hand to promote peace, happiness and complete harmony with nature - a world where we respect and revere every life - a Jain world indeed ! Scientific developments are not going to stop, nor should they. They need to be tempered by some moral and ethical values. Religions still have the power to reintroduce these values, but they must learn to work hand in hand with science instead of blaming it for all the woes and fighting it. Being on the winning streak, modern science is not likely to readily reconcile with the very religions with which it has battled for centuries. However Jainism, which has a history of harmony between the scientific and the spiritual, could blend the two. The contemporary world could do well to explore, and accept, elements of Jainism as a possible solution to its woes.

Jainism is a spiritually scientific or scientifically spiritual philosophy. Its message of the Triple 'A's - a*himsa*, a*parigraha* and *anekantavada* - is the need of the hour ! However, the Jains themselves must first undertake dedicated research and scholarship to understand and interpret their scriptures in the light of the modern science. Only then would they be able to convince the rest of the world that Jainism holds a promise.

15

15. Global Peace

We humans have waged more wars and killed more fellow beings in the 20th century than ever before. The 20th century has seen two world wars, a war in Korea, Vietnam, Chechnya, Bosnia, Ireland, China, India, Pakistan, Israel, Palestine, Iraq, Argentina, Columbia, and in almost every other part of the world. This was the century in which Moslems, Jews, Christians, Tutsis, Hutus, Serbs, and Croatians all killed their neighbors and friends in the name of race, religion, or color of their skin. Six million Jews were sent to gas chambers, and three million Hindus, Moslems and Sikhs were knifed or hacked to death during South Asia's struggle for independence.

In the 20th Century, the so-called civilized nations spent billions of dollars for building military academies to turn decent young minds into killing machines, and one nation dropped atomic bombs on another annihilating tens of thousands of men, women, and children in a fraction of a second. This was the century of human lust for power, greed, arrogance, bigotry, self-righteousness, and savagery. How can anyone be proud of the 20th century?

Now we are into a new century and a new millennium ! Will the new century be any different? Will global peace have any chance in this century? There are some hopeful signs, but the burden of our history is very heavy. The entire history of human race is full of wars, savagery, and unthinkable cruelty towards all other living beings. In the 20th century we have further improved our ability to kill each other more rapidly and efficiently. We have employed our genius in inventing and stockpiling weapons of mass destruction. Our wisdom has reached the depths of using passenger jetliners as weapons to destroy people and property. How then can we make the 21st century any different?

Global peace is a top priority for every contemporary thinker, but will peace festivals, street demonstrations, anti-nuclear protests, and pressures on politicians

There never was a good war, or a bad peace
Benjamin Franklin, Letter to Quincy, 11 Sept. 1783.

bring peace? Will speeches at the United Nations bring peace? Will sanctions, coercions and pressure from one nation over other work? Chances are that people and nations will continue to fight - and more savagely now than ever before - as long as human beings continue to be driven by bigotry, greed, lust, and ego. How then can we hope for global peace?

Root Causes of War

Wars have been with us ever since humans learnt to walk upright, and it is unrealistic or naïve to believe that analyzing the causes of war will stop us from fighting wars, nor are we suggesting that Jainism, or any other religion, has a magic wand to freeze the soldiers or the terrorists in their tracks. Nevertheless, a

Mark ! where his carnage and his conquests cease !
He makes a solitude, And calls it - peace !
Lord Byron, The Bride of Abydos, St. 20

close analysis of the soldiers or the terrorists in their tracks. Nevertheless, a close analysis of the causes would make us realize that a long-term solution is possible, that such solutions have been successfully tried in the past, and if applied widely can hopefully succeed in saving the world. Such a hope may appear optimistic, but giving up hope would be irresponsible.

Every war has its own special reason to start. In old days kings, wanting to expand their kingdoms, looked for a nearby weaker kingdom and pounced on it.

They make a wilderness And call it peace.
Tcitus 55 A.D.

Religious zealots organized military campaigns to forcibly convert 'unbelievers' to their own religion, and political ideologists built up worldwide alliances to look down upon the antagonists through the barrel of a gun. Regardless of the reason for starting a war, eventually the war stops when one party accepts defeat - not because it no longer believes in its original cause - but because it no longer has the strength and power to continue fighting. The temporary peace thus achieved leads everyone to believe that the use of power stopped the war therefore; peace lies in the balance of power - balance of terror ! A build up of arms soon follows, and peace lasts only until one party or the other starts believing that its killing machines are now better than those of its enemy.

Analyses of the causes of wars, indeed of all conflicts, reveal that the immediate, precipitating causes for starting wars may differ from event to event, but the root

causes are the same. Every party to the war treats its own action as 'just' or 'defense', and the enemy as 'unjust' or 'aggressor.' Certainly, senseless acts such as the terrorist attacks on New York's twin towers, killing more than 5,000 innocent people or attack on a nation's parliament, would generate rage and grief in any sensible human being, but is revenge the sensible response? Didn't Mahatma Gandhi - the modern apostle of peace - say, "An eye for eye would leave the entire world blind"? Was that the 'word of the wise,' or 'the idiocy of an idealist'?

Rage is a natural animal instinct, but human intellect lies in transforming rage into wisdom instead of allowing it to grip and over-power our mind. The adrenaline and energy generated by that rage should not be allowed to turn into revenge and further violence. A feeling of grief and loss when such events happen is inevitable but we must allow ourselves to transcend rage and step into wisdom. This may be easier said than done but it is possible to cultivate such equanimity at personal as well as community levels. It is possible to train our mind to control all our emotions through self-discipline. In fact, there is an age-old path that teaches us the technique of achieving self-control, equanimity and internal peace. It teaches how to transcend our emotions and transform them into wisdom. Without such wisdom conflicts will multiply, and we will destroy each other and our world. The wisdom, on the other hand, will enable us to truly understand and revere our fellow human being and the entire living world around us. Is this really possible? If so, how can this be done?

First Peace Movement

Some eight thousand five hundred years ago a man called Rikhava (known also as Rishabhadeva) pondered on this very problem. Moved by man's cruelty to man, he started, what may be, the world's first peace movement. He recognized that regardless of its immediate cause, *war really originates in the human psyche, and peace requires a massive change in that psyche.* He believed that bringing about such a change in human behavior may be a slow and arduous task, but it is not impossible. He believed that it is possible to train and discipline the human mind. Respect and reverence for life - not just human life but all life - can be etched into the human psyche, and a culture of peace can be developed through self-discipline. With this belief, 'King Rikhava' turned himself into a hermit and devoted rest of his life in pursuit of self-discipline and peace. Emerging from years of seclusion he, in effect, started a peace movement preaching that internal and global peace can be achieved through meditation, contemplation, and self-discipline.

Rikhava's peace movement survives today in the form of Jainism which is now a world community of about ten million people. Throughout their history, Jains have maintained their focus on self-discipline governed by a core code of conduct namely: (1) minimizing hurting and love for all living beings (*ahimsa*), (2) minimizing one's personal wants and possessions (*aparigraha*), and (3) minimizing chances of conflict by respecting different viewpoints as facets of the same reality (*anekantavada*). These Triple 'A's were developed by Rikhava, refined by Mahavira in the 6th century BCE, and have enabled Jainism to survive the turbulent history of India without ever going to war in the name of religion.

Peace Now

Jains have learnt that global peace is possible only through our own internal peace. Their triple 'A's - constitute a rigorously tested and refined formula for internal peace. They have succeeded in the formation of peaceful communities, but can their formula be universally applied for global peace? If applicable, it could be the planet's best hope for survival. Jains owe it to the world to investigate, refine if necessary, and bring it to the attention of the world. Global peace is a great burden, which the tiny Jain community may not be able to carry all alone. Jains owe it to themselves to conduct an audit of the community strengths and weaknesses in this regard and build interfaith alliances to revive Rikhava's peace initiatives. They have a very illustrious recent example to be inspired from. The example set by Mahatma Gandhi in applying Rikhava's concepts of nonviolence and love to political struggle in India has had worldwide effect. Leaders like Martin Luther King and Nelson Mandela have drawn inspiration from the Mahatma and have successfully applied his techniques to their movements.

> **Respect and reverence for life - not just human life but all life - can be etched into human psyche, and a culture of peace can be developed through self-discipline.**

All too often a question is asked, "Would Gandhi's *Satyagraha* and peace techniques of 1930s and 40s work in the violent world of the twenty first century?" The answer really lies in the question itself. If it worked then, why wouldn't it now? What has changed in the last fifty years? The real change has been in the culture and in our mindsets. During the past fifty years our mindsets have been collectively influenced to accept more violence. We need not go into the causes for this transformation, but the fact remains that the mass transformation of the mindset has happened, and is possible. Given this fact, let us imagine the state of our world today if fifty years ago we had consciously opted out for true peace instead of building war machines, nuclear stockpiles, and military academies ! Similarly, let us also imagine what would happen to our civilization in the next fifty years if we continued with our present course of violence and self-destruction instead of embarking, at least now, on a true peace mission ! In questioning the effectiveness of Rikhava's and Gandhi's techniques, we end up realizing the weakness of our own collective psyche and mindset.

Since the peace initiative is based on transforming the very psyche of the masses, our focus should be on the interfaith alliances. These could be very effective. Religions have great influence on human mind and emotions. They also have the means to explain the base dynamics of war and peace to their followers. However, could the faith leaders be persuaded to take the peace message to their congregations? Jains have a great tool in *anekantavada* with which they could patiently and peacefully engage in interfaith dialogues. Through such dialogues Jains could convince other religions to review their priorities. Would the Jains demonstrate the effectiveness of their Triple 'A' formula, and team up with major religions to generate momentum for peace?

Global peace is one of the major concerns for the contemporary thinker. It is also a component of the new spirituality. Young people in particular are desperately searching for peace. The stockpiling of nuclear weapons, increase in fundamentalism, and terrorism are making them desperate. This desperation is evident in street protests, peace rallies, and the number of peace organizations springing up all over the world. Even the United Nations organized a New Millennium Multi-faith Peace Conference at its headquarters in New York in August 2000. These protests, rallies and conferences have focused on the arms buildup and stockpiling of nuclear arsenals, but have had very little effect on world belligerency.

Peace Academy

Such a focus and agitation, may be somewhat useful in drawing the world's attention, but does very little for real peace. Since peace requires fundamental change in the psyche of the masses, the real focus of our peace effort should be on training and conditioning our minds to be receptive to peace. Governments spend billions of dollars annually on military academies to turn our fine young minds into efficient killing machines. We - including the peace activists - quietly pay for them through our taxes. How can we expect global peace unless this trend is reversed?

If Jains themselves are convinced of the possible application of their Triple 'A's to the issue of global peace, perhaps the first step for the Jain organizations would be to explore the possibility of developing a worldwide network of **Multi-faith Peace Academies.** They could use their expertise in non-confrontational dialogue (*anekantavada*), explain to their partners-in-peace that nonviolence begins with training, and self-disciplining, one's own mind. Rikhava's message that war is a symptom; greed, lust, ego, and pride are its causes; and our weak mind is the source of all these violent emotions; is not too hard to understand. Other faiths too have similar concepts. A genuine seeker of peace would readily blend these concepts and grasp the importance of training our minds, and get full control over our emotions instead of being controlled by them.

Can we train human mind to be strong and control itself? I believe that we can do so. After all, don't our military academies train and discipline the minds of our young men to turn them into fine killing machines and crusaders for war? Couldn't a 'Peace Academy' turn our youth into graceful ambassadors for peace? These academies could seek out peace initiatives in each faith and train people to become true messengers of peace by blending the Triple 'A's with multi-faith wisdom. One of the strengths of the Jain communities worldwide is their exceptional ability to raise funds for building temples. In the 21st century, Jains could regard Peace Academies as their new temples to honor Rikhava and Mahavira. Contemporary Jains, as a community, are often accused of lacking the vision, the spirit, the will, and the organizational skill to undertake a social project on a sustained long-term basis. If so, they can take the initiative and shore up this weakness through alliances with the major organized religions.

Jains already know and follow Rikhava's path. Confined to the borders of India, they have so far kept this path to themselves. Now they are in North America and Europe - the mightiest military regions on the earth. It is here that the Jain expertise for personal and universal peace is most needed. It is here that the ordinary Jains need to become peace activists. By working proactively in co-operation with the mainstream religions, these heirs of Rikhava's path can make a "Multi-faith Peace Academy" a reality and renew world's hope for survival.* By being proactive, can they not help build a culture of peace?

---

* The Government of Gujarat, India, at a Jain conference on December 26, 2001 in Ahmedabad , announced its intent to establish a " *Ahimsa* University". Hopefully, local Jain community would take initiative to promote and help establish first such university for peace, in Gujarat - the land of Mahatma Gandhi and home to majority of Jains.

16

16. Nonviolence and Vegetarianism

A Common Heritage

Almost every major religion preaches nonviolence. According to Jews and Christians, God says in The Ten Commandments, 'thou shalt not kill.' Simple and direct orders to the faithful! The Holy Koran of Islam preaches love, brotherhood, and kindness. Every one of its 114 *suras* or chapters starts with the phrase "In the name of Allah, the Compassionate, the Merciful." It teaches that God will not be affectionate to those who are not affectionate to God's creatures.

Upper caste Hindus, at some point in their history, abandoned sacrificing animals in the name of God, and adopted rituals of nonviolence. Hindu sages and seers denounced the killing of animals. Buddha, who was a contemporary of Mahavira, taught that desirable acts included those that abstained from stealing, lechery, and from taking life.

> *Nonviolence and kindness to living beings is kindness to oneself. For thereby one's own self is saved from various kinds of sins and resultant sufferings and is able to secure one's own welfare.*
>
> *-Mahavira, Saman Suttam: 151.*

Many religions advocate total or partial vegetarianism. For example, Christians are advised to abstain from eating meat during lent. Some Hindus follow a strict vegetarian diet, as do some Buddhist monks. Hindu, Buddhist and Jain scriptures repeatedly stress that virtuous individuals practice self-control, do not eat meat or consume liquor.

A disciple of Buddha shall not himself kill, encourage others to kill, kill by expedient means, praise killing, rejoice at witnessing killing, or kill through incantation or deviant mantras. He must not create the causes, conditions, methods, or karma of killing, and shall not intentionally kill any living being.
First Major Vow of Buddhism.

All scriptures seem to be essentially unanimous in denouncing violence. Scriptures form the basis for the ethical codes of every religion. If the message on violence is the same in all scriptures, shouldn't the ethical code of nonviolence be also essentially the same in all religions? Why then the difference? Why are Jains so committed to nonviolence that they will not kill even the tiniest of insects or dangerous creatures like snakes and wild animals, yet on the other hand, some religions accept the killing of animals not only for food, but also for fun and games? Why, according to some religions, it is all right to go to war and kill men, women, and children in the name of defending the faith - in the name of God?

Interpreting Scriptures

I think that the difference is because the scriptures and their interpretations often differ widely. Even if we accept that the scriptures are the words of the 'perfect' God, prophets, or that of the Omniscient Ones, the fact is that imperfect individuals receive them, and even more imperfect human beings interpret them. For example, three different versions of Ten Commandments - in Bible, Exodus, and Deuteronomy - and different interpretations - Jewish, Protestant, Orthodox, Roman Catholic and Lutheran - are currently available. Such interpretations shape the worldview and code of ethics for each religion. The practice of nonviolence and vegetarianism differs among different religious groups because those who interpret scriptures either lack understanding of true nonviolence, or because they misinterpret their particular scriptures and its concepts of the nature of the universe. Here are some examples.

I have a profound respect for Christian priests and nuns who provide selfless service, kindness and care to millions of poor, sick, and dying people around the world. Some even run animal shelters, or follow in the footsteps of such compassionate Christian saints as Francis of Assisi ! Almost every religion has some compassionate people like that. However, I am dismayed that some of these individuals lose their sense of empathy when they sit down at the table for a dinner of turkey, lamb chops or veal. How could these compassionate people 'enjoy' feasting on animals, or approve of killing animals in the name of sports? How could people justify, even to their own conscience, events like the crusades, the inquisitions, the jihads, the animal sacrifices, and wars in the name of God?

I raised the question about this apparent contradiction with a close friend a Catholic priest. The occasion may not have been the most appropriate one. We were having a dinner at a restaurant. I had ordered a cold bowl of fruit salad and the priest had ordered veal.

“Dr. Parikh, you don't know what you are missing !” The priest was the one who started the topic.

“ Missing? How can I miss something which I never have had before?”

“That's the point ! You don't even know what a pleasure it is to have a nice sizzling steak. It is heavenly !”

“Father, I am just an ordinary lay person brought up in the Jain tradition of self-restraint, and respect for ALL life. I really don't understand how anyone - let alone a priest - can derive pleasure in having an innocent little calf killed for his food. Isn't that calf your God 's beautiful creation like you are?”

“Yes, Dr. Parikh. God's creation indeed ! So is the rest of this universe. God created it all for our pleasure, our plate !” This interpretation of *“thou shalt not kill”* did not appeal to me. I lost contact with the priest for several years after that incident. However, during an accidental meeting at a pro-life rally he told me that he had become a vegan (a vegetarian who avoids ALL animal products including milk, cheese, butter, ghee, etc.) One up-man-ship was beaming through his chuckle.

Likewise, many Buddhists interpret Buddha's message of 'abstaining from taking life' as, 'Buddhist can eat meat but will not themselves slaughter animals.' They even claim that Buddha himself was a meat eater and the last repast, which the Master partook in the house of a metal worker, Chunda, was dried boar's flesh. (In the scripture, which describes the Master's death, the Pali word used can be interpreted as 'boar's flesh' or ‘boar's wart' - a kind of edible mushroom common in Northern India and Nepal.)

In Islam and Judaism also God's commands such as: “thou shalt not kill,” and 'be affectionate to all the Gods creatures,' is interpreted as, “our only obligation to animals is to give them a happy life and a painless death.”Such interpretation may have given rise to the practices such as '*kosher*' and '*halal*'.

Cruelty to Animals

How does one define cruelty? We are often told that the slaughterhouses use 'humane' practices in killing animals. What could be 'humane' about killing? Could killing painlessly a human being, just for our benefit, be justified as a 'humane' act? Why then toss thousands of two-day old chicks in a meat grinder, or cook lobsters by throwing them alive in boiling water, or take away a few days-old calf from its mother to produce tender veal for someone's table -- are these not cruel acts? Where does one draw the line? In the United States alone, the following animals are killed in slaughterhouses on an average day. (Source: J. Peder Zane: It Ain't Just For Meat; It's for Lotion, New York Times May 12, 1996, Reproduced in The Book of Compassion, Complied by P. Chitrabhanu and P. K. Shah, Oct. 2000)

Cattle	130,000
Calves	7,000
Hogs	360,000
Chickens	24,000,000

If we consume the products from this slaughter, could we really be absolved of the responsibility just because someone else - not us - killed the animals?

Jain Code

How do Jains interpret their scriptures in this respect? Violence and its consequences are very explicitly stated, as quoted below from the Jain scriptures.

Violence is always harmful and injurious to the perpetrator because it is a violation of his soul's path to liberation.
-Ayaranga Suttam, I.1.2

All living beings wish to live and not to die; that is why the wise are advised to desist from the terrible sin of injuring a living being.
- Dasavaikalika Sutra, 6/11

Knowing that all the evils and sorrows arise from injury to living beings, and knowing further that it leads to endless enmity and hatred, and is the root cause of great fear, a wise man, who is awakened and knows the reality, should refrain from such sinful activities.
-Suyagadang Suttam I.10.21

Even an intention of killing is the cause of the bondage of karma, whether you actually kill or not; from the real point of view, this is the nature of the bondage of karma.
-Saman Suttam, 154

As we can see from these quotes, the Jain code of ethics is based on their concept of reality. According to this concept, there are innumerable individual souls in the universe. In its purest form, each soul is omniscient, omnipotent, and eternal. However, all worldly souls are impure and undergo painful cycles of birth and rebirth because of their *karma* of the present and the past lives. The ultimate goal of each worldly soul is liberation (*moksha*) from this cycle.

Like us, plants and animals also go through this worldly existence and suffering. Regardless of their present form, their souls are potentially identical to ours and capable of achieving liberation. Therefore, they all deserve to be respected and revered. We humans are a species of animals with the special ability to think, reason, choose, calculate, and plan our course of actions. Unlike other life forms, we can progress towards liberation through rationalism - a combination of a rational worldview, rational knowledge, and rational conduct. Nonviolence is our rational conduct. We have a moral obligation to protect all life because we can make a rational choice.

What do Jains mean by 'violence' or '*himsa*'? It is important to note that the Jains have classified violence in two basic categories namely, actual hurting or killing (*dravya himsa*) and the intention of hurting or killing (*bhava himsa*). In our daily lives we hurt others - knowingly or unknowingly, intentionally or unintentionally and physically or verbally. It is easy to recognize this kind of violence, and often the victim of our violence feels the hurt and suffers immediate consequences. Even verbal hurting, such as insulting someone is easily recognizable as violence. These easily recognizable acts are instances of *dravya himsa.* However, how about someone who, while hiding his hatred, is sweet-talking to you, and praising you to your face? His actual act or words may not hurt you, might even be soothing, but his mind is wishing ill of you. Is this person performing a violent act?

Physical violence is invariably accompanied by mental violence of self undesirable thoughts and feelings.

Jain concepts of violence even include wishing ill of another living being. This is *bhava himsa* (mental violence). Jains consider this a more serious and potentially more damaging type of violence. Physical violence is invariably accompanied by mental violence of the self - undesirable thoughts and feelings. Our mental violence may or may not hurt another living being but the very emotions or passions involved in it will attract and bond karmic particles to our soul. If our ultimate goal is to free our soul from all *karma*, our mental violence works against it, sinks our soul deeper into karmic bondage, and in effect, harms us. Any action - mental, verbal, or physical - that knowingly or unknowingly hurts another living being, or violates our own chosen path to liberation, is violence. In the same sense violence is also classified as, 'pragmatic violence' (*vyavahara himsa*) and 'definitive violence' (*nischaya himsa*). Broadly speaking, *dravya himsa* is given pragmatic consideration whereas and *bhava himsa* is regarded as more serious 'real or definitive violence' as we can see from the following quotes from the scriptures:

A tiny insect may be trampled to death under the foot of an ascetic of restrained and careful movement. However, according to vyavhar, because there is no attachment or hatred (i.e. passion), no bondage whatsoever is created. Just as the sense of clinging to things, not the actual ownership has been declared in the scriptures as possessiveness; even so, it is only the passion that is said to be the cause of bondage and not the act itself if it is free of passion and laxity. -
-Pravacanasara, 3.16

Taking life away out of passion is violence. *-Tattvarthasutra, 7.8 or 7.13*

A creature may die or not (from an action), but it is a definite act of violence if the perpetrator has acted without restraint. Mere injury does not produce bondage in a self-restrained person acting with care and caution. -
-Pravacanasara, 3.17

Jains recognize that the process of living itself involves killing and destruction of some life. The air we breath, the water we drink, the food we eat and the ground we walk on, everything is full of micro-organisms. Violence is inevitable. The central determinant, however, is that we, unlike animals can make a self-conscious, rational choice ! Given the choice, could we not at least minimize, if not avoid hurting and killing? Breath we must, but can we minimize inhaling the microbes? Hence, some Jain monks and nuns wear nose masks. We must drink water; can we reduce the number of water-borne lives in our drinking water? Jains filter and boil their drinking water.*

TERMS TO REMEMBER

Bhava Himsa	Intentional violence
Dravya Himsa	Physical/verbal violence
Ekendriya	One-sensed organism
Nischaya Himsa	Definitive violence
Panchendriya	Five-sensed organisms
Sthula Himsa	Major violence
Sukshma Himsa	Minor violence
Vyavahara	Pragmatic

Recognizing the inevitability of physical violence (*dravya himsa*) in the process of living, Jains classify violence in yet another way. For example, ancient Jain philosopher-scientists classified living beings on the biological basis of the number of senses they possess. Humans and some animals possess five sense organs (*panchendriya*); some animals possess only four, some three etc. until we reach the lowest form of microbiological form having only one sense. While *bhava himsa* or intentional violence against any of these life forms is a strict no-no, the *dravya himsa* against the lowest form, being unavoidable, is permitted if we do so with due restraint and care. Thus physical violence against one-sensed organisms (*ekendriya*) is called *sukshma himsa* or minor violence, and acts against two or higher sensed living beings are called *sthula himsa* or major violence.

* Water borne microbes die when water is boiled. This is pragmatic (*dravya*) violence committed with the intention (*bhava*) to minimize killing of more microbes which otherwise would continue to multiply in water or in our body.

Vegetarianism

Our very act of eating food involves unavoidable acts of violence. However, we can choose to minimize it. By choosing to be a vegetarian, we choose not to hurt or kill animals. We choose empathy with another life which also experiences fear, pleasure, courage, love, dislike, and anger just like us human beings. Like us, animals also learn and acquire knowledge through their five senses. If we cannot be compassionate to such a highly evolved but helpless living being, can we really be empathetic with a less fortunate human being?

In this context Jains are often asked to justify eating even vegetables. Here again, the issue is conscious choice. The guiding principle is to minimize hurting and killing. Given a choice, we could carefully select foods with this principle in focus. For example, Jains avoid root vegetables because uprooting them likely involves killing the entire plant. The rainy season in India is the period when plant kingdom suddenly comes to life after nine months of draught. Every plant tries to complete its life cycle in the four rainy months. Hurting a plant during this growing stage is like hurting a growing child. Sensitive to the plant's natural cycle, Jains would avoid eating green vegetables during this season. Even fruits - Jains would rather pluck ripe fruits instead of the raw ones so as not to hurt the plant. Seeds being the plant's means of propagating life, Jains prefer a single seeded fruit (thus destroying only one potential life) to a multi-seeded one.

Finally, readers will find it interesting to read about an alleged conversation on the topic of nonviolence, between Lord Mahavira and one of his new disciples.

Disciple: I now understand my Lord that minimizing hurting and killing, is the supreme principle. I must therefore not kill animals and eat their flesh. However, if I should find an animal freshly killed by a hunter, can I partake the meat of such an animal?
Mahavira: Thou shall neither kill nor cause them to be killed by others.
Disciple: What if the animal had died accidentally?
Mahavira: That too is a forbidden food my dear *sravaka*
Disciple: Why so dear Lord? I have neither killed nor hurt the animal. It was a mere accident.
Mahavira: No, my dear *sravaka*. For man's lust makes him too clever for his own good. (That is, because of 'desire', he would cause many more 'accidents' to happen.)

The Jain scriptural definition of violence, its sub-classification, and the preaching that the intention of violence (*bhava himsa*) as the most serious act of violence, has had a great impact on the psyche of the Jain community. This impact has resulted in the formation of a peaceful community, which has adhered to the strict principles of *ahimsa* for thousands of years. It can be said that its doctrine of *ahimsa* has even managed to influence a majority within the Hindu religion in India to abandon its practice of animal sacrifices and become vegetarians. In the next Chapter we will see how this Jain concept of *ahimsa*, together with its associate concepts of *anekantavada* and *aparigraha* can be used to promote the much-needed social and economic justice, as well as environmental responsibilities in our times.

17

17. An Action Plan

The modern thinker is defining new spirituality in terms of a lifestyle, which cares for the future of our planet, our ecology, and for the rights, freedom and welfare of all living beings. To them a rational lifestyle (*samyak-charitra*) is to be active in the efforts to resolve the problems facing our civilization (Chapter 12). Since most of our current problems arise out of passions such as anger, pride, deceit, and greed, we suggested that the Jain system of dealing with these passions (*kasayas*) - through *ahimsa, anekantavada,* and *aparigraha* - could provide effective tools in dealing with these problems. We focused our attention particularly on nonviolence - *ahimsa* - (Chapter 16) because most of our problems stem directly or indirectly from our violent mindset. Let us take a stock of the ground realities about violence.

1 Nonviolence has become an important element of the new spirituality. As a result, many contemporary thinkers and social activists in various parts of the world have taken up the cause of nonviolence. Several organizations promoting vegetarianism and animal welfare (similar to '*pinjarapoles*' or animal shelters in India) are springing up in Europe, North America, and other parts of the world.

2. Transition from a violent to nonviolent individual or society, requires self-discipline and massive shifts in attitudes. The Jain spiritual path for self-discipline is an age-old tool effective in inspiring entire communities to adopt a nonviolent way of life.

3. Skills in inter-personal or inter-group dialogue are essential for effecting social change. Diverse interest groups could work together for social change if the arguments for change are non-aggressive, non-absolutistic, and made in a genuinely non-threatening and nonviolent manner. With a heritage of non-absolutistic philosophy (*anekantavada*), nonviolence, and self-discipline, Jains are eminently equipped with the skills needed for such inter-group dialogue.

The Challenge

In relatively recent times, leaders like Mahatma Gandhi and Martin Luther King have successfully used nonviolence as a tool for resistance to evil and violence, and to bring about social and political changes. Mahatma Gandhi took inspiration and guidance from a Jain guru - Srimad Rajachandra Mehta. However, as Joseph O'Connell points out, [21] "When we hear Jains and others speak of the Jains' influence on Gandhi, we may well ask if there has been reciprocal Gandhian influence on the Jains. In particular, is there any evidence that, through Mahatma Gandhi's influence, nonviolent resistance to evil - and not just passive nonviolence - has become a factor in a lay Jain ethics relating to public issues of major human import?" In effect, O'Connell's challenge to the Jains is that, "you commit yourselves - individually and collectively - to become the catalysts and leaders in a global dialogue on nonviolent stewardship of this endangered planet."[22]

Stewardship of this endangered planet is a challenge facing almost all religions today. Given the realities listed above, the challenge is more pertinent to the Jain community. Simply stated, the world is asking the fourfold Jain community of the the *sadhus, sadhvis, sravakas,* and *sravikas* a simple question: "Your long - standing experience with *ahimsa, anekantavada and aparigraha* could provide some solutions to the global issues. When you talk of these doctrines, are you willing - both individually and collectively - to help the world with these tools, or do you talk only in the abstract, whatever that might mean in practice?"

The world is asking the fourfold Jain community a simple question. "Your longstanding experience with *ahimsa, anekantavada and aparigraha* could provide some solutions to the global issues. When you talk of these doctrines, are you willing to help the world with these tools, or is that talk only in the abstract, whatever that might mean in practice?"

The Jain concept of *bhava himsa* (mental violence) is important for our contemporary concerns. Issues such as global peace, community violence, animal cruelty, ecology, etc. are all related to our mental attitude, our sense of empathy, and sensitivity to violence. Resolving these issues would require a shift in the mindset of a whole generation of people. It would involve sensitizing the masses to the effects of hurting other life on their own lives. Jain *karma* theory does that by emphasizing *'bhava'* or mental attitude as more important in determining the seriousness of a violent act. Such emphasis has guided the entire Jain community

21 Joseph T. O'Connell, "Jain Contributions to Current Ethical Discourse", in *Jain Doctrine and Practice: Academic Perspectives,* Toronto: Center For South Asian Studies, University of Toronto, 2000, p.215

22 Joseph T. O'Connell, in an address to the 9th Biennial Convention of the Federation of Jain Associations in North America (JAINA), July 1997

In to an empathetic nonviolent way of life. Jains now have a mammoth task of bringing this technique to the attention of the world. If they should succeed, they would have rendered the greatest service to humanity and to our planet.

An Action Plan

As stated, O'Connell's challenge gives an impression that the Jains are oblivious to, or have not been involved in, social issues. This is not so. Jain scriptures, for example, have repeatedly emphasized the positive aspect of nonviolence as universal love, helping others, or donating (*dana*) for social causes. For example,

> *The donor benefits (spiritually) by giving charity to the qualified persons (and causes)*
>
> -- *Tattvartha Sutra 7-33*

> *Even a small donation given to a suitable person (or cause) bears much desirable (spiritual) fruit for souls in due course, just as the tiny seed of a tree, sown in good soil, eventually gives magnificent cooling shade.*
>
> -- *Sravakachara 116.*

The scriptures describe four kinds of *karuna-dana* (compassionate donations) thus demonstrating concern not only for the humanitarian causes but also for the welfare of all living beings. These are: (1) gift of food, (2) gift of medicines, (3) gift of shelter, protection from danger, attack, intimidation, threat, etc., and (4) gift of books and/or useful knowledge. Jains are told that extending these gifts to all living beings contributes to their own spiritual progress, and is the part of their vows of *ahimsa* and *aparigraha.* This message has considerable influence on the community, and Jains are among the most generous philanthropists. This is evident not only in the thousands of beautifully carved Jain temples throughout India, but also in many educational institutions, charitable hospitals and clinics, animal shelters and hospitals, bird sanctuaries, pilgrim rest houses and free food centers for the poor - all built and run by charitable donations.

Jains certainly are serious with their compassionate donations: giving food to the hungry and poor, saving the lives of creatures in danger, distributing free medicines and spreading knowledge. However, the real motivation behind all this charitable giving is often a suspect. Just as non-Christians often criticize the charitable work of Christian missionaries in developing countries as "prosylatization - not charity", Jain motivation in giving is also often criticized by non-Jains as "donations - not to alleviate miseries of others, but to liberate one's own soul". Jains leave themselves open to such criticism because of the fact that historically Jains have rarely participated actively in social justice causes, except by giving generous donations. The new spirituality requires proactive physical participation in efforts to solve the social problems instead of just donating money. Volunteerism at the personal level and active projects in tune with the current global concerns would truly demonstrate Jain involvement with new spirituality.

Jains, particularly those outside India, are fast becoming aware of this new spirituality and a number of individuals are getting personally involved as volunteers with organizations actively working to solve global problems. For those who are wondering where to begin, given below is a partial list showing various fields of concerns in which, individuals, and organizations are trying to make a difference.

Regardless of your age, economic status, the country you live in and the community you belong to, such a list could help you find a niche where you could make a difference. Chances are that an organization dedicated to the topic of your interest may already exist in your area and you could begin to participate in it as a volunteer. Alternatively, if the field you have selected is important to you but no suitable organization - Jain or non-Jain - is present in your locality, you could start a new organization and motivate your community to be active. Additional information on many of the topics listed can be found on the Internet at: http://envirolink.netforchange.com/ Furthermore, for those who really want to be involved with these issues but are unable to find any support, I have given an "An Individual Action Plan" to illustrate how you can still make a difference.

In any case, with the powerful tools of social change they have inherited in the Triple 'A's, Jains could certainly take on the challenge mentioned above, work actively on these issues, and demonstrate to the world that Jainism - the world's oldest living religion - is compatible with the most contemporary concepts of new spirituality.

ACTIVITIES FOR COMMUNITY SERVICE

FIELD	ACTIVITY	MY CONCERN	
	(Areas of concern in which I can obtain more information and become active)	HIGH	LOW
Cruelty to Animals Issues			
Farm Animals	Factory farms, living conditions, use of hormones, ecological degradation, and ground water pollution.		
Dairy Industry	Milking machines, animal feed, calves, slaughter of male animals.		
Chicken Industry	Living conditions, using male chicks for animal feed, debeaking.		
Transportation	Cruelty involved in transportation of animals to slaughterhouses.		

Slaughter Houses	Slaughtering technology, use of animal by- products, economics of meat Industry.		
Working Animals	Farm animals; transportation animals - horses, camels, cattle, elephants, dogs; circus animals; animals in entertainment, racing.		
Hunting, Fishing and Trapping	Poaching, wildlife, endangered species, leg-traps, clubbing seal puppies, fur industry, trawling, whale hunting, fish-factories.		
Laboratory Animals	Animals in drug research, space research, animal dissection in laboratories		
Animal rescue, Shelters/sanctuaries	*Pinjarapoles, Goshalas,* building hospitals for sick animals, birds, etc.;		
Habitat	Forests, lakes, pesticides, ecosystems animal sanctuaries.		
Environmental Issues			
Agriculture	Soil conservation, leaching of fertilizers, herbicides, pesticides, etc. in ground water, genetically altered seeds, agriculture policy.		
Air Pollution	Internal combustion engines pollutants, industrial pollutants, alternate energy, sulfur dioxide and nitrous oxide levels, global warming, greenhouse effect, environmental legislation and policy.		
Corporate Accountability	Industrial emissions, chemicals in effluents, safe environment for factory workers and community, ethical practices, environmental economics, ethical investing, industrial waste.		
Energy	Energy conservation, solar/wind/geothermal energy, energy legislation.		
Education	Environmental education, neighborhood cleanliness projects, raising environmental ethics, consciousness and discipline among children.		
Forests	Rain forests, ecosystems, habitats for wild life, reforestation, human encroachment, clear cutting, biodiversity, and sustainable forestry.		
Genetic Engineering	Health issues, effects on marginal farmers in Developing countries, legislation.		

Green Design	Urban developments, city parks and playgrounds, planting and preserving trees.		
Ground Pollution	Chemical spills, pollutants in industrial soil, PCB, domestic waste, dump sites.		
Environmental Laws	Legislation and policies, enforcement of		
	environmental laws, justice, international issues.		
Water Pollution	Potable water, effects on aquatic life, water conservation, harvesting of oceans, leaching of chemicals in underground water, water tables, ground water protection.		
Human Issues			
Child Welfare	Orphanages, child labor, pornography, selling, children's' rights, run-away children.		
Human Health	Medicare, free/affordable hospital care, affordable medicines, air/water quality, Cleanliness issues, tobacco, alcoholism and narcotic drugs, childcare, mother's health, physically and mentally handicapped, long-term care, disabilities, old-age homes.		
Human Rights	Human dignity, racism and discrimination, freedom of political/religious beliefs, justice systems, rights of the poor and dispossessed, capital punishment, exploitation of people and nations, fundamental rights, corruption.		
Natural Disasters	Disaster preparedness, immediate/long term relief, fund-raising, volunteerism.		
Globalization	Economic domination of nations, powers of multinationals, unethical trade practices, flow of wealth from poor nations to the rich nations, and labor exploitation.		
Inter-faith Dialogue	Fundamentalism, religious riots, *anekantavada,* understanding different faiths, co-operative projects, Terrorism.		
Urban/Rural Life	Habitat, poverty, soup kitchens/food banks, literacy, appropriate technology, urban pollution, waste management, city parks and recreation areas, school systems, agricultural advances.		

Vegetarianism	Educating public, focus on cruelty to animals, sacrificial and ritualistic killing of animals, health, animal rights, vegetarian recipes and menus, Organizing and promoting vegetarian restaurants and eating-places.		
Violence	Violence due to: - living conditions, media, uneven income distribution, political situation, fundamentalism, gun-control legislation, and culture of hunting/fishing, Sensitization of public to violence. Violence counseling, meditation, stress control, *ahimsa*, violence against women.		
Wars	Arms race, nuclear issues, arms trade, exposing the underworld of arms dealers, national and International policies, promoting political debates, defense budgets and tax-revolts, inter-faith dialogue, Multi-faith/multi -party peace projects, Peace academy.		
World-cultures	Preservation and diversity of cultures, racism, tribal Wars, ethnic cleansing,		

The foregoing list gives us an idea of the scope of activities we can get involved into if we are truly spiritual in the modern sense. In some cases, Jain associations and organizations could initiate and run projects. In fact, JAINA - the Federation of Jain Associations of North America - has already undertaken some humanitarian projects, however, except for a few committed individuals, public involvement in these projects is limited only to donating some money. Direct participation by way of volunteerism and actual dedication of personal labor, time, and efforts is still missing.

Jain organizations worldwide can make considerable difference by nurturing and promoting the spirit of volunteerism. A prominent Jain layperson - Dr. L.M. Singhvi - former High Commissioner for India in the U.K. - brought this issue to the surface by issuing a call at the JAINA convention in Toronto, Canada in 1997. His appeal to Jains was to establish a youth volunteer organization called "Ecology Scouts" dedicated to environment.

Setup a new movement of Ecology Scouts in which boys and girls may establish an environmental program of education, outdoor activity, building up ecology trails, promoting tree planting, and preserving forests, wildlife and bio-diversity. I would like Jains to be in the forefront of this new worldwide movement, which will not be limited to Jains, but would advance the ecological and environment-friendly ways and perspective of Jains.

His Excellency Dr. L.M. Singhvi, High Commissioner for India in U.K.
in Keynote address at the 1997 JAINA Convention at Toronto, Canada

This call is perhaps the beginning of the Jain awareness of their connection to the New Spirituality. It may have inspired some individual response but for a collective action by Jain organizations and communities, a critical mass of awareness has yet to be reached. This could happen and Jains can truly be 'in the forefront' of the New Spirituality movement if such messages are carried, beyond the conventions, to the Jain masses. Fortunately, Jains do have the tools such as *ahimsa* and *aparigraha*, and also a highly efficient mechanism to carry these messages to the public.

When Mahavira reformed Jainism in 600 BCE, he organized the Jain community into a four-fold *sangh* of monks, nuns, laymen, and laywomen (*sadhu, sadhvi, sravaka* and *sravika*.) and mandated ascetics to be always on the move helping the laity in their spiritual pursuits. He also endowed the *acharyas* - the heads of the ascetic orders - with the exclusive authority to interpret the scriptures from time to time. There is a close relationship and mutual dependency between the Jain ascetics and the laity. Whereas the laity depends heavily on the ascetics for spiritual guidance, the dependency of the ascetic orders on laity for survival is equally heavy. This arrangement is a highly effective mechanism not only of adopting scriptural interpretations to meet the demands of the evolving universe but also to carry the message of change to the masses. Consequently, Jain *acharyas* and their ascetic orders could become harbingers of the new spirituality, generate the critical mass of awareness needed for activism in ecological, social and economic justice issues, and thus help Jainism recapture its lost vitality.

Individual Action Plan

We have seen in Chapter 2 that compassion and empathy for all souls is one of the characteristics of an awakened soul. Your urge to be compassionate and helpful to others is a sure sign of your spiritual progress to the fourth *gunasthana*. You may be dreaming of changing the world and making it a beautiful and happy place for all living beings. Perhaps, such a dream may be unrealistic and utopian, and no one around you is ready to share it with you. Nevertheless, you need not be frustrated because you can still begin to make a difference - if not to the entire planet, then at least in the lives of a few individuals in the neighborhood. A project described below would show how. This project -- let us call it "Compassionate Connection" - is simple. It requires very little funds, if any, and can be started by anyone - young or old, rich or not so rich, living in a city, town or a small village - anyone, anywhere, anytime, and you do not have to depend on anyone else !

Regardless of where you live, you are certain to come across a lonely, desperate elderly person who is in need of some help. Some may call him a beggar, some call him "homeless". You may even be walking by him everyday on your way to work, temple, or anywhere else. Next time you encounter him, try to think about your response. Presuming that you believe in *karma* theory, you could be responding in one of the four ways.

1. Your lazy response, based upon a very narrow (and wrong) under standing of the *karma* theory could be:"this person is suffering the consequences of his bad *karma*, he has to so suffer, and I do not have to do anything about it."

2. Your apathetic response could be: "the world is full of such wretched and miserable people, and anything I do is not going to change the world. So let me walk by."

3. Your generous response would be to throw a penny or two in his begging bowl and wash your conscience away in the hope that your *'dana'* (donation) has helped generate some auspicious *karma* (*punya*) on your way to personal liberation (or to a temple). OR

4. Your spiritual activist response could be: "my good *karma* have given me an opportunity to make a real difference in the life of this suffering individual and in so doing I will not only alleviate his suffering but would also shed some of my bad *karma* and accumulate some good ones."

In the truly spiritual response, what can be done next? How can you really make a difference in this unfortunate person's life? The "Compassionate Connection" project shows the way.* It is a five-step project for adopting an unfortunate fellow human being. In fact, the process really involves establishing only a connection - not a real adoption - and the level of it can be chosen according to your own comfort level. You can choose to stop at any level. In all circumstances, one should be careful.

1. The Greetings Connection: The lowest level of your activist response would be just to stop by this homeless/elderly/lonely person and greet him warmly. Do this daily, find out his name, and greet him by name every day, looking straight into

* Idea conceived by Mr. Ahmed Motiar of Toronto, Canada, and developed in co-operation with the "Interfaith in Action Group".

his eyes. You may or may not offer any financial help, and at first there will be very awkward moments because it is a new experience for both of you. The homeless person may have encountered several persons daily who would simply walk past him or would throw a penny or two at him, but the experience of someone actually stopping and showing concern may be new and unexpected. Perhaps the person you are trying to help may not appreciate this kind of intrusion, or may be suspicious of your intentions. On the other hand, for any personal reason, you may decide not to continue with this particular person, and may want to try with another homeless person. In any case, it is best to be open-minded and cautious about your approach at every step of the way.

2. The Chai Connection: When you feel comfortable with this person, you may want to move to the next level. It is now time to bring this person a warm cup of tea and something to eat. His accepting this is a sign of his trust in you, and now you can proceed to pry a little deeper into finding out more about him so that you may help him overcome his impediments. Perhaps he has no marketable skills, no self-confidence, or no education at all, may be he has family problems or problems with his health, mental problems. There could be as many problems as there are homeless people. Always remember that you are luckier and have less severe problems than he has, that is why he is there on the street, and you are not. Make a note of his difficulties and take your time to decide how you can help. If possible, talk to some of your friends who may have means and skills to help.

3. The Lunch Connection: By now you may have some ideas about the possible steps you can take to make a difference in the life of this homeless person. However, nothing will succeed unless your new friend has developed full trust in you and is willing to put some efforts into his own reform. Perhaps you have decided to teach him reading and writing, or to pay for his medical treatment, or help him find a simple job..., whatever your solution may be, it is now time to discuss it with your new friend on a one on one basis as true friends. Treat him with full human dignity. Decide on a day when you can take him to a nearby restaurant for lunch, if necessary, get him some decent well-fitting cloths, ask him to clean up and be ready, and personally escort him - walking shoulder to shoulder with him - to a nearby restaurant for a sumptuous meal. This may the first decent meal he has ever eaten but make sure that he feels himself to be important. Now it is time to talk about his future, making sure that he understands your plans and is willing to take its ownership. Listen carefully to his apprehensions, fears, concerns, and reservations of your plan. These may be trivial to you but they are very much real for him. Ask him how he thinks you can work jointly to overcome these fears, and follow - do not belittle - his suggestions.

4. Emergency and Stormy Day Connection: It is now important to monitor his progress along the plan you both agreed on in the Lunch Connection. While a smooth uninterrupted progress may be too much to expect, lack of effort or commitment on his part should not be too difficult to detect. Be prepared to provide occasional support to perk up his spirit. However, if you detect absolute lack of will and dedication to self-improvement on his part, you must take comfort in the thought that you have brought a few moments of joy to a fellow human being, and abandon the project. If your efforts are reasonably reciprocated and genuine progress is noticeable, you can, with full caution, decide to offer him further help. This includes giving him permission to contact you at the time of emergencies and stormy days in his life. You can now tell him where and how he can see you or contact you in real emergency. Explain to him why you had found it prudent to keep this information unavailable to him until now. If, in your opinion, he has progressed as planned, you both are now ready to enter the final level of connection.

5. Highest Level Connection: By now, your new friend has acquired the skill level, and has the self-confidence to attain the means of decent, self-respecting lifestyle. Now you can bring his full story to your friends and colleagues, find him a job, or raise some funds to help him start a small business, find a decent shelter, or reconnect him with his family.

CAUTION IN INDIVIDUAL ACTION PLAN

- Not everyone wants to be helped.
- Always be cautious never place yourself at risk.
- Whenever possible, be in the company of a friend.
- Abide by your comfort level.
- Do not make promises that cannot be kept.
- Exercise compassion, not sympathy.
- Understand the boundaries of your involvement.
- Make no effort to convert ones religious or political convictions.
- Giving money is not always the best response.
- Do not give your address or telephone number.
- Realize that not everyone wants to change his or her circumstances.
- Keep a personal diary of your connecting experience.
- Try to involve your friends, group, or organization in this project.
- Be prepared to encounter disinterest on the part of others.
- Be mindful of the spiritual strength you gain from this experience.

This was a small, individual project in the area of economic justice. You might feel that the project has not made even the slightest dent in the global problem, but in reality you have changed the entire world - the world of the person whose life you have rescued ! You may have also sparked the imagination of those who watched you struggle through this project. Who knows, to what heights the spirit you helped revive may soar because of the upward push you gave !

These details demonstrate how similar projects can be designed in any field of your interest. Is there any area in the list above that concerns you? Is it important enough for you to do something about it? Then you don't have to wait for someone else to come and help you start the project. If you feel strongly about it, and if you believe in yourself, go ahead and design a similar one-person action plan. At the initial stages you may face some ridicule, opposition and obstacles that might frustrate you. However, if your act is kind, honest, or sincere enough others would soon join you, funding will flow, and you may have started a quiet revolution. Of course, much of your energy would be better utilized if you could find an organization that is already working in the field, and you just join it. Alternatively, you could explain your concerns to your own organization, society, or friend's circle, and motivate others to participate. Jains have not only the obligation and responsibility to act, but also the tools and the effective mechanisms to successfully resolve the issues facing the 21st century. It is also an opportunity for them to plan, prepare and recapture their past glory. The question is, of course, "does the four-fold Jain *Sangha* have the needed vitality for such project?"

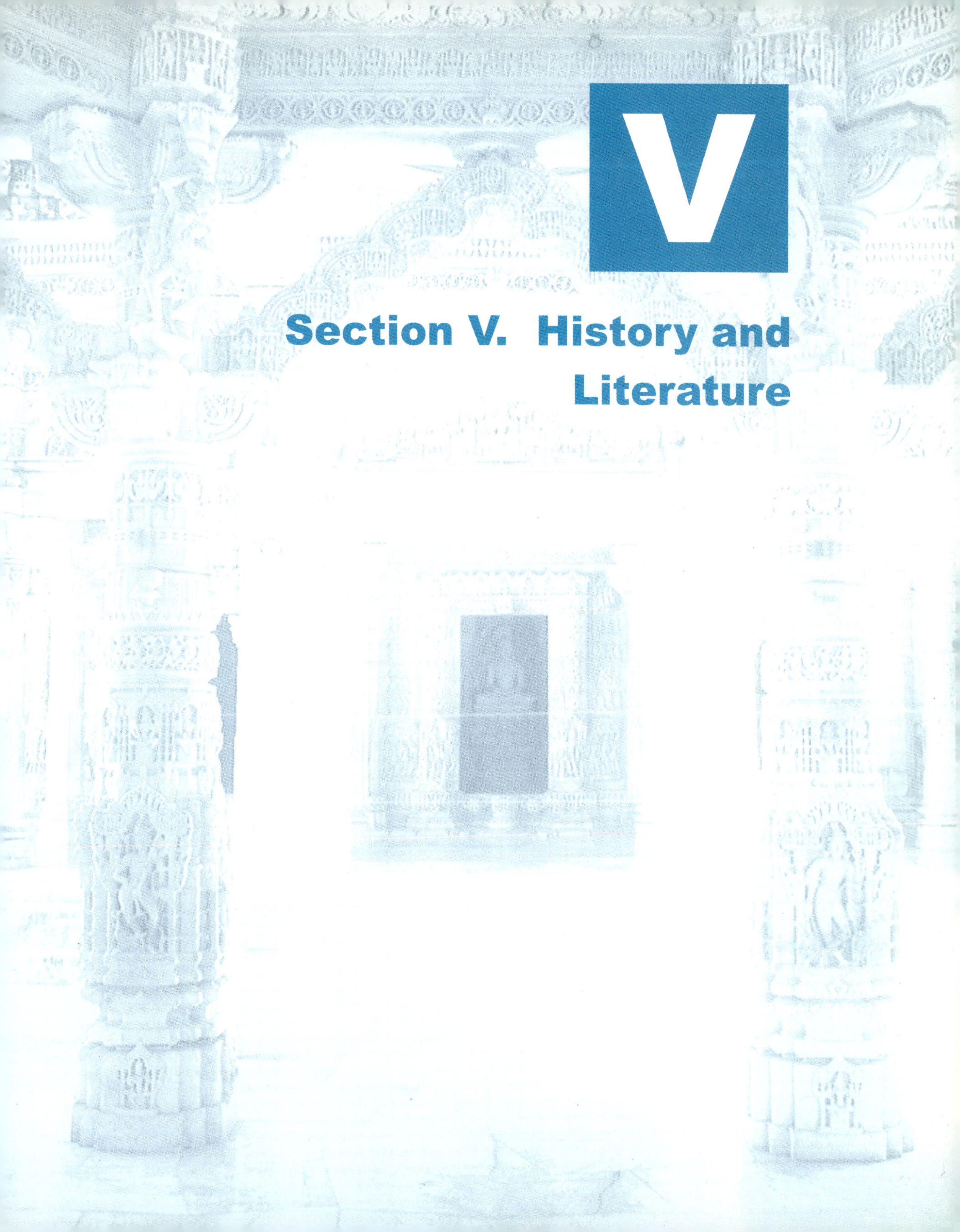

V

Section V. History and Literature

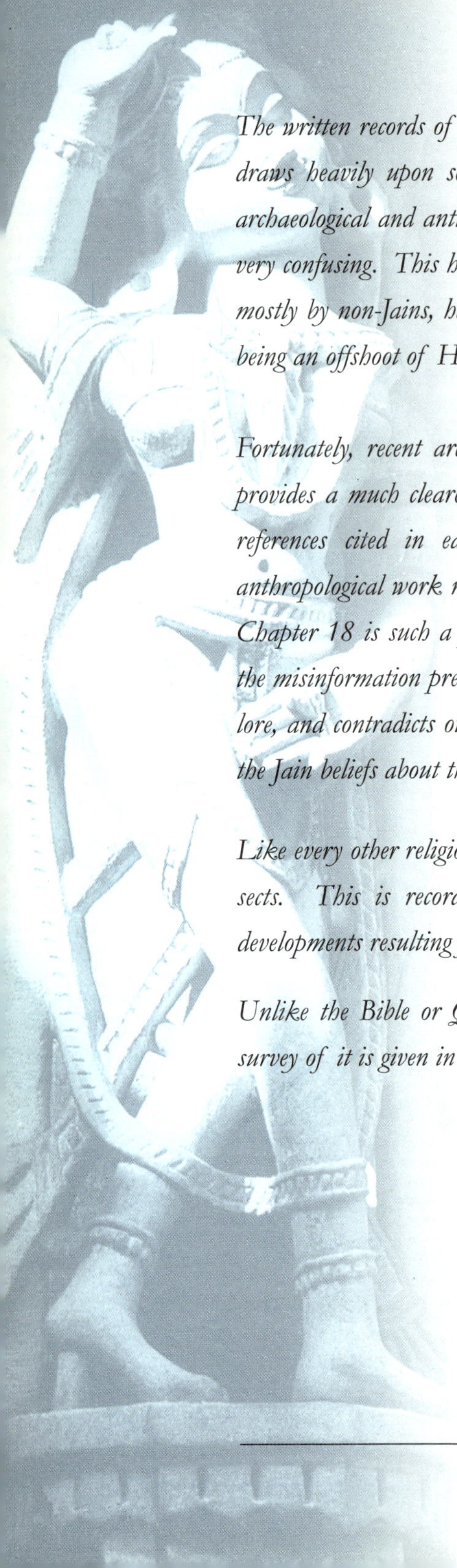

SECTION PREVIEW

The written records of ancient Indian periods are scarce. The history of ancient India therefore draws heavily upon secondary sources such as traditional lore, religious literature, and both archaeological and anthropological work. The conclusions drawn from such wide sources can be very confusing. This has been the case with the early history of Jainism. Erroneous conclusions, mostly by non-Jains, have varied from, "Jainism and Buddhism being the same religion, to both being an offshoot of Hinduism, to both being a primitive, animistic system."

Fortunately, recent archaeological research in Afghanistan, North-west India, and Pakistan, provides a much clearer picture of early Jain history. Integrating this research with Jain lore, references cited in early Hindu and Buddhist literature, and earlier archaeological and anthropological work now enables us to construct a much more definitive picture of Jain history. Chapter 18 is such a picture of Jainism before Mahavira. It attempts to deconstruct some of the misinformation presented as 'absolute fact' in many history books, confirms parts of the Jain lore, and contradicts other beliefs. However, this must not be construed as an attempt to negate the Jain beliefs about their past.

Like every other religion, Jainism has gone through several reform efforts, and has formed several sects. This is recorded in Chapter 19 -- not as acrimonious schisms -- but as healthy developments resulting from repeated attempts to keep Jainism true to its roots.

Unlike the Bible or Qumran, Jain Sacred literature is made up of many volumes. A short survey of it is given in Chapter 20.

18

18. Jainism Before Mahavira

A general belief that Jainism did not exist before Mahavira is both true and false. It is true because the word "JINA", from which the term "JAINISM" was derived, was coined well after Mahavira. However, the tradition and the philosophy that the Jains follow today, and Mahavira followed in his days, is far more ancient than Mahavira himself.

Jain Belief and Lore

Jains believe that Jainism is an eternal religion. This belief is in keeping with their fundamental assumption that time is eternal and cyclical, with an ascending and a descending period in each cycle (Page 52). The fourth division (unhappy-happy time) of either period produces twenty-four *Tirthankaras* who preach the Jain path of self-purification and liberation. Since there have been innumerable such cycles throughout eternal time, Jains argue that their religion is at the heart of this eternal cycle. They believe that we are currently in the fifth division of the descending period and that the situation for humans will continue downhill until our world ends catastrophically in the sixth division, an occurrence thousands of years from now, and marking the period of the ascending part of a new cycle.

Recorded history and archaeology are our only tools to verify any of these Jain claims. Unfortunately, these tools tend to be deficient in denying or accepting claims. Further complicating this issue is the fact that Jainism, being a minority religion, has received very little attention from historians. When Western Indologists started studying Jainism in the early 19th century, they erroneously believed that both Jainism and Buddhism were offshoots of Hinduism. This notion soon changed upon further study; however, they came across some parallels between the life-story of Buddha and Mahavira, and hastily concluded that the two histories are of the same person, and therefore, Jainism was only a variation of Buddhism. This error was also rectified in time, but left them with another incorrect assumption that Mahavira, like the Buddha, was the 'founder' of a 'new religion' called, Jainism.

It is only in the late nineteenth and early twentieth centuries that Western scholars took the study of Jain history seriously, and largely because of the pioneering work of Hermann Jacobi,[23] an impressive array of Western Jainologists have pieced together archaeological, historical, literary and religious information, to develop, what now appears to be, a plausible history of Jainism. Among them are Indologists such as J. G. Bühler, Jas Burgess, Carpentier, James Ferguson, A. Guerionot, N. R. Guseva, Hertel, Hurnle, Kuhne, B. C. Law, E. Leumann, J. E. van Lohuizen-de Leeuw, Louis Renou, Edward P. Rice, B. A. Saletore, Walther Schubring, Vincent Smith, F. W. Thomas, Albrecht Weber, Wilson, Maurice Winternitz, and Heinrich Zimmer. Indian scholars have also made significant contributions to our understanding of Jain history. Notable among these are: B. C. Bhattacharya, A. M. Ghatge, Banarasidas Jain, Kamta Prasad Jain, Jagmanderlal Jaini, H. R. Kapadia, P. C. Nahar, H. D. Sankalia, Chimanlal J. Shah, and A. N. Upadhye. Studies by these scholars support the claim that Mahavira, Parsva and Nemi - the twenty-fourth, twenty-third, and twenty-second *Tirthankaras* respectively - did walk this earth and preach a path to liberation that the Jains follow today. Nemi seems to have preached in Gujarat and to have been a cousin of Krsna, and Parsva and Mahavira have been verified as spiritual leaders in Bihar - Parsva born in c. 850 BCE, and Mahavira in 599 BCE. These three are the last of the present series of twenty-four *Tirthankaras*; the first according to the Jain tradition is Rikhava (or Rishabha).

It is the Jain literature that gives the details about Rikhava and his times,[24] about his birth, parents, achievements, and his reaching the state of *moksha*. Accordingly, most Jains believe that Rikhava was the pioneer of civilization, first to practice agriculture, and help a nomadic culture settle. He founded a social order, the institution of marriage and family, and the system of law, order, and justice. He abdicated his kingdom, renounced all worldly possessions, and lived a life of penance and austerity through which he attained omniscience. He preached that the root cause of happiness and misery is our own karmic bondage and that liberation from this bondage is possible through a path of self-purification by

[23] Jacobi, H.:(1) *Bhadrabahu's Kalpasutra*, Leipzig, 1879
(2) "Mahavira and his Predecessors," *Indian Antiquary*, 1880
(3) *Jaina Sutras Part I* (1984); Part II (1895)

[24] *Jambudvīpa-Prajnapati* a *Upanga* text forming the Jain subsidiary canon

means of meditation, penance, and austerity. This is the path that the Jains follow today and consider it to be the legacy of Rikhava - their first *Tirthankara* or spiritual leader of the present time cycle. The units of time used in Jain literature being different from the ones used today (e.g. years, months, days, etc.) it is difficult to ascertain the period when Rikhava preached, and therefore, Jains use the inexact term, "Rikhava lived thousands of years ago, and Jainism is millions of years old."

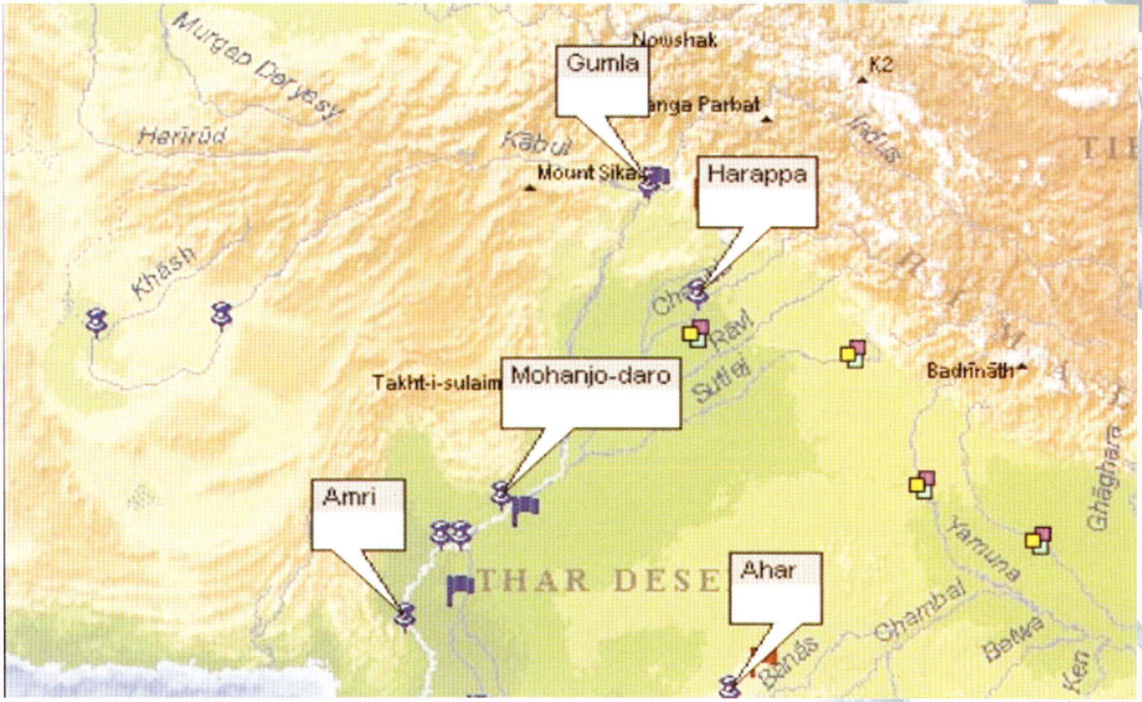

FIGURE 18.1: Some important cities in the 5000 years-old, pre-Aryan, Indus valley civilization.

The Indus Valley Civilization

Modern archaeological excavations, however, may provide some clues to the historicity of the Rikhava biography, his period, his achievements, and teachings. The food grains found recently in excavations in Afghanistan and along the Northern reaches of the Indus valley in Pakistan are carbon-dated to ca. 6500 BCE, and some archeologists have concluded, "The cultivation of grain started around 7000 BCE in southern Asia."[25] Perhaps, this is the proof of the earliest agriculture in Indian subcontinent. Excavations at Harappa and Mohenjo Daro in

[25] Kulke, H. and Rothermund, D., A *History of India,* Rupa & co., Delhi 1993, pg.5

India have also unearthed statues, seals and figurines in naked meditative poses - sitting in what appears to be a lotus position or meditating in a standing *kayostarga* position -- poses used by later *Tirthankaras* iconography, and unique to the Jain tradition even today. Based on these seals, some historians have suggested a possibility that a philosophy of the purification of soul by ascetic and meditation practices existed at least 5000 years ago during the Indus Valley period.[26] However, these conclusions have yet to be thoroughly justified.

The people of the Indus built cities, developed agriculture, fully developed commerce in conjunction with maritime navigation, formulated a script, and it appears, lived in a state of relative peace for at least 2000 years. Intensive archaeological excavations in recent years have shown that this civilization had as many as 1800 settlements encompassing an area of over 280,000 sq. miles (larger than Western Europe). Alamgirpur, in Meerut district in the center of the Ganga-Yamuna confluence, marks its eastern boundary, whereas Sutkagen-Dor, close to the border of present Iran, may have been its western out-post. Its southern borders reached as far as Lothal (near Ahmedabad) and Malwan (near Surat) in Gujarat. Rupar, in the foothills of Himalayas, was its farthest northern outpost. There is no evidence that these people ever engaged in aggressive warfare, but it is clear that they did have bronze weapons such as swords, bows and arrows, spears, daggers, and axes. Many large cities, like those at Harappa with estimated population of 80,000 people at its height of occupation, had surrounding walls; however, these walls do not appear to be fortifications to protect themselves from an aggressive enemy and may have served as possible entry checkpoints for commerce and taxation purposes only. Interestingly, some seals found in excavating these cities bear the mark of priests in remarkable detail, but few deities, as we would recognize them today are represented. There are, however, many clay figurines of 'goddess' images, and this would suggest a culture that has room for both a household deity religion, and a religion(s) that had a focus on a purification of the spirit (soul?) through some process of meditation and ascetic austerities.

What is quite interesting about these finds that - and this will obviously be controversial statement -- if the Jain account about Rikhava's invention of agriculture is augmented with the carbon dating of the earliest food grains found in the excavation sites of what is commonly called the Harappan culture, we could infer that Rikhava's period could be established as ca. 6500 BCE. This conclusion

[26] Kulke, H. and Rothermund, D., A *History of India,* Rupa & co., Delhi 1993, pg.20

is further strengthened by the fact that the Indus civilization had seals with images of a meditating person who, according to Jain traditional lore, could represent something akin to a 'historical' Rikhava. The controversy surrounding the issue, at least from a Jain perspective, is that Jains believe that Rikhava's period is much earlier than that of the Harappan culture. In other words, to suggest that Rikhava lived 6500 BCE places some tremendous pressure on traditional Jaina cosmology.

However difficult it may be to discuss or accept this historical scrutiny by the Jain community of today, they cite that in just one-century some historians have come long ways from not even accepting Jainism as a distinct religion, to fixing 6500 BCE as Rikhava's period. Jains claim that their religion is 'eternal' and thus beyond the capabilities of historian's craft. For the time being, this claim, like that of the Hindu revisionist's claim that the Harappan or Indus Valley culture was a 'proto-Shiva' culture, is an equally valid article of faith and should be accepted from that perspective only. Here is what we do know of the Indus Valley culture:

(1) Their civilization development included a social order, a system of marriage and family, law and order, justice and government.
(2) They had adopted an urban lifestyle with a well-designed public sanitation system. They used bricks to build large homes and well-planned cities as well as towns and villages.
(3) They had the ability to read and write. Their script is a mix of phonetic symbols and pictographs, and reads right to left.
(4) They knew land cultivation. They had artistic talent in drawing, sculpture, figurines, jewelry, pottery, and arts and crafts.
(5) They knew metallurgy of gold, copper, bronze, lead and silver (but not iron). Finely crafted articles were exported as far as Mesopotamia, Iran, and Central Asia.
(6) Archaeological evidence shows that they used offensive weapons made of stone and wood, but had no defensive shields, coats, helmets, etc. This indicates a non-aggressive, peaceful life style in which people did not have to go to wars. They were without a standing army. Not a single depiction of a military act, of conquest, of taking prisoners, or of a human killing another human is found. Human remains from the early period show no signs of violence.
(7) Their domesticated animals included bulls, cows and elephants but no horses. Their seals bore images of these animals, and were probably emblems of different clans.
(8) Intensive craftsmanship and trade enabled Indus valley culture to

spread over a region twice the size of Mesopotamia without a trace of military domination.

(9) Theirs could have possibly been a matriarchal society.

(10) Their spirituality included purification of soul through meditation. They believed in transmigration of soul.

A Moment of Speculation

Knowing full well that this hypothesis is quite speculative in nature, I would like to offer a plausible interpretation of the Harappan archaeological data I've outlined above. Again, it is a controversial interpretation, but one made in the spirit of opening new avenues of discussion, and hopefully, will provide some new insights into those cultural images that a particular culture projects of themselves to others. From a Jain perspective of the Harappan data, the people of the Indus Valley civilization tried to follow a path to liberation based on self-control through meditation, yoga, nonviolence, and other ascetic practices. From some of the 'seal' evidence, it appears that, these peoples worshiped images that we could possibly identify as Rikhava.* The statues unearthed at Harappa are remarkably detailed and show facial features, which are distinctly non-Aryan, but appear to be similar to those of one of the indigenous peoples of India - the Dravidians.♦ In this context, the evidence - albeit very limited evidence - demonstrates that these peoples had some reverence for an ascetic figure (the seal evidence) and when combined with a Jain oral tradition that describes Rikhava as being the first to introduce both meditation as a spiritual practice and such things as agriculture and a distinctively different social order to South Asia than that of what is called 'Aryan culture,' then let us call the peoples of the Indus Valley culture, 'Rikhavites'.

Aryan Arrival

The original homeland of Aryan tribes may have been around the Caspian Sea (a salt-water lake, land-locked by what is today known as Azerbaijan, Russia, Kazakhstan, Turkmenistan, and Iran. The word Iran actually means the Land of the Aryans.) Around 1500 BCE, they invaded the Indus valley from Central Asia.

* The meditative figurines of Harappa could not be of the Hindu god Shiva because Hinduism started after Aryan arrival in 1500 BCE. Furthermore, the concept of soul, meditation, etc. did not appear in Hindu sacred literature until much later.

♦ Aryans arrived in India much later in 1500 BCE. They subjugated the local people. Vedas- the Aryan literature refers to the indigenous people by such derogatory terms as *'dasyus'* (slaves), *asuras* or *rakhashas* (demons), etc. We use the term 'Rikhavites' because of their spiritual practices. The term 'Dravidians' was coined much later and is in use today for the people in Southern India. The features of the human figures on the Harappa seals, being similar to those of the present-day Dravidians, suggest that they are possibly the indigenous peoples of India.

According to Jain traditional lore, these invasions took place just after their ninth *Tirthankara* - Pushpadanta(fig.18-2). Although the 'Rikhavites' lived peacefully with their neighbors (this is supported by the lack of evidence for any sustained battles or wars), the nonviolent 'Rikhavites' had no chance against the waves of migrating, arms-bearing Aryan tribes. Most of the surviving 'Rikhavites' retreated eastward and settled in several small kingdoms (*janapadas*) along the Ganges, and those who stayed in the Indus region were enslaved by the Aryans, and according to their texts, called *'dasyus'* (slaves). In due course, the 'Rikhavites' re-established themselves in the East - in the present state of Bihar.

One picture of the Aryan life-style in 1500 BCE, and for a few centuries after that, emerges from the *Vedas* - the earliest literature they composed. It suggests that:

(1) Theirs was a rural, nomadic, pastoral lifestyle.
(2) They settled mostly in forests creating smaller new communities of bamboo huts with thatched roofs.
(3) They knew the use of gold, copper, bronze, and iron but not of silver and lead.
(4) Their weapons were both aggressive as well as defensive and were made of wood, stone, and iron. They used chariots, defensive shields, helmets, and coats of nails.
(5) The horse was their most domesticated animal and was used in warfare. Other domesticated animals included cows and sheep.
(6) They had virtually no achievement in arts and writing skills. However, once they settled in the Indus valley, they developed verbal poetry.
(7) Their spiritual development was limited to the invocation of powers of nature to bestow favors, and worship involving the use of fire and an exhilarating drink called *soma*.
(8) Their pantheon of naturalistic and functional gods had mythological counterparts in Iran, Greece, and Rome.
(9) Their religious concepts included neither soul nor one God. However, later they quickly assimilated religious notions encountered in the Indian subcontinent.
(10) In order to prevent assimilation with the dark-skinned indigenous people, they limited their religion to persons of Aryan birth, and fully observed the traditions of genealogical count, transferring the names of their own ancestors from generation to generation. This practice resulted in dynasties such as Solar and Lunar (*Surya-vanshi* and *Chandra-vanshi*)

One logical conclusion from the comparison of the Indus Valley and Aryan culture of 1500 BCE is that the *Rig Veda* culture (an evolution out of the Aryan civilization), although established later, was unrelated to the Indus culture and had an independent origin outside India. Furthermore, the facts that the cultural and racial characteristics of the urban dwelling 'Rikhavites' are different from the rural, nomadic culture of the Aryans, and Rikhavite religious practices appear to be closer to a proto-Jain belief and practice, gives more credence to the Jain claim, that the their tradition dates back to the pre-Aryan period when an indigenous people flourished in the Indus Valley in North-western India, and built cities like Mohenjo Daro, Lothal, and Harappa.[27]

Brahmanic Religion

We have traced the origin of 'Rikhavites' to the years of the Indus Valley culture based on the archeological evidence and Jain traditional lore. Their history during the 800 years after the Aryan arrival can be learnt only through the references to them in the Vedic literature and through the Jain lore. The Aryan immigrants composed hymns, which formed the basis for the new Aryan religion called Brahmanic religion. Their entire literature can be grouped into three groups:

(1) The Vedas: The process of accumulation of Vedic hymns was gradual and proceeded in the course of many centuries after the arrival of Aryan settlers in India. The four *Vedas* or (*Samhitas*) are (i) *Rig Veda*, (ii) *Yajur Veda*, (iii) *Sama Veda*, and (iv) *Atharva Veda*. They were composed during a period of ca. 1300 to ca. 1150 BCE. The Rig *Veda,* which is the earliest collection of hymns in praise of the Aryan functional gods (Varuna, Indra, Agni and Surya), refers to 'Rikhavites' as *vrata dharmi* (ascetics who live by vows) or *yogins*. The Rig *Veda* does not seem to be concerned with the basic philosophical curiosity about the 'meaning of life'. There is no evidence yet of the caste system, although the indigenous dark-skinned people are referred to as *'dasyus'*.[28]

(2) The Brahmanas and Aranyakas: Several expository ritual texts attached to each of the *Vedas*, are called *Brahmanas and Aranyakas*. These texts were composed between 1000 BCE and 700 BCE. In these texts we witness some insecurity, and skepticism of the mythical powers of Aryan gods. The *Brahmanas* and *Aranyakas* also mark the transition from the metrical hymns of the *Vedas* to

[27] Kulke, Hermann and Rothermund, Dietmar, *A History of India*, Rupa & Co., New Delhi 1993

[28] Dandekar, R.N., "The Brahmanical Tradition: The Vedic Period", in *Sources of Indian Tradition*, Volume 1, Embree, A.T. ed., Columbia University Press, New York 1988

elaborate prose stressing the need for sacrificial ritualistic offerings. "These magical rites must be performed exactly as prescribed, any mistakes would invite the wrath of the gods," we are told. This transition from mythical gods to magical rituals, and the need for the expertise to perform rituals as prescribed seems to have given birth to the caste (*varna*) system in which the ritual experts - the *Brahmin* priests - occupied the top social position.

Although meditation, yoga, and penances were not yet prescribed for the common man, some wise men of the Brahmanic faith had begun adopting the 'Rikhavite' practice of dropping out from the society and heading into the forests. Unlike the 'Rikhavites', however, their motivation was to seek magical powers from their gods through extreme penances. It is possible that that these sages, in their attempt to practice penances may have adopted Rikhava as their ideal, and in the process may have transformed him into Mahadeva (Great god), Shankara (source of auspicious and beneficial *karma*) and Shiva (Pure).* Nevertheless, these sages seem to have initiated a fundamental transition in the Brahmanic religion, from the mythical gods of nature (*Rig Veda*) to the magical sacrificial rituals (*Brahmanas* and *Aranyakas*), and ultimately to the mystical philosophy of salvation as seen in the later Vedic literature. "The world-view in the late Vedic age was totally different from that in the early period of migration. There was also doubt about the almighty power of the gods. In its place grew an increasing awareness of an immutable law according to which everybody was accountable for his deeds (*karma*) not only here and now but also in subsequent births (*samsara*). These two ideas of *karma* and *samsara* became the key elements of Indian religious life. They may have been derived from the religion of the indigenous people with whom the Aryans became more and more involved.[29]

It is interesting to note that in the great Hindu epic, the *Ramayana*, which is set in about 1000 BCE, the great Aryan king Rama, upon banishment from his kingdom, lives in the forests South of the Vindhya mountain range in central India. According to the Ramayana, when Ravana - the mighty Dravidian king of Sri Lanka - kidnaps Rama's wife, Rama invades Sri Lanka with the help of an army of monkeys (*vanara*) and defeats Ravana. Although, the use of "an army of monkeys

---

* There are uncanny similarities between the Jain image of Rikhava and the Hindu image of Shiva. For example, Rikhava practiced meditation, penances, and austerities; Shiva is the only god in Hindu pantheon that practiced these techniques. Jains believe that Rikhava invented agriculture and used bull as a farm animal, therefore they use bull as a symbol of Rikhava; bull is also the symbol for Shiva. In the end, Rikhava left the society, went into the Himalayas for his intense meditation, and achieved *moksha* on the top of the Kailash Mountain; Hindus regard Kailash to be the home of Shiva. Hindu idols of Shiva & Krasna are usually blue in color, suggesting their Dravidian (darker-skin) origin.

29 Kulke, Hermann and Rothermund, Dietmar, *A History of India*, Rupa & Co., New Delhi 1993 page 48

led by their chief monkey - Hanumana" - appears to be illogical, a logical explanation could be that Rama was able to get help from the local forest dwelling Dravidians. The Sanskrit word *vana* means forest, and *nara* means men, the forest dwelling men are thus *vana-nara.* The Aryan author of the *Ramayana*, unwilling to acknowledge the Dravidian help, conveniently joined the two words (as is the common grammatical practice in Sanskrit) to read *Vanara* - the monkeys. Similarly, the author states that Ravana was the worshipper of Shiva, and possessed magical powers resulting from years of his practicing austerities and penance.

As we have seen earlier, the original people of India followed the 'Rikhavite' practices of meditation, penances, etc., and since the Aryan sages had renamed Rikhava as Mahadeva or Shiva, the author may have identified Ravana as a Rikkavite and has demonized him as a *raksha* (devil). Rama - the Aryan hero of *Ramayana*, - and - Munisuvrata - the 20th *tirthankara* of the Jains - appear to be from the same period. A reconciliation attempt between the *Brahmana* (Vedic) and *Sramana* (ascetic) systems seems to have been attempted during their time. *Satapatha Brahmana* also records the Aryan march eastward (towards the present-day Bihar) along the river Ganges.

It is remarkable that in the Vedas and the earlier Brahmana literature the doctrine of transmigration is nowhere clearly mentioned, and there is no good reason to believe that the Aryans of the Vedic time accepted it. It first appears, in a rather primitive form, in the early Upanishads as a rare and new doctrine, to be imparted as a great mystery of master-hermits [Rikhavite monks] to their more promising pupils... The rapid spread of belief in transmigration throughout the whole of Northern India is hard to account for; it may be that the humbler ['Rikhavites'] strata of society had always believed in some form of transmigration.

-R.N. Dandekar, in Sources of Indian Tradition, Edited by A.T. Embree, 2nd Edition, Volume 1, Columbia University Press, New York 1988

(3) The Upanishads: The *Upanishads* (800 to 500 BCE) refer to the 'Rikhavite' as *Arhant Dharmi* (followers of the liberated one). The *Upanishads* mention about an *arhant dharmi* named Parsva (877 to 777 BCE) as the son of the King of Kashi, and another one called Nemi as the cousin of the dark-colored Hindu god Krshna. The *Upanishads* represent a reaction to the glorification of the ritualistic sacrifice. The Brahhmanic authors now seem to be paying greater attention to *sramana* philosophy of *karma* and *samsara*. For the first time, during this period, the mystico-spiritualistic thoughts such as identity of the individual soul (*Atman*) with the soul of the universe (*Brahman*),[30] the idea of rebirth and transmigration, the concept of purification of soul through yoga, penances and austerities begin to officially appear as valid Brahmanic practices in the *Upanishads*. For example,

[30] *Chandogya Upanishad*, 6.1-3, 12-14

the *Mundaka Upanishad* states that sacrificial rituals are ineffectual as a means to understand the highest reality and to spiritual liberation. "The fools who delight in the sacrificial rituals as the highest spiritual good go again and again through the cycle of old age and death… . Those who practice penance (*tapas*) and faith in the forest, the tranquil ones, the 'knowers' of truth, living the life of wandering mendicancy - they depart, freed from passion, through the door of the sun, to where dwells, verily, the immortal *Purusha*, the imperishable soul (*atman*)."[31]

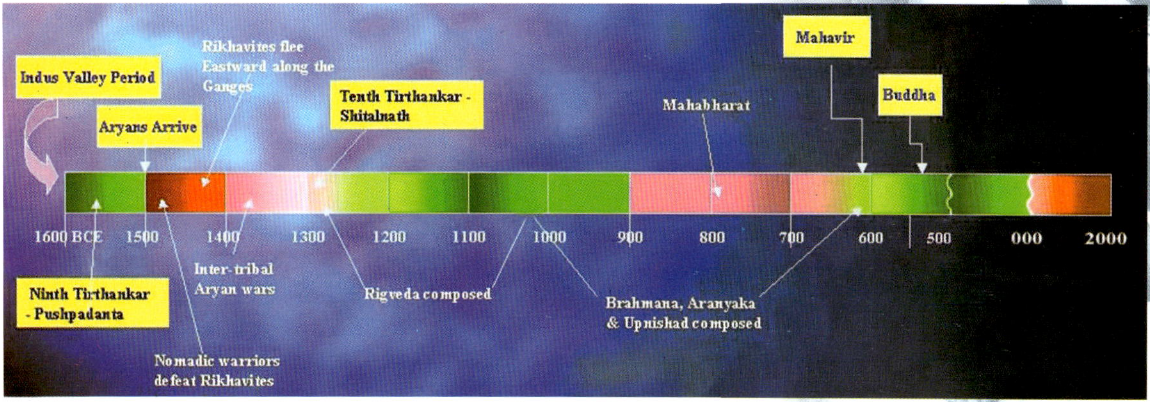

FIGURE 18.2: A time chart showing the major developments between 1,600 BCE and 2000 CE

The Eastward March

The birth, development, and stratification of modern Hinduism, which evolved out of the Brahmanic religion, happened during the 800 years between 1500 BCE and 700 BCE. The stratification was mainly due to the hierarchy of the caste system, which made one caste inferior to the other. This stratification became a serious problem when the Aryans were on the move again.

This time the move was eastward along the plains of the Ganges River. The kings and the republics of the indigenous settlements along the Ganges tried to stop Aryan advances, but the powerful war machine of the Aryans, with their horses and chariots, could not be stopped. The Aryans readily destroyed the wooden walls and the fortifications built around the towns (*purah*) of the Gangetic nations. Vedic hymns describe this march and praise Indra (*Purandara*) as the god who could break fortifications. By the eighth century BCE, the Aryans had reached River Sadanira (now Gandak) to the Northeast of Patna with the help of their god

---

31 *Mundaka Upanishad*, 1.2.-7,11

Agni-Vishvanara who burnt everything to prepare for the advances of Aryans. The *Satapatha Brahmana*, records Aryan march eastward and the founding of Videha to the northeast of Patna by prince Videgha-Mathava. Videgha marched eastward burning Dravidian kingdoms.The kingdom of Magadha - to the East of the river Sadanira - was yet to be conquered and was therefore considered to be impure by the contemporary (8th century) *Brahmins*. This is where the 'Rikhavites,' by now referred to by the Aryans as *Niganthis* (unattached), were settled.

"Agni thence went burning along this earth towards the East… and Videgha Mathava followed after him. He (Agni) burnt over (dried up) all these rivers. Now that river, which is called Sadanira (modern Gandak), flows from the Northern mountains: that one he did not burn over. That one the Brahmins did not cross thinking, 'it has not been burnt over by Agni-Vishvanara'. Videgha said to Agni, 'Where am I to abide?' 'To the East of this river be thy abode!' said he.
"Nowadays, however, there are many Brahmins in the East of Sadanira. Brahmins have caused Agni to taste (purify) it through sacrifices. Oh Lord Vishvanara, purify thy now the land of Niganthis to the South"

-Satpatah Brahmana, Translation by J. Eggeling - Sacred Books of the East (1882-1900)

Sramana evival

The threat to the kingdom of Magadha was obvious, but this time, the *sramana's* religion was also being threatened. Many scholars believe that this danger was responsible for the sudden revival of *sramana* religion by Mahavira and the founding of Buddhism by Gautama Buddha within few years of each other.With the Aryan forces concentrated to the Northwest, the Niganthis may have realized that an armed conflict with the Aryans was not a choice for them. Their conviction of the moral superiority of their nonviolent, ascetic way of life was a great morale booster. Furthermore, the Niganthis may have sensed that the Aryan fighting force, which was mainly of the *Kshtriya* caste, was unhappy with their secondary position in the caste setup. In spite of their might, *Kshtriyas* were relegated to a secondary position to the *Brahmins* (priestly caste).

The *sramanas* therefore may have launched a two-fold counter attack. On the one hand, they rejuvenated their religion through Mahavira, Gautama and many other *sramana* religious leaders and tried to re-establish their moral superiority by re-emphasizing that salvation and eternal bliss is attainable through their system. On the other hand, they, might have encouraged mass defections of *Kshtriyas* from Aryan ranks by emphasizing that *sramanas* revere all life. "ALL are equal, and anyone - even a *Kshtriya* - can reach *moksha* by following the *sramana* path." This was a very powerful message. It appears that even the *Brahmins* recognized the moral threat of the principles of the equality of life, and non-violence. *Brahmins*, who until now were carnivorous and consumed the animals slaughtered in their sacrificial rituals, now attempted to take the wind out of the *sramana* argument by adopting nonviolence and vegetarianism as their own creed. Hindu Gods, nevertheless, continued to carry weapons, and animal sacrifices continued to receive Brahmin blessings.

19

19. Post-Mahavira Jainism

In the previous chapter we learnt of the circumstances which generated a flurry of activities to revive the 'Rikhavite's' *sramana* religion. Within some 800 years after their arrival, Aryans were well setteled in the Indus Valley and had composed a large collection of hymns of Nature Worship. Their new Brahmanic religion had evolved into a more sophisticated philosophy, and the 'Rikhavite' ideas of soul, its transmigration and its purification by ascetic practice were incorporated into the latest Brahmanic literature the *Upanishads*. Brahmanism had developed a rigid caste system and a system of sacrificial rituals in which animals and even humans were sacrificed to please the gods.[32] 'Rikhavites' had retreated to the plains along the Ganges river where they had organized themselves in small kingdoms and built cities, but by 700 BCE Aryans had destroyed these cities. Bihar, in the Eastern region was now their spiritual centre.

Early Reforms

The social and historical background of the *sramana* reform efforts cannot be traced with great accuracy because of the small amount of 'concrete evidence;' however, the event that seems to have precipitated the reforms is the eastward march of the Aryans into the mostly *sramana* territory in Eastern India. The *Sramana* tradition was a religion of strict asceticism founded (according to the Jain tradition) by Rikhava - the first *Tirthankara*. Parsva, the twenty-third *Tirthankara* seems to have made some effort, in about 850 BCE, to bring back strict self-discipline by formalizing a code of ascetic behaviour. He organized the

32 The practice of sacrificial killings of the Dravidian tribes of Nagas and Rakshasas by Aryans was called *purushmedh*. Cases of this are repeatedly described in the *Vedas*, e.g. *Atharva Veda*, 6.56 and *Mahabharata* a Hindu epic. Reference: N.R. Guseva, *Jainism*, Institute of Ethnography, Academy of Sciences, Moscow, 1970; English translation by Y.S. Redkar, Jainism, Sindhu Publications, Bombay, 1971, pp. 28)

community and prescribed four basic vows (namely, restraint from injuring other beings, being truthful, taking only what is given, and minimizing possession of worldly goods). However, not until the eastward march of the Aryans in late 700 BCE, was there an urgency and intellectual fervour to reform the *sramana* philosophy. At least seven attempts - all in Eastern India - to reform non-Vedic concepts of that period (ca. 700 BCE) have been recorded in great details in the extant Buddhist scriptures.[33]

One of these seven attempts is by **Kassapa** who preached that conduct, virtuous or otherwise, had no effect on a soul's transmigration and all *karmas* must come to frution. Kassapa's faith in the rigidity of the *karma* theory was such that he questioned the efficacy of any human act to escape its consequences.

The second was **Mikkhali Gosala** founder of the 'Ajivika' sect. He preached the same doctrine of *karma* as did Kassapa, and coined the word *niyati* (fate) for the principle which controlled the rigid pattern of transmigration. His was a totally fatalistic approach. He preached that a soul's destiny is completely controlled by the rigid laws of *karma* and that there is nothing one can do about it.

The third reform school mentioned in the Buddhist literature is that of **Ajita Kesakambala** who was a complete materialist. He did not believe in soul or in any cosmic power. To him, a living being was formed of four elements; and earth returns to the aggregate of earth, water to water, fire to fire, and air to air, upon death. No soul, no transmigration ! Enjoy life as you go along, for there is no afterlife. However, such a totally materialistic outlook, similar to that of the modern science, could not explain life's ups and downs or inequalities and injustices, and was promptly rejected by his contemporary intellectuals.

The fourth reformist was **Pakudha Kacchayana** whose teachings were later absorbed by what was to become the Hindu tradition, and was to give rise to the Hindu Vaisheshika school. He preached the doctrine of seven fundamental elements. According to him, life, earth, water, fire, air, joy and sorrow are the fundamental universal elements which are neither made nor governed, neither caused nor constructed, neither originated nor destroyed, and one element has no effect on the fundamental qualities of another.

The fifth was **Sanjaya Belathiputta** whose main thesis was that no one is capable of knowing the absolute truth. Truth is beyond human comprehension. Therefore, all

[33] *Digha Nikaya*, 1.47 ff.

theories ranging from the existence or non-existence of God to any 'reality' are just that the theories. Consequently, he surmised, “let us not even debate the existence of God or of any other perceived reality”.

The sixth reformer was **Vardhaman Mahavira** who is called Nigantha Nataputta in the Buddhist literature. Typical of his *'anekantavada'* approach, he examined all the arguments of the contemporary reformers, and incorporated most of the valid ones into his reformed version of *sramana* philosophy. One can see some commonality between his teachings and those of the five mentioned above. Mahavira's reforms have survived in the form of Jainism.

The last reformist, some 60 years after Mahavir, was **Gautama Buddha**, who like others, rejected the existence of God, tried ascetic life in search of liberation, but gave it up claiming that it was too extreme a path, and adopted a middle-of the road approach. He also rejected the permanence of soul.

Several other reform attempts were made but, only Jainism and Buddhism have survied todate. Whereas, Mahavira acknowledged and maintained his connections with the past and thus became a 'reformer', Buddha severed the links with his *sramana* roots and became the 'founder' of a new religion.

Mahavira

Mahavira was born in 599 BCE in Kundalgram, Bihar, which was then the centre of *sramana* religion. His parents Siddhartha and Trishala belonged to the royal family, followed the *sramana* religion, and named their son Vardhamana. Prince Vardhamana left his kingdom at the age of thirty to seek salvation through self-purification by retreating into a nearby forest, and living a rigorous ascetic life. He achieved full enlightenment (omniscience) twelve years later at forty-two years of age. Jains believe that omniscience results when one manages to get rid of all destructive and deluding *karma* through total control over ones' own mind. Since, gaining total control over the self is the greatest victory one can achieve, Vardhamana was given the title Mahavira (Great Victor) by the community when he returned to tell about his experience. He was also called the *'Jina'* (conqueror), a title from which his followers derive the name, Jains.

Mahavira modified Parshva's ascetic code of conduct by adding the vow of celibacy to the four of his predecessor, and until his death in 527 BCE, preached the 'Jaina path of purification of the soul.' During his life, his teachings became widely known throughout the eastern region, and the rulers of many eastern Gangetic kingdoms supported Jainism. He had eleven direct disciples (*ganadhara*) who propagated Mahavira's teachings. He attracted 527,000 followers - 159,000 *sravakas*, 318,000 *sravikas* and ordained 14,000 monks with *Acharya* Indrabhuti Gautama as a head monk, and 36,000 nuns.[34] with *Acharya* Chandanbala as a head nun. Many in this congregation made great spiritual strides by following the path preached by Mahavira. *Kalpasutra* records that 314 achieved absolute mastery over the language, 400 monks achieved complete mastery over Jina's philosophy, 1300 achieved clairvionce, 700 attained omniscience, 700 attained peace and happiness similar to those in heaven (*devaloka*), 500 gained the mind-reading ability, and 700 monks and 1400 nuns achieved total liberation (*moksha*).[35]

Antiquity and Perceptions

It is a tribute to the great organizational skill of Mahavira that his four-fold Jain community now became a powerful force in the religious history of India. With Mahavira's achievements in focus, we can now revisit the controversy over the antiquity of Jainism. In the true spirit of *anekantavada*, we can assess various claims. The Hindus claim that Mahavira started Jainism. From their perspective, the claim is valid because, strictly speaking the word Jain was coined only after Mahavira's great enlightenment. Therefore Jainism cannot be older than Mahavira. From the Jain perspective however, it is not the word but the basic religious philosophy associated with it that is important. Mahavira simply reformed and refined a *sramana* philosophy of purification of soul - a philosophy, which goes back not only to Parsva but also all the way to Rikhava. From this perspective the Jain claim is also valid. For the time being however, let us accept this claim also as a mere article of faith.

Spread of Jainism

Only two of the eleven *ganadharas* - Indrabhuti Gautama and Sudharman - survived their teacher. Indrabhuti achieved omniscience immediately upon Mahavira's death and Sudharman twelve years later. Both continued to preach the Mahavira's message until they died at the age of 92 and 100 years respectively. Sudharman's student - Jambuswami - mastered the canon and achieved omniscience. Jambuswami is considered to be the last of the omniscient teachers (*Arhat kevali*). The canon was then passed on to four successive generations of ascetics, the last among them, 116 years after the passing of Mahavira, was Bhadrabahu I.

---

[34] *Kalpasutram* 133 135

[35] *Ibid*: 138 - 144

The spread of religion in ancient India depended mostly on the royal patronage. Of the sixteen major kingdoms (*Mahajanapadas*) in northern India, those in the eastern region followed the non-vedic *sramana* religion and the royal families in four of them (Kasi, Magadha, Vajji, Malla) were the devotees of Parshva. Mahavira the Jina from Vijji, being their own, had immediate following in these four kingdoms. In other *sramana*-type kingdoms, Mahavira may not have been as successful because of the simultaneous rival attempts by other *sramanas*, viz.Ajivikas, and Buddhists. By 150 BCE, just as had happened with the Aryan's arrival in the Indus Valley in 1500 BCE, the *sramanas* were once again on the move. This time, it was the victory of the Brahmanical kings of the Sung dynasty over the *sramana* kingdoms in the eastern regions. Life was now becoming difficult for the Jains in this region, and whereas some Jains moved to the South-east along the coastal route, others followed the trade routes to the North-west along the Ganges. The group that migrated to the southern lands were well received, the community grew with royal patronage, and attained dominance in present-day states of Andhra, Tamilnadu, Karnataka, and Maharashtra.

The Split

Perhaps the most serious blow to Mahavira's efforts was from two of his own followers several centuries later. North-eastern India, particularly the Maghada region, which was the stronghold of Jainism, was hit by a severe draught and famine in 360 BCE. A group of Jain monks led by Bhadrabahu therefore decided to migrate southwards to what is now Karnataka state, while others led by Sthulabhadra stayed back in Patliputra (modern Patana in the state of Bihar). With the spread of the religion in new regions, its preachers incorporated their own versions of the unwritten Jain canon, and made changes in ritualistic practices. Alarmed, after Bhadrabahu's death Sthulabhadra called a 'Council of Monks' in Patliputra in 327 BCE, and invited Bhadrabahu's chief disciple Balabhadra to participate. However, he could not attend the meeting.* Serious differences therefore arose amongst the community of monks, some accepting the scriptures organized by Sthulabhadra, and others rejecting its authority. Each claiming that the other has deviated from the original words of Mahavira.

This was the beginning of a split in the Jain community. By the first century CE, the Jain migration and dispersal of monks in various parts of the country resulted in major differences in rituals between the two groups. It appears that in 82 CE,

* According to another version, Bhadrabahu - who knew all the *Agamas* - was in Nepal and Sthulbhadra was sent from Patliputra to learn *Agamas* from him. However, he was able to learn full import of only a part of the scriptures. Later, Sthulabhadra called Council of Monks to prepare a unified version of the scriptures, but Balabhadra could not attend.

Shivakoti established a separate order of naked monks, thereby increasing the rift between the two groups.[36] However, the final falling apart of the two sects may have happened in Valabhi in Gujarat as a result of King Lokpala's decree for all monks to be fully clothed. Those unwilling to comply with the decree migrated south along the west coast to meet with the group that had migrated along the East coast. Jainism thus split into two major sects, viz. the sky-clad Digambara, and Svetambara in which the monks use plain white clothes only. This division persist even today.

Both sects continued to subdivide further, almost independent of each other, in to subsects, each differing from the other in minor details. Yet, there are no major philosophical differences between the two sects. An independent student of Jainism could easily conclude that the minor differences that have persisted so long between the two sects are petty, and reflect on the ego of the monks and the ignorance of their followers. On the other hand, one may also conclude that the splits demonstrate *'anekantavada'* in action, where different interpretations of Mahavira's path are encouraged, respected, and honestly followed by all sects.

The central point of difference between the two sects is in the practice of *'aparigraha'* or minimization of possessions. The Digambara sect, which stands for the ritualistic nudity for its monks, maintains that a monk can become truly free of shame and sexuality and thus hope to attain *moksha* if his *aparigraha* means "possessing nothing", including clothes. "Total nudity demnostrates absolute non-attachment required for *moksha,*" they maintain. The Svetambara sect permits its monks and nuns to cover themselves with two pieces of simple, white, unstiched cloth but do not consider that as *parigraha.* They point to the peacock feather brooms and water gourds, which the naked Digambara monks carry, and suggest that these too must not be viewed as *parigraha.* A seventeenth century monk Yashovijayji - clarified the situation by saying, "attachment is a state of mind (*bhava*) and draping ones body with a simple functional piece of cloth, or carrying a peacock-feather broom does not necessarily mean that the monk is emotionally attached to it."[37]

A consequence of such interpretations of *'aparigraha'* is the position of women in the two sects. Digamabaras believe that women, being incapable of going about

36 Schubring, Walther, *The Doctrine of the Jainas,* tr. from German by Wolfgang Beurlen, Motilal Banarasidas, Delhi, 1962, § 26,27

37 Muni Yashovijayji, *Dharmasangraha-tika*, a Seventeenth Century work.

nude in public, cannot observe fully the vow of *'aparigraha,'* and hence cannot achieve *moksha*. Apparently, this atttude towards women may be a much later development. Third and fourth century important Digambara texts clearly state that both men and women can achieve *moksha*.[38] Svetambaras state that men and women are equally capable of the same spiritual accomplishment. In fact, they point to Malli, who was a woman, and became the nineteenth *Tirthankara*.

Another evidence of this difference in interpretation of *'aparigraha'* is seen in the Jain temples. Digambara idols of *Tirthankaras* are unadorned and in the form of an asctetic in the meditating position, whereas the Svetambara idols are adorned as a king, often with a crown.

The *'aparigraha '* debate is extended even further into the nature of the omniscient Jina. According to Jain *karma* theory, the state of omniscience is reached when a soul has shed all its destructive (*ghatiya*) *karma*. The soul is then free from all passions and does not attract any karmic particles. In most cases, non-destructive *karma* are also elimnated immediately. The soul thus freed from all *karma*, leaves the body, and reaches *siddha-loka*. The souls of omniscient Jinas however, continue to remain in the present body because their nondestructive *Tirthankara karma* are not immediately eliminated. According to the Digambara, such omniscient beings, though still in their human form, do not engage into any kind of bodily function such as eating, talking, etc. Unaware of their physical form, they remain seated in detached meditation, and a 'magical divine sound' (*divya-dhwani*) emanating from their soul carries their message to the receptive minds. Svetambaras reject the notion of magical divine sounds and maintain that all *Tirthankaras* indeed talked and walked, and preached their creed. What makes Jinas different is that being omniscient, the infinite energy of their soul prevents any destructive *karma* from touching their soul ever again.

By insisting on their own interpretation of the doctrine of *'aparigraha,'* both sects seem to overlook *'anekantavada,'* a doctrine which is a great tool of reconciliation. Digambara and Svetambara versions of the scriptures differ only slightly, but the hardliners in both the sects continue to reject the authenticity of each other's scriptures. There is some disagreement over whether or not Mahavira was married before leaving it all in search of *moksha*. Such a purely academic debate should not affect lay Jains, but they too often get carried away by the influence of their monks. Nevertheless, cordial and cooperative relationship does exist between the two sects, and much publicized dispute over the ownership of shrines and holy

[38] See (1) Schubring, W., *Kleine Schrifen*, Wiesbaden, 1977, pp. 344-61, and (2) Malvania, Dalsukh, *Jainism: Some Essays*, Jaipur, 1986, pp.8

places in a few communities in India must not be viewed in purely adversarial terms. Furthermore, Jains outside India are steadily growing in number without much interaction with their orthodox ascetics. They don't see much sense in maintaining sectarian boundaries in an extra-Indian context; however, it may be too early to predict if they will be able to erode and break down these boundaries.

Digambara Developments

The process of dividing into subsects continued among both the Digambaras in the South and the Svetambaras in the North-west. Monks of both sects claimed to have an authentic and only link to the 'original community' (*mula sangha)* through a lengthy lineage of gurus dating back to Mahavira's time. The *mula sangha* was so called because it was seen as the basis of the true path to deliverence as established by Mahavira and those who did not belong to it were looked upon as pseudo-Jains.[39] For example, a tenth century Digambara text by Devasena calls Buddhists (described as a followers of Parshva), Svetambaras, and Yapaniyas[40] (a Jain sect trying to reconcile the differences between Digambaras and Svetambaras) as 'sectarian miscreants.' He strongly criticized other Digambara subsects such as the Mathura, Dravida, and Kastha *sanghas* founded respectively in the second century by Ramasena, in the fifth century by Vajranandin, and in the seventh century by Kumarsena. The reason for his wrath was that the monks of these subsects did not carry peacock-feather brooms. Devasena insisted that a peacock-feather broom was mandatory for true (*mula*) Digambara monks.

The *Bhattarakas*

Earlier, we have seen that Jainism florished in the South with royal patronage. With this, the influence of its monks on the royalty, and the land endowments to the religion increased substantially. Many forest-dwelling monks gradually started accomodating themselves to a quasi-householder mode, apparently to provide spiritual guidance to the laity. Some senior monks even took to being carried in palanquins attended by escorts of soldiers in a show of authority. Such practices, unworthy of a Jain monk, were no doubt periodically stigmatised as a sign of decadence and drew bitter criticism. Unfortunately, such hardline criticism discouraged contacts between the monks and the lay community, and deprived the community of spiritual guidance.

---

[39] Soni, Pannalal (ed.): Shrutasagara's *Shatprabharit Adisamgraham,* A Sixteenth Century text, Bombay 1920

[40] Upadhye, A.N. "Yapaniya Sangha: A Jaina Sect," in *Journal of the Uni. Of Bombay*, I, no.4, 224-231. Upadhye, A.N. "More Light on the Yapaniya Sangha," in *Annals of the Bhandarkar Oriental Research Institute*, LV, 9-22, Pune.

This situation created a need for some respectable authority who could guide the community in spiritual matters, and administer the gifts of funds, buildings and endowed lands. A new religious authority, in the institution of *bhattarakas*, soon emerged to fill this need. For all practical purposes, a *bhattaraka* was supposed to be like a monk, learned and celibate, but not having taken the vows of monkhood or formally ordained, was free to live among the laity as an administrative authority. A *bhattaraka* thus became a lay authority conducting rituals, administering monasteries and other properties, preserving scriptures and libraries, representing Jainism at king's courts, negotiating with kings and other religious authorities on behalf of his Jain constituents, supervising religious education, and generally adjucating the affairs and conduct of his sect.

With such a role and authority, it was inevitable that this office also succumbed to trappings of having a throne, and a great deal of pomp and ceremony. Such *granduer* did not initially attract much criticism from the community because of the fact that a *bhattaraka* was not a cleric but only a lay authority. Nevertheless, the pomp and the laxity of this office eventually proved to be too much for the simplicity-minded Jains, and a challenge to their authority was mounted from northern India. Banarasidas was a sixteenth century Jain poet in Agra who was convinced that *bhatattarakas,* like Hindu Brahmins, have monopolised rituals and thus exercise powerful control over the masses. [41] Furthermore, he also believed that ritual offerings of flowers, fruits and sweets during Jain temple worship involved large-scale violence against plants and was similar to the sacrificial rituals of Hinduism. His reformist efforts resulted in de-emphasizing the importance of the *bhattarakas*, their number dwindeling from about thirty-six in the medieval period to only four now. Attempts are afoot to revive this institution, and six more *bhattaraka* seats are under consideration.

Marginalization

Jainism once attained a position of dominance in the Southern states of Andhra, Tamilnadu, Karnataka and Maharashtra. However, Jains in this area are now a marginalized community. Several factors can be attributed to this decline, among which 'secterian infighting' and 'lack of effective leadership' could be the internal factors, and a 'militant Hindu Renissance' and 'Muslim invasions' the external factors. From the eighth century onwards Jains often met with violent reprisals, mass conversions to Hinduism, and the destruction or takeover of their shrines and temples in the South. Some Hindu temples, including the great Minakshi temple in Madurai and a shrine to Murugan in Kalugamalai (Dist. Tirunelveli),

[41] Jain, Ravindra Kumar, *Kavivara Banarasidas* (in Hindi), Bharatuya Jnanapitha Publication Varanasi.

even today display vivid murals of the massacre of Jains. Destruction of three hundred fifty-two Jain temples by Muslim invaders is noticable in the ramparts of Belgaum Fort (Karnataka), built with pieces of carved stones from these destroyed temples. And graphic proof of conversion of Jain temples to Hindu shrines is visible in the walls, plastered-over steeples, and the courtyards of the famous Mahalakshmi temple in Kolhapur (Maharashtra), and in the Murugan and Aiyanar shrines in Kalugamalai. The fact that Jains cannot seek legal redress for such obvious cases, even in the secular and human-rights culture of the 21st century, is an eloquent proof of the marginalization of Jainism that has occurred in the South.

One of the reasons for such marginalization is presumably the prevelance of orthodoxy and coservatism in the community. We have seen earlier that Devasena ridiculed some Digambara subsects even for minor attempts to reform the external trapping of carrying a peacock broom. Such orthodoxy not only discouraged reform, but deprived the community of effective leadership because monks gradually chose to stay away from the community. The institution of *bhattaraka* also did not prove to be much help in these matters.

Two fortunate developments during the last century, however, may help the community regain its vitality. One such development is the foundation and leadership role of an organization called *Dakshin Bharat Jain Sabha* (South Indian Jain Society). Through this organization, eminent Digambara Jain lay persons voluntarily took over almost all the responsibilities which were formerly in the domain of the *bhattarakas*. This Society has already achieved commendable progress in Digambara publications, education, temple managements, community representation, and even in bringing about social reforms.

Digambara Subsects

KANJI SWAMI PATH

Another major development took place not in the South, but rather, in the Svetambara stronghold of West Gujarat. Kanji, a powerful learned Svetambara monk, who had a significant following in the reform-minded Sthanakvasi subsect, (Page 189) embraced the Digambara philosophical perspecitve of Kundakunda. Born into a Sthanakvasi family, he was ordained as a Sthanakvasi monk at the age of twenty-four, and rapidly rose to prominance because of his scholarship and charismatic preaching. At the age of forty-five, however, at a public ceremony in Songadh near Palitana, Gujarat, Kanji Swami, as he was already being called, announced that he has found true spirit of Jainism in the teachings of Kundakunda - a third century teacher of mystical tradition in the Digambara sect, and as a result is leaving the order to become a Digambara layman.[42]

Kanji Swami de-emphasized rituals, dietary codes and merit-making practices of Jainism and preached that the soul is an eternal reality. Therefore, we should strive to fully understand the nature of the soul without the emphasis on rituals. Whether his reformist preaching will have a long-lasting effect on the orthodox and conservative attitudes in the South is yet too early to judge. However, the fact that he is merely restating the views of Kundakunda, whose book *Samayasara* (Essence of Doctrine) holds a quasi-scriptural place within the Jain tradition,[43] and that Kanji Swami and his message received warm welcome from Shanti Sagar - the most venerated Digambar teacher of the 20th century - has caused the greatest stir in the Digambara sect.

For the present, he and his followers, which includes some 300 families in Songadh, are looked upon as another subsect - called "Kanji Swami Panth" that is spearheading the Digambara reform movement. Until his death in 1980, Kanji Swami refused to accept any sectarian lable claiming that he was merely advocating the true path of Jainism as preached by the *Tirthankaras*. However, his devotees have built a massive structure called the '*Digambara Svadhyaya Mandir*' (Digambara Study Centre) in Songadh, and unlike his early 'Sthanakavasi' belief of not worshipping any idols, the Digambara images of *Tirthankaras* are worshiped here. His critics however, ridicule Kanji's claims that he, in a previous existence, had met Kundakunda, and that he - Kanji - would be reborn as a *Tirthankara*.

Svetambara Developments

Mathura - the ancient city of the Parsva time - was the first major stop for the Jain group moving North-west from Bihar. Inscription on a recently excavated funerary monument (Kankali *stupa*) in Mathura, dating from 157 CE, suggests that the monument was built in Parshva's time by a laywoman.[44] Mathura then was already a vigorous city. Here Jain monks had organized themselves into several groups (*gana*) on the basis of their lineage - a system which continues today with Svetambara monks. Another influence of that era - Jains becoming traders and businessmen - continues to date. Mathura was located at the junction of trades routes to the West, East and South, and the Jains migrating to the North-west took to trading in the absence of any royal patronage.

42 Bharill, H., *Yugapurusha Shri Kanji* Swami, Jaipur, 1981.

43 Kundakunda, *Samaysara*, Ardhamaghadi text with translation by A. Chakravarti, Bharatiya Jnanapitha Publication, Varanasi, 1925.

44 Srinivasan, D.M., *Mathura: The Cultural Heritage*, Delhi, 1989

Mathura remained a great Jain holy place for centuries, but trade took Jains westward to the coastal areas of Gujarat where ship-building and overseas trade had developed (Mathura is landlocked). By the fifth century, Jains were well settled in Gujarat, Rajasthan and as far north as Punjab. It is in Valabhi, of the fifth century Gujarat, that the Jain monks now felt stable enough to call a conference to reconcile various versions of their scriptures and to produce written copies of the Jain canon. For the following few centuries, the Jains continued to thrive, established themselves into influential positions such as big business owners, bankers, scholars and ministers or advisors to the kings. A twelfth century Jain *acharya*, Hemachandra, was even able to engineer the succession of King Kumarpal to the throne.[45] The reign of Kumarpal and his Jain minister Vastupal is considered to be the golden-age of Jainism in the West. The duo built many temples, including the famous temple complex at Mount Abu, and at Taranga Hill.

Meanwhile, Islam had arrived in India with Mahmud Ghazni's raids during the period of 999 - 1026 and Ghor's invasion in 1151. Kumarpala's rule succumbed to Islam in 1165, and during the next three and half centuries, the Turkish sultanantes caused havoc in the countryside by forcing the local population to convert to Islam, destroying idols and temples, taking Jain monks as slaves, and establishing provincial sultanates. Though a minority religion, Jainism survived and was even able to blunt Islam's sword by its nonaggressive and peaceful message. Jains, being traders, merchants, bankers, and expert managers, were also able to wield considerable influence over the sultans.. For example, in 1313 the Turks (Moghuls) severely damaged the great "Adinath" temple on Mount Shatrunjaya (Palitana), but by 1330 the Jains had managed to wield enough influence over the Turkish governor of Gujarat - Alp Khan - who ordered his minister Samara Shah to restore the temple, and granted financial assistance for the project. A memorial built built to honor a Moslem clergy who cooperated in this restoration still stands among the Jain temples on the mount.

A major source of early Svetambara history is a text -- the *Prabhavaka Charitra* (Lives of the Jain Masters) -- by Prabhachandra.[46] This text has compiled biographies of twenty-two Jain *acharyas*, starting from Vajrasvamin (fourth century), who was supposedly the last *acharya* to have memorized the ancient *Purva* scriptures, to Hemchandra (1089-1172) whose knowledge of Jain scriptures was

[45] Buhler, G., *The Life of Hemchandra Acharya*, Shantiniketan, Varanasi, 1936

[46] Jinavijayji Maharaj, *Prabhachandra's Prabhvaka Charitra*, Ahmedabad, 1940

unsurpassed. Others listed in this text are: Siddhasena Divakara (fifth century), Haribhadra who has written hundreds of volumes on Jain philosophy and has been a pivotal figure in the Svetambara monk lineage (sixth century), Kalka (seventh century), Mahadeva of Taxila (ca. 980 CE), and Abhayadeva Suri (eleventh century). This work sheds some light on the lives of the *acharyas* and their contemporary Jain community, and provides important information on the old *gana* system and the lineages of *acharyas.*

Svetambara Subects

TAPA AND KHARTARA GACCHA

In the fourth century, Vajrasvamin's four pupils - Chandra, Nagendra, Nirvriti and Vidyadhara - may have replaced the term *gana* (group) with *kula* (family). Prabhachandra claims his lineage to be with Chandra whereas that of Haribhadra is with the Vidyadhara family*(kula).* This classification seems to have been soon replaced by another term, *gaccha* (subsect), which is used even today by the two groups of Svetambara monks, namely, the Kharatara *gaccha* and Tapa *gaccha.* Although the exact origin of the Kharatara subsect cannot be traced, it seems somehow to be linked to Abhyadeva Suri because many monks of the later period use the term 'Suri' as an appendix to their name e.g., Jinavallabha Suri (eleventh century), Jinadatta Suri (1075 - 1154), Jinachandra Suri I (1139 - 1165), Jinakushala Suri (1279 - 1331), and Jinachandra Suri II (1537 - 1612).

The Tapa *gaccha* also links its roots with Abhayadeva Suri. It was started by Jagachandra Suri in 1228, who belived in greater austerities (*tapa*) than those followed by his contemporary monks.[47] Over the centuries, Tapa ascetics have been successful in exercising great influence not only on Jain laypersons but even on the Moslem rulers. For example, Jain principles were first introduced and explained to the Moghul emperor Akbar (1556 - 1605) by a monk called Padmasundara who also gave him a gift of a large number of Jain manuscripts. Later, Akbar invited Hiravijaya Suri (1527 - 1595) - head of the Tapa *gaccha* - to be one of his religious advisors. So influenced was Akbar by Hiravijaya and his disciple Shantichandra's message of nonviolence that Akabar ordered the freeing of caged birds, banned killing of animals, and lifted the tax on non-Moslems. Later, in 1591, Jinachandra Suri II of the Kharatara *gaccha* was also able to persuade Akabar to protect Jain temples from Moslem rampage.[48] Akbar's successor emperor Jahangir, who was also prevailed upon by a Jain monk of the Tapa *gaccha*, had taken a vow of nonviolence and appointed a Jain monk to teach his son.

---

[47] Klatt, J., "Extracts from the Historical Records of the Jains." *Indian Antiquary*, 1882

[48] Desai, M.D., *Bhanuchandra Charitra*, Ahmedabad, 1941.

There has been considerable rivalary between the two subsects however, and the Kharatara *gaccha*, which is mostly located in Rajasthan, seems to be in decline with less than 20 monks and 200 nuns remaining in the order today. The Tapa *gaccha*, by contrast, now claims to have nearly 2,000 monks and 4,000 nuns.

Like their southern counterparts, the Svetambara monks faced an intense debate about their role in the community. Should monks live in the towns and villages and interact with the lay society, or should they be relatively isolated and stay in the forests? A ninth century acharya, Silanka, had strongly defended the interaction by citing that Mahavira did not confine himself to one abode, instead he travelled, stayed in the towns and villages, and preached to the masses.[49] Nevertheless, two groups of monks - forest-dewlling (*vanavasin*) and temple-dwelling (*chaityavasin*) - had emerged in the fourth century, and the issue seems to have bubbled up in the eleventh century in the form of an intense debate. Whereas, the group opposed to social-interaction emerged victorious, and gave birth to the institution of *bhattarakas* in the Digambara tradition, the temple-dwelling group prevailed in the Svetambaras. By the eleventh century however, the reformist movement, led by Jineshvara Suri, had reduced the influence of the temple-dwelling monks. A compromise has prevailed to date whereby Svetambara monks are neither required to retreat to the forests nor are they allowed to stay put at one place. Instead, they are to maintain contact and preach to a maximum number of people by being constantly on the move from community to community. Except in the four months of rainy season, a Svetambara monk is expected to be criss-crossing the country on foot.*

LONKA GACCHA

The first major reform effort in Svetambara tradition was to take place in the fifteenth century, ironically because of Moslem rule in Gujarat. Lonka (1418 - 75) -- a lay Jain, working as a scribe to copy manuscripts in Ahmedabad -- was saddened by the destruction of Jain shrines which Muslim iconoclasts were carrying out in Gujarat. He was also disturbed by the highly ritualistic and temple-oriented behaviour of the ascetic community. He felt that such behaviour was contrary to that described in *Ayaranga Suttam* and *Dashavikalika*, the two scriptures

49 Muni Jambuvijayji, *Acharangsutram Aur Srutkritangasutram*, (Acharangsutra with Shilanka's Commentry), Agamodhaya Samiti Edition, Delhi, 1978

* A new trend challenging this requirement has emerged in the 20th century. Achrya Amarendra Muni and his disciples led by Acharya Chandanaji have started Western Missionary- style humanitarian work by building hospitals, schools and residences for the poor, aged and sick. This, according to them is the true message of Mahavira's nonviolence. However, their critics have decried this move as "unsuitable for a Jain ascetic." See section on Acharya Chandanaji later in this chapter.

dealing with monastic law that he was copying at the time. Furthermore, he found statements in the scriptures pointing to the destruction of life-forms entailed in the construction of any building.[50] Lonka therefore came out with a message denouncing image-worship. Lonka never took ascetic initiation but became a wandering preacher. His followers formed a separate group called the Lonka *gaccha* but continued using the meeting halls (*upasraya*) attached to the temples, without paying their respects to the temple deities. Monks of the Lonka *gaccha* also rejected the authority of some thirteen scriptures on the grounds that these prescribed image-worship. All this had enraged the image-worshipping community. The Lonka *gaccha*, however, suffered a great setback about a century after Lonka's death, when one of their prominent monk - Acharya Meghji - and hundreds of his pupils, publicly converted to idol-worship.

STHANAKVASIS

Lonka's ideas were revived in Surat, Gujarat, by two merchants - Lavaji and Dharmasimha in about 1730. They re-emphasized the monastic behaviour found in the *Dashavaikalika*, and suggested that instead of the temple halls (*upashrayas*), monks should use old abandoned buildings (*sthanaka)* for lodgings. The Lonka group thus became Sthanakavasi. This new subsect started permanently wearing a strip of cloth across the mouth (*muhapatti*) as an identifying device.

Like the Lonka *gaccha*, the Sthanakavasis also suffered some serious setbacks. Within a few decades Bhikanji - a Sthanakvasi monk - broke away and formed a separate subsect called Terapanth (see below). A major setback however, was to come a century later when several Sthanakvasi monks, Atmaramji and Buterayaji being the prominent among them, declared that they found the image-worship justified in the scriptures, and are therefore joining the Tapa *gaccha* of the image-worshipers. Atmaramji, who was re-initiated in the Tapa *gaccha* as Vijayananda Suri, attained eminence as a great Jain scholar. In spite of such setbacks, the Sthanakvasis survive to date as a vibrant Svetambara subsect. Mental-worship (*bhava-puja*), instead of image-worship (*murti-puja*) is their basic thrust, and several of their monks have also achieved wide recognition. Muni Sushil Kumarji - a Sthanakvasi monk - who immigrated to the United States in 1975, along with Chitrabhanuji, a former image-worshipping monk, are credited with the establishment of some 16 Jain temples and a place of pilgrimage in North America.

TERAPANTHIS

Another setback to the Sthanakvasis group was in Rajasthan in the form of

[50] Mahaprajna, Yuvacharya, *Ahimsa Tattva Darshan*, Jain Viswabharati Press, Ladnum, 1988

Bhikanji (1726 - 1803) who was initiated as a Sthanakvasi monk in 1751. Unhappy with the lax practices of his contemporary monks, he, along with six of his collegues, formally broke away from the Sthankvasis in 1759 and started a new subsect. This new subsect came to be known as Svetambara Terapanth[51] to distinguish itself from the similar sounding name of the Digambara Terapanth, which was formed earlier as a protest to the authority of the *bhattarakas*. Though the new subsect denied any link to the Sthanakvasis, Terapanthis continued to follow certain Sthanakvasi practices such as the rejection of image-worship, the denial of the authority of thirteen scriptural texts, and permanently wearing of the *muhapatti.**

Bhikanji's Terapanth did not initially make much headway, perhaps because of his extreme views. Not only did he refuse to initiate those who he felt to be unfit to stand the rigor of his exacting standards, he also interpreted scriptures to maintain that, "being concerned with his own spiritual development through austerities, meditation and penances is the true code of an ascetic's conduct. Therefore, monks and nuns should not get involved with compassionate activities."[52] Such extreme views were unacceptable to the majority Jains who believed that compassion and meritorious activities (*punya*) further spiritual progress. So profound was his concern for the ascetic behavior that he prepared a list of 'Limits of Behavior' (*maryada*) and required that all monks and nuns in his order recite it daily. This list grew bigger with each succeeding *acharya* in his order. The fourth *acharya*, Jitmalji, produced a condensed version of all these *maryadas* and started a practice requiring every ascetic to read and sign a copy daily to pledge his/her allegiance. Terapanth movement is beleived to have survived because of the great organizing skill of acharya Jitmalji.

ACHARYA TULSI

Tulsi, initiated as the ninth *acharya* in 1936, reformed the Terapanth and put it on the world map. Tulsi must have studied Jain history well for he knew that moderating Bhikanji's strictures may encourage laxity in ascetic behavior, but not doing so would amount to the continued marginalization of his subsect. He had to find a solution that would retain an ascetic's ideal code of behavior and increase his sect's involvement in the social activities. He must have learnt from

[51] Rampuriya, S., *Acharya Bhikshu: Jivan Katha Aur Vyaktiva*, Jain Vishva Bhariti Press, Ladnum

* Whereas, the Sthankvasi *muhapatti* is a square piece of cloth, that worn by Terapanthis is an elongated Strip.

[52] Mahaprajna, Yuvacharya, *Ahimsa Tattva Darshan*, Jain Viswabharati Press, Ladnum, 1988

the Digambara experiment of creating an instituion of *bhattarakas* to serve the social needs, and the subsequent revolt of Banarasidas. He conceived a brilliant idea. Mahavira had recommended two sets of vows, a set of introductory vows called *'anuvrata'* for laypersons and the stricter set, *'mahavratas'* for the ascetics (Chapter 3). In practice however, while ascetics do take *'mahavratas'* and are subject to a very strict code of behavior, the laity generally follow a somewhat relaxed lifestyle in the spirit of *anuvratas* without ever taking any vows. He decided to create a new class of laity --*samans* and *samanis* - who would actually take *anuvrata* vows and thus be bound by these vows, but not being ordained, do not have to follow the very demanding strictures of an ascetic's life.

In 1949, he started the *'anuvrata'* movement and decided to take it beyond the normal sphere of Jainism. He opened the movement to the people of all religions, color, creed, nationality and language. His stated goal was to bring about a global moral reformation by rekindeling the values of unity, peace, friendship, morality and ethical behavior.[53] Anyone joining the movement is advised to take the *anuvrata* vows and practice them as described in Chapter 3. However, those who are ready to enter the ascetic life-style are first asked to take the "Five Great Vows" (*mahavrata*) and live a slighly less rigid life for some years before being fully ordained. Unlike the ordained ascetics, these *samans* and *samanis* can travel out of the country in order to provide spiritual guidance to the laity abroad, accept food, which is specially prepared for them, and participate in social activities designed for the moral and ethical reform. Another important activity, they are expected to practice and teach, is a special kind of meditation called *'prekshadhyana'*. This is perhaps the revival of a practice which Kundakunda, the great Digambara *acharya*, started nearly 1700 years ago but had been quite forgotten. *Prekshadhyana*, like the Buddhist *'vipakshana'* is designed to 'engage the mind fully in the perception of subtle, internal and innate phenomenon of consciousness.'

The '*anuvrata*' movement has since flurished. *Samans* and *samanis* have travelled the world, established *'prekshadhyana'* centers in a number of countries and are promoting Jain values of justice, unity, peace, friendship, morality and ethical behavior. Acharya Tulsi's efforts will be viewed as a reform to bring Jain values to the attention of the world, to revive Kundkunda's *prekshadhyana,* and to help us live according to Mahavira's basic message of justice and kindness towards all living beings. After Tulsi's death, the movement is now headed by his successor Acharya Mahaprajnaji.

53 Bhatnagar, R.P., (ed.), *Acharya Tulsi: Fifty Years of Selfless Dedication*. Jain Vishwabharati Press, Ladnum, 1985, also, *Acharya Tulsi, Anuvrata: Acode of Conduct for Moral Development*, New Delhi, 1988.

SRIMAD RAJCHANDRA

The essence of Jain philosophy lies in the path leading to *moksha.* In Mahavira's time, Sanskrit was the language of the scholars but Mahavira preached in Ardhamaghadhi the local language of the masses. The Jain canon - the *Agamas* - were also composed in Ardhamaghadhi and used by successive generations of monks to bring Mahavira's message to the masses. Although ancient Ardhamaghadhi evolved into more contemporary languages, none of the *Agamas* were translated into any of the modern Indian languages until recently, and the Jain laity had to depend on the ascetics to understand the essence of Jainism.

In 1883, a sixteen year old boy from Gujarat - Lakshminandan Mehta (who later became known as Shrimad Rajchandra) - changed all that by publishing a book called "*Mokshamala.*" This small composition of 108 sections in a simple Gujarati language tries to "explain the philosophy of Jainism to young prople and to prevent them from being corrupted by false ideals" (preface). By reading it and contemplating on its contents, "faith will be established in the essence of Jain philosophy," states the author in its preface. The book is neither a translation of nor a commentary on any canon, instead it emphasizes actual spiritual experience of self-realization - a message more commonly found in Hindu mysticism than in Jain ascetic tradition. A second century Digambara Jain monk - Kundakunda - was the only major Jain ascetic to profess similar mystical experience.

Rajchandra's prolific letter writing (about 800 letters to his friends and followers on spiritual matters)[54] and his later book *Atmasiddhi* (Self-Realization of the Soul)[55] emphasizes this mysticism again and again. For him, there was no difference between 'the direct experience of the self' or 'self realization' and liberation of the soul. In the *Atmasiddhi* and in an elaborate letter sent to his long-time friend Sobhagbhai, he has stressed that the soul has eternal existence, it is the agent of its actions, and experiences its consequenses, the state of *moksha* exists and the means of gaining it is through self-realization with the help of a guru. Jain tradition, on the other hand, distinguishes between the realization of the soul (awakening or *samyak-darsana*), and liberation of soul (annihilation of all *karma* or *moksha*). Rajchandra regarded self-realization to be central to a true religion and viewed idol worship, rituals, monkshood, sectarianism, etc. as unnecessary.

---

54 *Shrimad Rajchandra*, Shrimad Rajchanra Asram, Agas, India, 1985

55 *Self-Realisation* (An English translation), Mehta, D.C., Bharatiya Vidya Bhavan, Mumbai, 1978.

The Jain path to *moksha* is essentially the ascetic path, which one follows after gaining *samyak-darsana* at the 4th *gunasthana.* The path lays equal emphasis on both internal purity of soul and its external manifestation in ascetic's self-discipline. The Svetambara tradition believes that while asceticism is critically important for *moksha*, a layperson also may, as an exception, attain *moksha* on the basis of mere internal purity. The Digamabara tradition however, considers nudity and asceticism as absolutely essential for liberation, and rejects any possibility for a house holder to ever attain *moksha.* This, in spite of the fact, that the most revered Digambara Acharya - Kundakunda - has stated in Samayasara:

"The ignorant persons say that the adoption of the external marks of asceticism…is the only way to liberation. The mark is never the way to liberation, because the arhats who have given up an attachment to the body and ignored the mark, have realized right belief, knowledge and conduct which is the path to liberation.

The Hindu Vedic system does not consider asceticism as a must for liberation. Rajchandra too in emphasizing realization of the self through experience has discounted the requirement of asceticism although in reality, after gaining self-realization or *samyak darsana* (4th *gunasthana*) at an early stage in his life, he was already well on his way along the path to asceticism and appears to have reached the 6th or almost the 7th *gunasthana.* Rajchandra maintained that the religion of the self (*atma dharma*) is the root of all philosophies, and that even today we can realize the self through the mere acquisition of knowledge under the guidance of a worthy teacher. He claimed to have attained memory of his former births at the age of seven, and made a grand claim that he - a layman - achieved a state of self-realization (his concept of *moksha* or *siddhi*) in 1890. In the last days of his life, he openly declared to his few monk disciples such as Lalluji and Devakaranaji that they should not distinguish between himself and Mahavira. In a letter addressed to Mr. Chaturbhuj Becara, he writes:

I am the second Mahavira. This I have realized through the power of my soul. ..I am omniscient, full of detachment. I am going to establish the supreme religion by following Mahavira. .. I have prepared disciples and a moral code of conduct for them. .. For propagating this religion I would renounce the world and make my disciples omniscient. ..I am distinct from everything in all respects. I am only most pure consciousness, most exalted and unthinkable and an unadulterated pure experience self.[56]

Born of a Hindu-Vaishnava father and a Jain mother, Lakshminandan was a child prodigy studying and absorbing both Hindu and Jain philosophies at very young age. He was renamed Raichand at age four and later became known as Shrimad Rajchandra. The Hindu Vedic influence of his childhood is evident from his early writings (*Pushpamala, Bodhavachana, Anupreksha*) where he emphasizes the

56 Mehta S.R. and Seth B.G., *Shrimad Rajchandra: a Great Seer*, Shrimad Rjchandra Ashram, Agas, 1971

importance of good religious assembly (*sat-sanga*), a good mentor (*sat-guru* or *sat-purusha*), and his right teachings (*sat-sruta*) in achieving self-realization.

He continued to emphasize the importance of these three things for the rest of his short life. By the age of 22 he introduced another Hindu concept - *bhakti* or devotion - and raised the status of a guru almost to that of a deity. In an exchange of 9 letters between himself and his Hindu devotee - Mansukhram Suryaram - Shrimad states that "Scriptures describe only the pathways leading to *moksha*, but the secret of the same rests in the heart of a *sat-guru*. For realizing God one should look upon the guru as God himself ! There is no distinction between God (*purusottama*) , a *sat-guru*, and a saint." Similarly, in a letter addressed to Muni Lalluji, Shrimad advises: "Be absorbed in devotion to the *sat-purusas*. Reflect upon the biographies of the *sat-purusas*. Ponder over the characteristics of the *sat-purusas*. Concentrate on the faces of the *sat-purusas* and perceive them through your inward eye. Brood upon their each and every mental, verbal and physical act repeatedly and accept whatever they hold ...This is ..the pathway to the abode of god." In the *Atmasiddhi* - his most revered book - Shrimad has devoted 31 out of 142 verses to describe the importance of having and devoting oneself to a *sat-guru*.

Jain tradition, while acknowledging the role of a guru in seeking spiritual progress, does not accord similar importance to a guru as did Shrimad Rajchandra. Shrimad's 'guru-bhakti or devotion to a guru' stems from the Vedantic, Vaishnava influence on him. He asserts repeatedly that Jainism is the supreme religion. However, his consistent emphasis on devotion to a guru, his use of Vedantic terminology such as hari, brahman, sat, chitta, ananad, etc. and his statements such as, "consciousness is the substratum (*adhisthana*) of this universe" - a Vedantic monist concept diametrically opposite to the Jain dualistic viewpoint of both jiva (consciousness) and ajiva as real constituents of the universe - display the extent of the Vaishnava influence on him. This was natural not only because of his upbringing in a Hindu/Jain family, but also because of Shrimad's voracious reading of non-Jain religious literature such as the Dasbodha, Bhagvat Gita, Guru Gita, Yogavasistha, etc.

In summary, Rajchandra's greatest contribution to Jainism appears to be his compositions - letters and books. poetry and prose - explaining Jainism in a simple understandable modern Indian language. His deep understanding of both Jain and non-Jain philosophies and his consistent emphasis on devotion to a *sat-guru* earned him (and ultimately to Jainism) a large number of Jain as well as non-Jain followers. Even Mahatma Gandhi, in his early years, declared himself to be one of Shrimad's followers. Shrimad's admirers believe that he was a liberal reformer attempting to blend Vedic and Jain philosophies. However, his detractors see this as a confused vacillation between the two philosophies from which Shrimad could not truly emerge. To them, it was also a failed attempt to challenge and reform the traditional Jain dogma of ascetic path.

In reality, Shrimad seems to have started a "devotion to Guru" (*Guru-bhakti*) movement in Jainism. His declaration that he has achieved omniscience and self-realization (implying *moksha*) even as a layperson, and that he is the "Second Mahavira" has fanned this movement. Since his premature death in 1901, many of his disciples have declared themselves as having achieved self-realization through absolute devotion to a *sat-guru.* Shrimad's closest disciple Lallu, and Lallu's appointed successor Brahmachari Govardhandas have claimed this and the consequent authority, on the basis of direct (*pratyaksha*) guru lineage.

Others have also made similar claims based on verse eleven in the *Atmasiddhi*, in which Shrimad classifies *sat-gurus* as both presently-living (*pratyaksha*), and non-living (*paroksha*). For example, Ladakchand Vora (1903-1997) declared himself to be an independent guru based on his devotion to his *paroksha guru* Shrimad, and established '*Raj Saubhag Satsang Mandal*' in Sayla, Gujarat. Dr. Mukund Sone (Atmanand Maharaj) claimed self-realisation in 1969, and established an *ashram* called '*Shrimad Rajchandra Adhyatmik Sadhan Kendra,*' currently located in Koba, Gujarat. Similarly, Dr. Rakesh Jhaveri, who was recognized as a guru in 1980 by his followers, established '*Shrimad Rajchandra Adhyatmik Satsang Sadhana Kendra*' in Mumbai.

Rajchandra may have tried to ensure the continuation of his tradition by preaching *guru-bhakti* and suggesting that lay persons can also achieve *siddhi*, but he may also have opened doors to internal conflicts and power struggles within the movement by enabling too many followers to independently declare themselves to be *gurus.* It is too early in the movement to predict the outcome. Meanwhile, by declaring himself to be "Second Mahavir" Shrimad may have given reasons for his conservative Jain critics to be skeptical.

GURUDEV CHITRABHANU AND ACHARYA SUSHIL KUMAR

The 20th century has been marked by two global conflicts (World War I and II), more than a few regional wars, several genocides and the holocaust. Intellectuals around the world have agonized over these horrible events and have sought various avenues of peace. One such avenue has been the interfaith dailogue through spiritual conferences. In 1970, a Spiritual Summit Conference was being organized in Geneva, Switzerland, by the U.S.-based Temple of Understanding, and a Jain monk in India was invited. The monk - Muni Chandra Prabha Sagar (later to be known as Gurudev Chitrabhanu) - was torn between his strong urge to take Mahavira's peace message to this conference, and equally strong travel restrictions placed on him by the tradition.

Tradition dictated that Jain monks do not undertake vehicular travel, and for 28 years, Muni Chandra Prabha Sagar had covered nearly 30,000 miles walking bare foot to bring Mahavira's message to the villages, towns, and cities in India. However, now he felt that it was important to participate in an international dialogue involving all the religions so that Mahavira's message of universal peace, fraternity, compassion, nonviolence and reverence for life in all its forms can be explained to the rest of the world. He also felt that travel restrictions on monks were depriving thousands of overseas Jains from spiritual guidance. Jains were migrating to Africa, Europe and North America in increasing numbers each year, but in the absence of Jain monks they were fast losing their spiritual identity. Muni Chandra Prabha Sagar decided to travel to Geneva.

His travel abroad as a monk created a storm of protests in the Jain community in India, but his visit to Geneva had now given him a new vision of a universal mission. In response, the *muni* decided to renounce his monkhood and travel again as a lay-Jain under the name Chitrabhanu - a pen-name he had already been using to write books and poems. His 1971 travels took him to Kenya, England, The Hague and then to the United States where he gave a series of lectures. New York was to be his new arena of activity. With the intellectual fortitude of a monk, dogged determination of a maverick and the zeal of a missionary, he opened America's first Jain Meditation International Centre near the United Nations building in New York. No longer a monk, he soon became popular as a spiritual leader and equally loved and admired by Jains and non-Jains, who affectionately call him "Gurudev Chitrabhanuji".

Muni Chandra Prabha Sagar's bold decision to travel abroad proved to be a an important and timely step towards Jain reform efforts.[57] With his sponsorship in 1975, another Jain monk - Acharya Sushil Kumar - followed his lead, arrived in the United States and joined Chitrabhanuji in his efforts to bring Mahavir's message to the West. Acharya Sushil Kumarji established "The Mahavir Jain Mission", and a pilgrimage center - Siddhachalam - in North America. In 1981,

57 Jain, D.P., *The Wave of Bliss: Impact of Chitrabhanu On The Western World*, Swadhyay Mandir Charitable Trust, Ahmedabad. Also, Rosenfield, Clare, *Gurdev Shree Chitrabhanu: A Man of Vision*, Jain Meditation International Centre, New York, 1981.

these two mavericks inspired nearly 80,000 Jains living in various parts of North America to come together to form an umbrella organization JAINA - Federation of Jain Associations of North America. Together, they have presided over the establishment of 57 Jain Centers and 16 Jain temples. Chitrabhanuji travels extensively each year to Europe, Africa and India bringing Mahavira's message to the ever-increasing number of participants. His global mission is for the young Jains to continue the heritage of *ahimsa* and *anekantavada.*

ACHARYA CHANDANAJI

Perhaps the most contraversial ascetic of the modern reform movement in Jainism is Acharya Chandanaji. Born in 1937, her parents Manek and Prem named her Shakuntala. She was ordained at a very young age of 14 by Acharya Anandrishi. She was impressed by the fact that Mahavir did not confine himself to personal spiritual perfection, but dedicated his life to the cause of social reconstruction through *ahimsa*, *aparigraha* and *anekantavada.* Convinced that Mahavira's central message of *ahimsa* is in reality a call for the service to humanity and all living beings, in 1972 she decided to join a group of nuns under the guidance of a reform minded guru Amar Muniji. True to the spirit of *anekantavada*, she studied Jain as well as non-Jain scriptures rapidly. In 1986, at the age of 49, her spiritual progress was recognized in the form of a promotion to the monestic rank of "*Darshan-Acharya.*"

Another fact which impressed upon her is Mahavira's message of equality. Mahavira's four-fold *sangha* was a community of equals where there was no barriers of caste or sex. Mahavira readily admitted high or low caste Hindus men or women into his *sangha* and promted them through the ascetic hirearchy purely on the basis of their scholarship and spititual progress. He chose men as well women to head the ascetic orders, and the head of all nuns during his time was, significantly, a nun called Acharya Chandanbala.[58] Unfortunately, as it has also happened in other faiths, with the male dominanance in the society the hirearchchcal positions of Jain nuns later became secondary to those of the monks. A Digambara author - Prabhachandra[59] - went as far as stating that women cannot be truly Jain. Although a contemporary Svetambara author, Shakatayana strongly attacked this position claiming that women are equal members of

[58] Jacobi, H., "The leader of the nuns (in Mahavira's *Sangh*) was Acharya Candana," *Jaina Sutras,* Part 1, Oxford.

[59] Prabhachandra, *Nyayakumudacarita*, Jain, M.K., ed., Bombay, 1941 pp. 865-70.

humanity with men, and therefore capable of enlightenment,[60] Svetambaras had also yielded to the patriarchal attitudes. According to their monastic hirearchy, a junior monk pays homage (*vandana*) to a senior monk, a newly initiated monk (regardless of his age) pays homage to all those initiated before him, and laypersons pay homage to all monks. However, the great medieval Svetambara *acharya*, Jinadattasuri, tried to ban women from worshipping the main *Tirthankara* image in temples,[61] and the Svetambara too adopted a new monastic law according to which a nun, regardless of how long she has been in the order, and regardless of her title of seniority in her order, must pay homage to even a newly initiated monk.[62] They developed a new set of monastic titles. The ranks for the monks became: (i) *Sadhu* or *Muni*, (ii) *Ganivarya* (iii) *Pannyasa* or *Pravartaka*, (iv) *Upadhayaya*, and (v) *Acharya*, the ranks for the nuns became *Sadhvi* or *Ganini*, *Pravartani*, and *Mahattara*. Only the "*Acharyas*" came to be recognised as "heads of the order." The fact that, for a long time in Jain history only men were allowed to head the order, was not lost on the young *sadhvi* Chandanaji.

In assuming the title "*Acharya*", instead of "*Mahattara*" - almost a non-title by now - both Chandanaji and her grantor Amar Muniji broke the tradition. They were, in effect, inviting the *sangha* to re-examine Mahavira's message of equality. With Mahavira's true message and history on her side, becoming an a*charya* was Chandanaji's act of self-assertion and defiance - a character trait evident in almost all her later activities.

Mahavira's message of compassion (*jiva-daya*) was another issue, where she felt compelled to act. Jain *karma* theory and the ascetic path, she felt, were being misinterpreted. A Jain ascetic takes five great vows (*maha-vrata*) as a personal commitment to dedicate the rest of his/her life to liberating his/her soul from all *karmas*. Since good as well as bad activities are all likely to bond a soul deeper with *karma*, many ascetics interpret their vows as "remaining aloof from all non-essential activities." They advise their lay followers to take up compassionate causes but would themselves remain uninvolved in order to avoid "attachment to the cause, and its resulting karmic bondage." Such interpretations have a serious negative effect on social-justice causes in a poor country like India. Jain laypersons generously donate to temples and support hospitals, animal shelters, schools and places of pilgrimage. However, a culture of physical and personal involvement as volunteers

60 Shakatayana, *Strinirvanakevalibhaktiprakarane*, Jambuvijayji, Muni, ed.., Bhavnagar, 1974.

61 Dundas, Paul, The Jains, Routledge, London, 1992 p. 52.

62 *ibid*, pg. 27.

in humanitarian causes has not adequately evolved in the Jain communities, especially in the absence of direct involvement of their ascetics.

Chandanaji was quick to recognize the seriousness of the lack of direct involvement by the Jain ascetics. She was aware of the globally evolving new concept of spirituality in terms of social justice, human rights and the rights of all the living beings - a concept which Mahvira preached nearly 2500 years ago.

Personal salvation as well as upliftment of ordinary person's mundane life is the mission of my initiation. In it, I am drawing inspiration from Bhagwan Mahavira's basic sutras.[63]

She reportedly started pressuring her *guru* to take on the social justice causes. Her *guru*, Upadhyaya Amar Muniji, in turn ordered her to undertake a very difficult and dangerous humanitarian mission. In 1973, Chandanaji and four other nuns were asked to go to the remote areas of Bihar and help the poor. Bihar was then, and still is, the most poor, underdevelped, and dangerous province in India. Twenty five hundred years ago, Bihar was the hub of Jainism, twenty-two out of twenty-four *Tirthankaras* had once roamed this land and had achieved *moksha* in this region. Mahavira meditated for fourteen years in this land at a place called Rajgiri, and preached nonviolence, love and compassion. Now however, there were hardly any Jain families in Bihar, and these nuns were to establish here a humanitarian mission called. 'Veerayatan.'

Initial attempts to build Veerayatan met with very little support and considerable hostility from the locals. The mission, operating out of a small hut, was vandalized, ransacked and looted several times in its early days, often endangering the lives of the nuns. Now, some 30 years later, the dedication and perseverance of Chandanaji and her 10 Jain *sadhvis* has transformed Veerayatan into a leading Jain socio-religious organization operating a 200-bed free hospital, clinics, relief centres, a research institution and schools in Rajgir, and Pune. When the earthquake struck Gujarat in 2001, Chandanaji and her nuns arrived on the scene within weeks and opened a school at which nearly 6000 children get free education and meals.

Chandanaji personally manages and supervises Veerayatan. Not only does she personally get involved in its activities, she also askes her nun deciples to get professionally trained in such fields as medicine, philosophy and business management, and get more involved in humanitarian work. Ordained nuns are sent to universities overseas to study comparative religion and to establish Jain

[63] *Amar Bharati* A Veerayatan Publication, Volume 4, January 1988 pg. 6.

TERMS TO REMEMBER

Gaccha	Ascetic lineage
Maryada	Limits of behavior
Muhapatti	Cloth for covering mouth
Paroksha	Indirect, non-living guru
Pratyaksha	Direct, Living guru
Prekshadhyana	A type of Jain meditation
Saman	A quasi-ascetic male
Samani	Aquasi-ascetic - female
Sat-Guru	Right guru
Sat-Sangha	Religious assembly
Sat-Sruta	Right teaching
Sthanaka	A hall for religious assembly
Tapa	Penance
Upashraya	A hall in a temple complex
Vipakshana	A type of Buddhist meditation

Educational centres. Chandanaji is also constantly on the move briniging her message of humanitarian service, social justice, education, and spiritual fulfillment to the growing number of her followers in Africa, Europe, and Americas, and encouraging them to get involved in the social justice issues.

The problem, is that active management role involves many trappings of the mundane lay life such as raising and managing funds; interacting with government officials, professionals and workers; and travel abroad. Chandanaji's decisions enrage conservative elements in the community who see her activities as the betrayal of the five great vows of ascetic life. They believe that ascetics must fully engage themselves in spiritual activities such as studying scriptures, meditation, and freedom from the karmic bondage. Any other activity is a deviation from the vows to follow the prescribed Jain path of purification.

Chandanaji's daily routine does include meditation and studying scriptures, but she maintains that bringing Mahavira's message of *ahimsa*, *aprigraha*, and *anekantavada* into action is the true spirituality. "All *Tirthankaras* have given this message through personal examples," she contends, "they did not turn away from the society upon enlightenment, instead they dedicated themselves to the creation of healthy social values." Her reform efforts are in keeping with the current global movement to rediscover true spirituality and redefine it in the terms of human rights and the rights of all living being (Chapter 13). Her reform movement has attracted worldwide attention from progressive thinkers, activists, and youth. Nevertheless, she also continues to attract strong criticism, opposition, and heat from conservative Jains. Several large signs on Gaya railway station near Rajgir warn travellers, "DANGER!". "Because of the rampant lawlessness in the surrounding areas, travellers are warned NOT to leave the perimeter of the railway station before dawn and after dusk." When I asked Chandanaji about the dangers of working in such a dangerous area, and the bitter criticism she often faces from other Jains, a gentle smile appeared on her face and she recited a line from a poem written by her *guru*, "*Path-darshak bananare balavoo pade che*" ("Only by burning, can a candle show the path.").

20

20. The Sacred Literature

Although the archaeological evidence, combined with the Jain lore, fixes Rikhava's period to be at least 8,500 years ago, there is no written literature from that time. Not until several centuries after Lord Mahavira that the first Jain sacred text was ever written.

The Oral Tradition

Ancient Indians had a great system of memorizing verbatim the teachings of their masters and passing these on to the next generation who then would transfer it orally to their next generation. The first written words in a script understandable today appeared in India approximately in 1300 BCE.* In the absence of paper, these were written on dried palm leaves. However, the *sramana* monks (predecessors of the present-day Jains) of this period did not adapt to the method of using palm leaves because of two major problems.

Firstly, because of their vows of minimizing hurting of any living being, the idea of cutting and drying palm leaves for writing was not acceptable. Secondly, even if the books were so written, the monks, who were always on the move, could not carry the books with them because of their vows of non-possession (*aparigraha*).

Furthermore, the infestation of dried leaves with millions of tiny insects, in the hot and humid weather of India, posed additional problems for the *sramana* monks who practiced nonviolence.

The concepts and ideas developed by Rikhava were memorized, improvised, and orally passed on to successive generations by *sramana* monks and *Tirthankaras*, and

* The seals and carvings from the Mohenjo-Daro period - 3500 BCE - do have writings. However, scientists have not been able to decipher these until recently. A first success in this respect has been reported in February 2000.

Were finally organized by the last *Tirthankara*, Mahavira, in about 600 BCE. His chief disciple, Indrabhuti Gautama, then codified and classified the teachings of his master into twelve parts called, *Dvadasanga Suttam*. This is the Jain canon; it was still only in the oral format and was to remain so for centuries to come.

The Written Texts

The first written scriptures of Jainism therefore did not appear until 453 CE - nearly 1,000 years after the death of Mahavira. Until then, Mahavira's words were transmitted orally by a succession of monks. Bihar was the center of learning in the fourth century BCE, but when Bhadrabahu passed away, and his disciples returned from southern India, their version of 'Mahavira's Words' (*Agama*) did not quite agree with that of Sthulabhadra's group, which had stayed back in Bihar.

Sthulabhadra had called nationwide 'Council of Monks' in Patliputra, Bihar in 327 BCE to reconcile the differences and to come up with an official version. The monks were now aware of the danger of losing Mahavira's words if they continued with the tradition of transmitting their knowledge by oral means only. A decision was perhaps taken here to commit the sacred words to writing and to exclude the scriptures from the vows of non-possession. However very little, if any, was committed to writing at this time. Meanwhile, debates continued about the authenticity of 'Mahavira's Words' as remembered by different groups of monks. A major debate in 82 CE on the issue of whether or not scriptures allow ascetics to wear clothes widened the split between the two camps. Although *Agamas* were yet to be redacted, several monks started writing independent treatises on various topics based on the knowledge they had orally received. The major works of that era is by *Acharya* Kundakunda (second century) whose texts such as *Samayasara*, *Niyamsara* and *Pravachansara* have attained quasi-scriptural status among the Digambara sect.

The second and third 'Councils of Monks' (Mathura in 340 AD, and Valabhi 453 AD) finally produced an official version of the *Dvadasanga Suttam*. It was written under the leadership of a monk, Ksamasramana, and called the *Agamas*. Since this version resulted from a conference at which hundreds of monks recited each *sutra* and the version memorized and recited by a large number of monks was written down. Svetambaras believe that the texts produced at this Council are very close to the exact words of Mahavira. Most of the pre-Mahavira teachings - called '*Purvas*' - from the time of the twenty-third *Tirthankara*, Parshva, were lost by this period. This first wave of books is called, the "*Anga-Agama*" literature (*Anga* means Original or Main and *Agama* means sacred canon). Its contents are claimed by Svetambaras to be the authentic teaching of 'Lord Mahavira.' The Digambaras however, did not accept these as Mahavira's authentic words. All agree, however, that Mahavira's essential message, if not actual words, have now been preserved.

The Main Canon

Unlike the Bible or Qur'an, Jain sacred literature is made up of many volumes. The Svetambara community accepts 45 volumes as Agama. This number includes 11 volumes of the main canon (Volume 12 was a collection of 14 books of *Purva* but is lost) and 34 subsidiary canon texts. The Digambaras maintain that all of Mahavira's authentic work is lost, and accept only two later works (2nd century AD) as their canon.

At the time of Mahavira, Ardhamaghadhi was the language of the masses in the region of the Ganga Plain, whereas the lingua franca of the contemporary scholars (mostly Brahmins) was an early form of Sanskrit. Mahavira preached in Ardhamaghadhi - the people's language. Therefore, later the *Anga-Agamas* were also written in that language. Much of the information on Jain metaphysics, epistemology, etc. given in earlier chapters can be traced back to these volumes. These 12 volumes can be roughly classified into four groups based on their content. For example, volumes 1, 7 and 10 are on Rational Conduct (*samyak-charitra*). Volume 2 compares Jain world-view with those of other contemporary philosophies. Rational worldview and Rational Knowledge (*samyak-darsana* and *samyak-jnana*) are discussed in volumes 3, 4 and 5. Volumes 6, 8, 9, 11, and 12 are narratives either to explain the philosophy or to induce followers to continue making progress on the path to moksha. Volume 12 is lost, but all others except volumes 3 and 4 have now been translated in either German or English, and all have been translated in Gujarati.

A brief introduction of each volume is given below. Sanskrit names of the original Ardhamaghadhi titles are given in the parenthesis.

Vol. 1 - Aayaramg Suttam (Acharanga Sutra)

By describing Mahavira's ascetic life, this volume serves as a model of behavior or conduct for Jain monks and nuns. It contains minutest details of the three core principles of Jain conduct (Triple 'A's)

Vol. 2 - Suyagadamg Suttam (Sutrakrtanga Sutra)

This volume is essentially a debate over Jain philosophical ideas in contrast to other contemporary worldviews such as fatalism, *Sankhya* externalism, agnosticism, etc. All these other philosophies being one-sided are considered inadequate or incomplete and judged inferior by the *anekantavada* standards of Jain philosophy.

Vol. 3 - Thanamg Suttam (Sthananga Sutra)
This volume is like a learning manual on Jain principles and worldview for the newly ordained monks and nuns.

Vol. 4 - Samavayamg Suttam (Samanvayanga Sutra)
Volumes 3 and 4 are written in a bulleted/tabular form. Its main purpose, it appears, is to help learners to memorize the details of Jain principles. Chronologically these volumes may be the last ones because they describe the detailed contents of all the 12 volumes.

Vol. 5 - Viyah Pannati Suttam (Vyakhya Prajnapti Sutra, Bhagavati Sutra)
This volume is the largest of all the *Anga-Agamas*. The format used in this volume is that of questions, asked by the chief disciple Indrabhuti Gautama, and the answers given by Mahavira. Over 36,000 questions and answers explain the minutest details and subtleties of topics such as: soul, matter, *karma*, *syadvada*, and others. These detailed discussions are so valuable in understanding Jainism that this volume is also called 'Bhagavati - the Most Revered One'.

Vol. 6 - Nayadhammakahao Suttam (Jnatra Dharma Kathanga Sutra)
This is a volume of narratives. Mahavira extensively used examples and stories to illustrate his point during his sermons. The importance of this style of telling stories to explain a subtle point can be readily appreciated from the fact that the Jain monks use it even today. For example, the famous stories like "The Elephant and the Seven Blind Persons" (to illustrate *anekantavada*), or "The Man in the Well" (to illustrate the importance of seeking permanent bliss instead of trivial pleasures) come from this repertoire.

Vol. 7 - Uvasagdasao Suttam (Upasaka-das-anga Sutra)
Whereas the first volume sets a code of conduct for the monks by describing Mahavira's ascetic life, this volume does the same thing for the laity. Stories of the conduct of ten of Mahavira's lay followers, their trials and tribulations, and their steadfastness are given.

Vol. 8 - Anatagaddasao Suttam (Antahkrida-das-anga Sutra)
This volume is essentially a storybook for the sravaka and sravikas. Jain literature is rich in stories and narratives used for the purpose of explaining the intricacies

of Jain concepts to lay persons. Jain ascetics even today use many of the stories from this volume in their public sermons.

Vol. 9 -Anuttarov Vaiya Dasao (Anuttaropa-patika-Dasanga Sutra)
These two volumes are designed to induce the laypersons to make progress through all the vows and *pratimas* to becomes monks, and achieve the goal of liberation. To this end these two volumes narrate stories about how ten venerable monks, from the time of Nemi (the twenty-second *Tirthankara*), achieved total liberation and how ten other monks did not achieve their goal but nevertheless attained rebirth in the top-most heaven.

Vol. 10 - Panha Vagarana Suttam (Prasna Vyakarana Sutra)
Whereas a layperson takes twelve minor vows (*anuvratas*) to begin his/her journey on the path to liberation, initiation into monkshood requires taking five major vows (*mahavratas*). This volume discusses these major vows, lays down a code of conduct for the ascetics, and warns the followers of the five worst sins.

Vol. 11 - Vivagsuyam Suttam (Vipaka Sutra)
This is a narrative on the Jain Theory of *karma*. It contains stories describing how, eventually, one reaps good or bad rewards of his/her *karma*. By describing how some people received benefits of their *karma,* and some are paying in this life for their past bad *karma*, this volume serves as a powerful deterrent to wrong doings.

Vol. 12 - Ditthivaya Suttam (Drstivada Sutra)
Although this volume is supposed to be totally lost, enough references to it exist in a subsidiary canon called *Prajnapana* to give us an idea of its contents. It was supposed to be divided into five parts and part 3 was believed to consist of 14 '*Purvas*' containing information and stories about the period before Mahavira. Digambara tradition believes that part of this has survived and was written down by Bhutabali, in the 2nd century CE, in a work known as *Satkhand-agama*. Another work based on the same information was soon composed by Gunabhadra, and is called, *Kasaya Prabhrta*. Digambaras, while respecting all the literature, accept only these last two works as valid scriptures.

The Subsidiary Canon

The main canon the *Anga-Agama* is generally accepted by Svetambaras as Mahavira's authentic teachings compiled by his direct disciples. Later, many other monks wrote supplements to *Anga-Agama* to provide detailed explanations. These books too are considered sacred or '*Agama*' but are given subsidiary - *Anga-bahya* (outside the main) status. There are 34 *Anga-bahya agama* texts classified as:

Upanga - (12 texts.) These texts are written for the laypersons to understand important Jain concepts. For example, The *Uvavaiya (Aupapatika)* emphasizes the importance of adherence to vows. The *Raya Pasenaijja (Rajaprasniya)* compares Jain ideas about soul with those of other schools in the form of a dialogue between Jain and non-Jain proponents. Whereas, non-Jain schools maintain that the soul, being non-material, is limitless and all pervasive, Jains believe it to be, though non-material, confined to shape and size of the body when it is in its bonded state. The *Jivajivabhigama* presents Jain ontology in a dialogue form. *Pannavana (Prajnapana)*, besides giving a summary of the contents of the 14 lost *Purvas*, discusses various aspects of bonded soul. Jain cosmology is discussed in the *Sunya-pannatti (Surya-prajnapati), Cand-pannatti (Chadra-prajnapati),* and *Jambudvipa-pannatti (Jambudvipa-prajnapati).* Furthermore, the *Jambudvipa-panatti* also explains Jain concept of time cycle and how Rikhava started civilization. The Jain claim of Hindu icons Krshna and Balarama being related to Neminath - the 22nd *Tirthankara* - is based on the accounts given in *Vanhidasao (Vrsnidasha).*

Chedsutra - (6 texts). These are the texts on Jain monastic laws describing the discipline, conduct, and behavior of monks and nuns, and rules for the atonement of their mistakes. The six texts are: *Ayaradasao (Achardasah)*, *Bihakappa (Brhatkalpa)*, *Vavahara (Vyavahara)*, *Nisiha (Nisitha)*, *Mahanisiha (Mahanisitha)*, and *Jiyakappa (Jitakalpa).*

Mulasutra - (4 texts). These texts are the required reading for all ascetics in the earlier stages of their monastic life. They describe the strict conditions under which the monks and nuns are to live. The four texts are: the *Dasaveyaliya (Dasavaikalika), Uttarajjhayana (Uttaradhyayana), Avassaya (Avasyaka), and Pimdanijjutti (Pindniryukti).* These texts describe, in minute details, permitted and restricted activities for ascetics under various conditions in daily living. The *Uttarajjhayana* is believed to be the last thirty-six lectures of Mahavira.

Prakirnasutra - (10 texts). These ten short texts describe the rituals for holy death (*santhara*). Topics such as taking refuges, renunciation by the sick, preparing the deathbed, renouncing food, retaining consciousness at the moment of death, praise of Mahavira and other Jinas, etc.

Culikasutra - (2 texts). The *Namdi-sutta* (*Nandi-sutra*) explains five types of knowledge - *mati, sruti, avadhi, manhaparyaya*, and *kevala-jnana.* It also gives elaborate description of *Tirthankaras* and *Ganadharas.* The other text - *Anuogaddaraim (Anuyogadvara-sutra)* contains section-by-section summaries of the topics discussed in most of the other canonical texts.

Expositions *(Anuyoga)*

Jain literature is equally rich in post-canonical compositions by monk-scholars. Several topics ranging from biographies of Jinas, hymns in praise of Jinas, logical and scientific work exploring not only the spiritual and philosophical topics but the material universe as well, and ascetic discipline are covered in this literature over the past 2,000 years. Given below is a small sample of works by well-known monk-scholars. Traditionally, Jain temples and *mathas* (religious places administered by *bhattarakas* have preserved a large number of manuscripts in their basement libraries called '*Bhandars*'.

AUTHOR	WORKS	TRANSLATIONS
Divakara, Siddhasena (5th Century)	*Nyayavatara* *Sanmatitarka*	Upadhye A. N., Jaina Sahitya Vikas Mandala, Bombay 1971 Sanghvi, Sukhlalji and Doshi, Bechardasji, Jaina Mahavira Jain Vidyalaya, 1939
Gunabhadra (9th Century)	*Uttarapurana*	Pannalal Jain Bharatiya Jnanapitha Publications, Varanasi 1954
Haribhadra (8th Century)	*Sambodhaprakarana* *Saddarsana - Samucchaya* *Yogabindu* *Youga-dristi-samucchaya* *Yogasataka*	Jaina Grantha Prakashak Sabha, Ahmedabad 1915 Jain M. K., Bharatiya Jnanapitha Publications 1969 Dixit K. K., L. D. Institute of Indology, Ahmedabad 1968
Hemchandra (12th Century)	*Trisastisalaka -purusacharitra* *Yogasastra* *Pramanmimasa* *Anyayogavyava-cchedika* *Parisistaparva* *Sabdanusasana*	1. Helen M. Johnson, Lives of Sixty-three Illustrious Persons, (6 volumes), Oriental Institute, Vadodara, 1962 2. Charanvijaya Muni (ed.), Jain Atmananda Sabha, Bhavnagar, 1933. Bharil, Shobhachandra, Delhi, 1963 1. Mukarjee, Satkari and Tatia, Nathmal, Tara Publications, Varanasi 1970 2. Sanghvi, Sukhlalji, Singhi Jaina Series, Calcutta1939 1. Thomas F. W., The Flower Spray of the Quodammodo Doctrine, Akademie-Verlag, 1960 2. Jain J. C., Rajchandra Jaina Sastramala, Agas 1970 Jacobi, H., Bibliotheca Indica no. 96, Calcutta, 1932 Himamsu Vijay Muni, Ahmedabad 1934

Jinasena (8th Century)	*Adipurana* *Harivanshapurana*	Pannalal Jain, Bharatiya Jnanapitha Publications, Varanasi 1963, 1965 (2 volumes) Pannalal Jain, Bharatiya Jnanapitha Publications, Varanasi
Kundakunda (2nd Century)	*Niyamsara* *Pravachansara* *Samayasara*	Maganlal Jain, Digambara Jain Svadhyaya Mandir, Sonagadh, 1965 Upadhye A. N., Rajchandra Jain Sastramala, Agas, 1934 Chakravarti, A., Bharatiya Jnanapitha Publications, Varanasi, 1925, Reissued in 1971 Bhore, D. G., Mahavira Jnanopasana Samiti, Karanja, 1968
Somadeva (10th Century)	*Nitivakyaamrita* *Yasatilaka-campu*	Malaviya, R. Chowkhambha Vidyabhavan, 1972 Shivadatta Mahamahopadhyaya, Kavyamala no. 70, Bombay 1901-1903
Umasvati (2nd Century)	*Tattvartha-sutra*	Tatia, Nathmal, That Which Is, Harper Collins Publishers, The Sacred Literature Series, San Francisco 1994 Siddhantsastri, Phoolchand, Varni Granthmala, Varanasi 1949 Sanghvi, Sukhlalji, Jaina Samskriti Samsodhana Mandala, Varanasi, 1952 (2nd edition) Vohora, Sunanda, *Tattvamimasa*, (Gujarati)
Yasovijaya (17th Century)	*Jaintarkabhasha* *Jnanabindu* *Nyayaloka*	Bhargava, D. Motilal Banarasidas 1973

Bibliography

Some Abbreviations used:

BJ: **B**haratiya **J**nanapitha Publications, Varanasi
LDII: **L**albhai **D**alpatbhai **I**nstitute of **I**ndology, Ahmedabad
MB: **M**otilal **B**anarasidas, Delhi

Babb, L. A. — Absent Lord: Ascetics and Kings in a Jain Ritual Culture, University of California Press, Los Angeles 1996

Banks, M. — Organising Jainism in India and England, Oxford University Press, New York, 1992

Bhadrabahu Swami — Kalpa-Sutra (Hindi Translation by Devendra Muni), Amara Jaina Agama Shodhasthana, Shivana 1968
Shree Kalpsutram (Gujarati Translation by Kheem Vijay Ganiji), Mehta Family Trust, Stoughton, MA, USA 1998
Kalpa-Sutra of Bhadrabahu Svami (English translation by Lalwani, K.C.), MB, Delhi 1979

Bhargava, D. — Jaina Ethics, MB, Delhi 1968

Bhattacharya, H. — Anekatavada, Jain Atmanand Sabha, Bhavnagar 1953

Bhattacharya, Harisatya — Reals in the Jain Metaphysics, SSK Charitable Trust, Bombay 1950
The Philosophy of the Jainas, Jain Literature Society, Bombay 1958
The Jain Prayer, University of Calcutta Press, Calcutta 1964
Jain Moral Doctrine, Jain Sahitya Vikasa Mandala, Bombay 1976
Sri Namaskara Mahamantra, Jain Youth Forum, Madras 1979

Bhattacharya, N.N. — Jain Philosophy, Historical Outline, Munshiram Manoharlal, Delhi 1976
Jainism and Prakrit, Manohar Publishers, New Delhi 1994

Bothra, P. — Jain Theory of Perception, MB, Delhi 1976

Buddhisagar Surisvarji Muni — Shree Anandghanapada Samgraha, (Gujarati)Adhyatmajnana Prakashan Mandala, Bombay 1954

Caillat, C.,Upadhye, A.N., and Patil B. — Jainism, Macmillan Company of India, Delhi 1974

Carrithers, M. and Humphrey, C. eds. — The Assembly of Listeners, Cambridge University Press, Cambridge 1991

Chakravarti, A. — *Samaysara* of Shri Kundakunda, Tr. with Introduction, BJ, Delhi 1971
Pancastikayasara, BJ Delhi 1975

Chapple, C. K. — Non Violence to Animals, Earth, and Self In Asian Traditions, State University of New York Press, Albany 1993

Chatterjee, A.K., — Comprehensive History of Jainism, (2 Volumes), Firma KLM, Calcutta 1978 and 1985

Chaudary, G.C. — Political History of Northern India from Jaina Sources, Amritsar 1963

Cort, J. E. ed. — Open Boundaries: Jain Communities and Culture in Indian History, State University of New York Press, 1988

Dasgupta, D.C. — Jaina System of Education, MB, Delhi 1999

Deepratnasagar Muni — *Agamadeep: 45 Agama Gurjarchaya*, Gujarati translation of Agama Scriptures, Agamadeep Prakashan, Ahmedabad 1997

Deleu, J. — *Viyah Pannati Suttam (Bhagavati Sutra)*, (Critical Analysis of 5th Agama, MB 1996

Desai, P.B. — Jainism in South India and Some Jaina Epigraphs, Jivraja Jain Granthamala, Sholapur 1957

Desai, R.C. — Srimad Rajachandra Volumes I & II, Srimad Rajacjandra Ashram, Agas 1976

Devendra Muni — Source-Book in Jaina Philosophy, Sri Tarak Guru Jain Grnathalaya, Udaipur, Hindi, 1973, English - 1983

Divyakirti Muni — *Visva Vijnana: Prachin Ane Navin* (Universal Science: Old and New) Ch. 5 of Tattvarthsutra (Gujarati), Sanmarg Prakashan Ahmedabad 1994

Dixit, K. K. — "A New Contribution to the Discussion of Jaina Monastic Discipline," in *Sambodhi*, V, No. 2-3, pp. 13-48. LDII, Ahmedabad 1976

Early Jainism, LDII, Ahmedabad 1978

Jaina Ontology, LDII, Ahmedabad 1971

Dundas, P. — The Jains, Routledge Press, London 1992

Dwivedi, R.C. ed. — Contribution of Jainism to Indian Culture, MB, Delhi 1975

Fischer, E. and Jain J. — Art and Rituals: 2500 Years of Jainism in India, Sterling Publishers, New Delhi 1977 (translation of German original in 1974)

Folkert, K. W., — "Jaina Studies: Japan, Europe, India", in *Sambodhi*, V, No. 2-3, pp. 138-147. LDII, Ahmedabad 1976

Scriptures and Community, Collected Essays on the Jains, ed. By John Cort, Scholars Press, Atlanta 1993

Gandhi, V.R. — Religion and Philosophy of the Jainas, Edited by Nagin Shah, Jain International, Ahmedabad, 1993

Glasenapp, H. V. — Doctrine of *Karma*n in Jain Philosophy, English translation from German by G. Barry Gifford, P.V. Research Insitute, Varanasi 1991

Gopalan, S. — Outlines of Jainism, Wiley Eastern New Delhi 1973

Gopani, A.S. (Tr.) — *Saman Suttam*, translated by Gopani A.S. Yajna Prakashan Samiti, Vadodara 1976

Saman Suttam, translated by Tukol, T.K. and Dixit, K.K., Sarva Seva Sangh Prakashan, Varanasi, 1993

Guseva, N.R. — Jainism, English translation from Russian by Y. S. Redkar, Sindhu Publications, Bombay 1971

Jacobi, H. — "On Mahavira and His Predecessors", in Indian Antiquary, IX, pp. 158-163, 1880

Jain Sutras, (2 Volumes) originally published by Clarendon Press, Oxford in the Sacred Books of the East Series, XXII and XLV in 1884 and 1895. Reprinted in Dover Publications, New York 1968

Jain, S. K. ed. — Glimpses of Jainism, MB, Delhi 1997

Progressive Jains of India, Shraman Sahitya Samsthan, New Delhi 1975

Jain, B.C. — Jaina Logic, University of Madras Press, 1992

Jain C. R. — Fundamentals of Jainism, Veer Nirvan Bharati, Meerut 1974

Jain Hiralal and Upadhye, A.N. — Mahavira: His Times and His Philosophy of Life, BJ, Varanasi 1974

Jain Jyoti Prasad — Jainism: The Oldest Living Religion, Cultural Research Society, Varanasi, 1951

The Jaina Sources of the History of Ancient India, Munishiram Manoharlal, Delhi 1964

Religion and Culture of the Jains, BJ, New Delhi 1983

Jain K.C. Lord Mahavira and His Times, MB, Delhi 1974

Jain L.C. The Essence of Attainment *Labdhisara*, Acharya Vidyasagar Research Institute, Jabalpur 1993

Jain N.L. Glossary of Jaina Terms, Jain International, Ahmedabad 1995

Scientific Contents in Prakrit Canons, Parsvanath Vidyalaya, Varanasi 1996

Biology in Jaina Treatise on Reals, (translation of Tattvatika Rajvartika by Akalanka), P.V. Institue, Varanasi 1999

Jain R. K. *Kavivara Banarasidas* (in Hindi), BJ, New Delhi 1966

The Universe as Audience: Metaphor and Community Among the Jains of North India, Indian Institute of Advanced Study, Shimla 1999

Jain S.C. Structure and Functions of Soul in Jainism, BJ, New Delhi 1978

Jain Sagarmal An Introduction to Jain Sadhana, (Jaina Way of Living), Parsvanatha Sodhapitha, Varanasi, 1995

Jaini, P.S. The Jaina Path of Purification, University of California Press, Berkeley 1979

Gender and Salvation Jaina Debates on the Spiritual Liberation of Women, University of California Press, Los Angeles, 1991

Johrapurkar, V.P. *Bhattaraka Sampradaya* (in Hindi), Jivraj Jain Granthamala, Sholapur 1958

Joshi, G. N. *Atma and Moksha* Gujarat University, Ahmedabad 1965

Joshi, L.M. Facets of Jain Religiousness in Comparative Light, LDII, Ahmedabad 1981

Kalghatgi, T.G. *Karma* and Rebirth, LDII, Ahmedabad 1971

Jaina View of Life, Jaina Samskrti Samraksaka Sangh, Sholapur 1984

Kapadia, H.R. A History of the Canonical Literature of the Jainas, Surat

Kapashi, V. J. In Search of the Ultimate, V.K. Publications, Harrow 1984

Khushaldas, J. ed. *Yogasastra*, Sri Mahavir Jain Vidyalaya, Bombay 1972

Kuhn, Hermann The Key to the Center of the Universe, Crosswind Publishing, 2000

Kulke, H. et. al. A History of India, Rupa & Co., Calcutta, 1993 (2nd edition)

Laislaw, J. Riches and Renunciation: Religion, Economy and Society Among the Jains, Oxford University Press, Oxford 1995

Lal R.B. Religion in the Light of Reason and Science, Bharatiya Vidya Bhavan, Bombay 1978

Law B.C. Some Jaina Canonical Sutras, Royal Àsiatic Society Monograph No. 2, Bombay 1949

Marathe, M.P., et. al. Studies in Jainism, I.P.Q. Publications, Dept. of Philosophy, University of Poona, Poona 1984

Mardia, K.V. The Scientific Foundations of Jainism, L.S.L. Jain Research Series, MB, Delhi 1990

Marett, Paul Jainism Explained, Jain Samaj Europe Publications, Leicester 1985

Matilal, B.K. The Central Philosophy of Jainism, LDII, Ahmedabad 1981

Mehta, Mohanlal Jaina Psychology, Sohanlal Jaindharma Pracharak Samiti, Amritsar 1955

Jaina Theory of Knowledge, Gujarat Vidyapith, Ahmedabad 1995

Mookerjee, S. The Jaina Philosophy of Non-Absolutism: A Critical Study of Anekantavada MB 1978 (2nd edition)

Nair, V.G. Jainism and Terapathism, Adinatha Jain Temple, Banglore 1970

Nathmal Muni Acharya Bhiksu: The Man and His Philosophy, Adarsha Sahitya Sangha Churu, 1968

Nemichandra Siddhantideva *Dryva-Sangraha*, translated by Sarat Chandra Ghosal, Shri Chandraprabha Digambar Jain Mandir Trust, Bombay 1986 (3rd ed.)

Nevaskar, B. Capitalists Without Capitalism: The Jains of India and the Quakers of the West Greenwood Publications,Westport, Conn. 1971

Nyayavijayji Muni — Jaina Darsana, Original 1956 Sanskrit text translated by Nagin J. Shah as: Jaina Philosophy and Religion, MB, Delhi 1998

O'Connell, J.T. ed. — Jain Doctrine and Practice: Academic Perspectives, University of Toronto Press, Toronto 2000

Padmarajiah, Y. J. — Jaina Theories of Reality and Knowledge, Jaina Sahitya Vikas Mandala, Bombay 1963

Pal, P. — The Peaceful Liberators: Jaina Art from India, Los Angeles County Museum of Art, and Thames and Hudson, Los Angeles 1994

Pandey, V., ed. — The World of Jainism, Published by the author, Bombay 1976

Rajchandra Srimad — *Atmakatha*, Srimad Rajachandra Asharam, Agas 1929

Mokshamala, Srimad Rajachandra Asharam, Agas

Ramachandran, T.N. — Harappa and Jainism, Kundakunda Bharati Prakashan, New Delhi 1987

Rosenfield, C. — Gurudev Shree Chitrabhanu A Man with a Vision, Jain Meditation International Centre New York 1982

Roy, A. K. — History of the Jains, Gitanjali Publishing House, New Delhi 1984

Salter, E. — "Unity and Diversity Amongst the followers of Srimad Rajacandra," in *Jinamanjari*, Vol. 23, No. 1, pp. 32-51

Sangave, V. A. — The Jaina Path of Ahimsa Bhagawan Mahavir Research Centre, Sholapur 1991

Aspects of Jain Religion, 3rd ed., BJ 2001

Sanghavi, Sukhlalji — *Samdarshi Acharya Haribhadra* (in Hindi), Rajasthan Puratan Granthamala, Jodhpur 1963

Darshan Aur Chintan Part 1 & 2, Gujarat Vidyasabha, Ahmedabad 1957

Schubring, W. — The Doctrine of the Jainas, translated from German by Wolfgang Beurlen, MB, Delhi 1962

Isibhasiyaim, text and commentary, LDII 1974

Settar, S. — Pursuing Death, Brahmi Society Publication, Mississauga 1991

Shah, D.M. and Pungaliya, U.K. — "Srimad Rajacandra on the Role of the *Sadguru* for Self-Realization" in *Jinamanjari*, Vol. 23, No. 1, pp. 1-31

Shah, Hemant — Jain Theism, Academy of Philosophy, Ahmedabad 1997

Sharma, A. — A Jaina Perspective on the Philosophy of Religion, MB, Delhi 2001

Sharma, J.P. — "Hemchandra: The Life and Scholarship of a Jain Monk," in *Asian Profile* III, no. 2, pp 195-215, Hong Kong 1975

Shukla, R. And Mishra, S.M. — *India as Known to* Haribhadrasuri, Kusumanjali Prakashan, Meerut 1991

Studies in Bhagavati Sutra, Muzaffarpur 1964

Sikdar, J. C. — "The Fabric of Life as Conceived in Jaina Biology," in *Sambodhi* III, No. 1, pp 1-10 Ahmedabad 1974

Singh R.J. — The Jaina Concept of Omniscience, LDII, Ahmedabad 1974

Singhavi, L. M. — Jain Declaration of Nature, Presented to H.H. Prince Phillip, 1990

Smart, N. — The Religious Experience of Mankind, Collins, London 1969

Smith, V. A. — The Jain Stupa and Other Antiquities of Mathura" Indological Book House, Varanasi 1969 (reprint of original in 1901)

Sogani, K.C. — Ethical Doctrines in Jainism, Jaina Samskriti Samrakshaka Sangha Sholapur 1967

Stevenson, S. — The Heart of Jainism, Munshiram Manoharlal, New Delhi 1970 (reprint of 1915 publication by Oxford University Press)

Sudharma Svami — *Bhagavati Sutra*: Volume III, Jain Bhavan, Calcutta 1980

Sushilkumar,Muni — Songs of the Soul An Introduction to the Namokar Mantra and the Science of the Soul, Siddhachalam Publishers, New Jersey 1987

Talib, G.S., ed. Jainism, Punjab University, Patiala 1975

Tatia, Nathmal Studies in Jaina Philosophy, Jaina Cultural Research Society, Varanasi 1951

That Which Is, commentary and English translation of Umasvati's *Tattvarthasutra*, Harper Collins Publishers, San Francisco 1994

Titze, Kurt Jainism: A Pictorial Guide to the Religion of Nonviolence MB, Delhi, 2000

Tiwary, B.K. History of Jainism in Bihar Academic Press, Delhi 1998

Tukol, T.K. *Sallekhana* Is Not Suicide, LDII, Ahmedabad 1976

Compendium of Jainism, (Original *Jain Darsana* translated by Shukla, C.P.), S.P. University, Vallabha Vidyanagar, 1978

Tull, H.W. The Vedic Origins of *Karma*: Cosmos as Man in Ancient Indian Myth and Ritual, State University of New York Press, Albany 1989

Tulsi Acharya My Religion, Adarsa Sahitya Sangh, Churu 1969

Illuminator of Jain Tenets, (Original *Jaina-Siddhanata Dipika* translated by Satkari Mookerji and edited by Nathmal Tatia), Jain Vishwa Bharati University, Ladnum 1985

Upadhye, A. N. et. al. Lord Mahavira and His Teachings, 2nd ed. Shree Vallabhsuri Smarak Nidhi, Bombay 1983

Nayayavatara, Jain Sahitya Vikas Mandal, Bombay 1971

Wagle, N.K. and Qvarnstrom, O. eds. Approaches to Jain Studies: Philosophy, Logic, Rituals and Symbols, University of Toronto Press, 1999

Warren, H. Jainism in Western Garb, as a Solution to Life's Great Problems, 2nd ed. with notes by N.J. Shah, Shree Vallabhsuri Smarak Nidhi, Bombay 1983

Williams, R. Jaina Yoga MB Delhi 1983

Zaveri, J.S. Microcosmology: Atom in Jain Philosophy and Modern Science, Jain Viswabharati University, Ladnum, 2nd edition 1991

Web - Sites on Jainism

www.atamvallabh.com
www.atmadharma.com
www.atmadharma.com
www.arham.com
www.atmasiddhi.com
www.angelfire.com
www.anekant.org
www.bhaktisangeet.com
www.beliefnet.com
www.cs.colostate.edu~malaiya/jainhlinks.html
www.ccsr.cms.dmu.ac.uk/resources/faith/jainism.html
www.digambarjain.com
www.globaljains.org Ê
www.geocities.com/Athens/3861
www.geocities.com/Athens/7592jain.html
www.intra-tech-5000.com/jain/convention.htm
www.jain-friends@onelist.com
www.jainworld.com
www.jcnc.org
www.jaintirth.org
www.jainheritage.com
www.jainism.org
www.jain-champapur.com
www.jain-padmaprabhu.com
www.jain-tijara.com
www.jainmahavirji.com
www.jaintriloktrith.com
www.jainsammedshikharji.com
www.jaindarshan.com
Www.jainacharyadevendramuni
www.jainstudy.org
www.jaina.org
www.jainism.org
www.jainspirit.org
www.jain-germany.de

www.jainojago.com
www.jain-astrology.com
www.ldindology.org
www.mantraonline.com/religion/mantra-religion.html
www.naples.net/~nfn02090
www.old.veg.org
www.pitara.com
www.snowcrest.net/dougbnt/jain.html
www.samyakinfotech.com
www.shantivijay.org
www.snowcrest.net/dougbnt/jain.html
www.sunsite.unc.edu/jainism
www.scerc.org
www.terapanth.com
www.umich.edu/%7Eumjains/jainismsimplified/jainsimp.html
www.veg.org/veg
www.vegsource.org
www.vegdining.ocm
www.vegeats.com
www.vegsource.org
www.webdunia.com
www.wizard.net/~ethan/ahimsa.htm
Www.yja.org

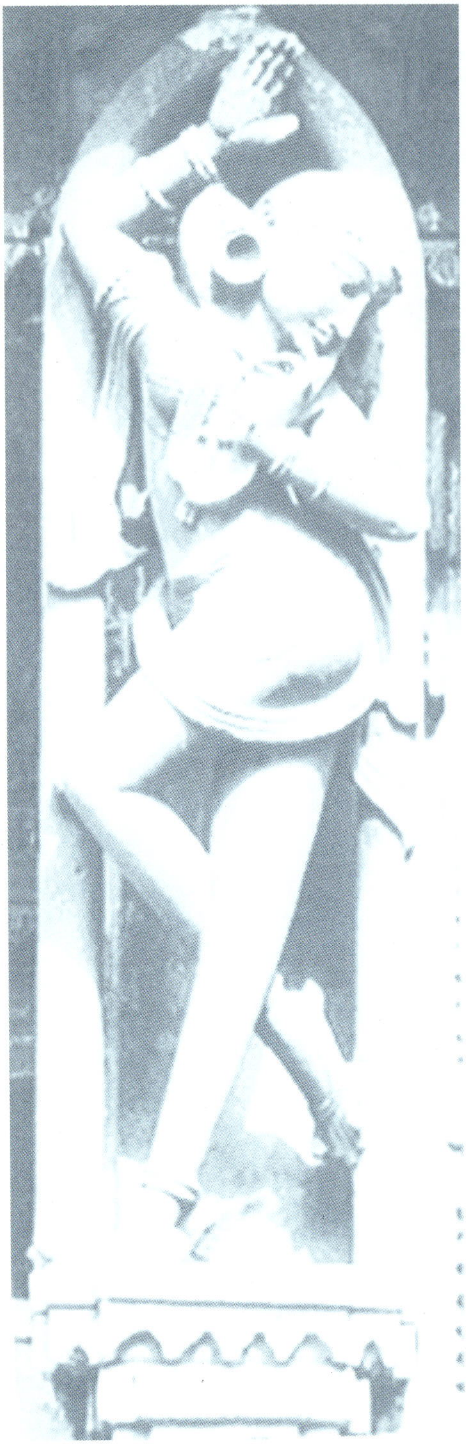

Glossary of Terms Used

Acharya	Leader of an ascetic order
Adharma	Medium of stability or rest
Agama	Sacred canon, scriptures, Mahavira's words
Ahimsa	Doctrine of non-hurting, non-killing
Ajiva	Non-living
Akasa	Universe, space
Aloka-akasa	Space that is not inhabited
Anekantavada	Doctrine of Multiple viewpoints
Anendriya	Non-sensuous
Anga	Original, main
Anitya	Non-eternal, impermanent, transitory
Anu	Indivisible, sub-atomic particle
Aparigraha	Doctrine of Limiting possessions
Arahant	Omniscient ones
Arahat	Omniscient ones
Asrava	Inflow of *karmic* matter
Avadhi	Clairvoyant knowledge
Avarniya	Obstructing
Aviriti	Non-restraint
Avasarpini	Declining period of cyclical time
Ayariya	Head of the religious order of monks or nuns
Bandha	Bondage of soul with *karmic* matter
Bhattaraka	An administrator-cleric
Bhava	Mental, psychical, feeling
Bhava Himsa	Intentional violence
Bhava Puja	Mental worship, psychical worship
Charitra	Conduct, behavior, lifestyle
Chedasutra	Scriptures prescribing ascetic behavior
Chouvihar	Eating before sunset
Dana	Donation
Darsana	Intuition, worldview, viewing with reverential feelings
Deva	Heavenly beings
Dharma	Medium of motion
Dravya Himsa	Physical/verbal violence
Dravya	The six 'Real Elements'
Ekendriya	One-sensed organism
Gaccha	Ascetic lineage
Ganadhara	Mahavira's eleven direct disciples
Ghee-boli	A fund-raising technique for the temples
Guna	Quality, attribute,
Gunasthana	Stage of spiritual progress
Indriya	Senses
Jina	One who has achieved total victory over the self
Jiva	Soul, consciousness energy and bliss
Jnana	Knowledge
Kala	Time
Karman-vargana	*Karma*-forming
Kasaya	Passions
Kayotsarga	Standing posture for meditation, relaxation
Kevali	One who has attained omniscience
Ksama-yachana	Asking for forgiveness
Loka-akasa	Space inhabited by the Existents
Mula-sutra	A group of texts belonging to the subsidiary canon
Muni	An ascetic
Namo	Reverent salutation
Namokara	A holy litany of reverent salutation
Naraki	Hellish beings
Navatattva	Nine operating principles of the universe
Naya	Logical viewpoint, logical standpoint
Nirjara	Dissociation or shedding of *karmic* matter
Nirvana	Death of holy person, reaching ecstasy
Nischaya Himsa	Definitive violence
Nitya	Eternal, permanent, constant
Panchendriya	Five-sensed organisms
Papa	Inauspicious or unwholesome bondage

Paryaya	Mode, modification, format
Pramada	Carelessness, non-vigilance
Pramana	Instrument of valid cognition,
Pratikramana	Confession
Pratima	Steps for spiritual progress for laypersons
Pudgala	Matter
Puja	Worship
Pujari	Usually a caretaker of idols in a temple
Punya	Auspicious or wholesome bondage
Purva	An early canon text (now lost
Ratnatraya	Three jewels, threefold path
Sahu	Monk, nun, ascetic
Sakahara	Vegetarianism
Saman	A quasi ascetic male follower of Acharya Tulsi
Samani	A quasi ascetic female Follower of Acharya Tulsi
Samayika	Equanimous meditation
Samsara	Cycle of transmigration, birth and death
Samvara	The stoppage of *karmic* influx
Samyak	Rational, logical, correct, right
Sapta-bhangi	Seven-fold predication
Siddha	One who has achieved omniscience
Sravaka	A lay man
Sravika	A lay woman
Sruti	Articulate
Sthanak	Lodging hall for Sthankvasi ascetics
Sthanakvasi	A Svetambara sub-sect
Sthula Himsa	Major violence
Sukshma Himsa	Minor violence
Suri	A prominent acharya
Sutra	Short mnemonic rule, scriptural text
Syad	In a certain sense or viewpoint
Syadvada	Doctrine of qualified assertions
Syat	Same as Syad, also Relatively
Terapanti	A sub-sect in Digambara and Svetambara sects
Tirthankara	Liberated one who shows path to liberation
Tiryancha	Animals and plants
Unodarika	Light eating, Semi-fasting
Upanga	A group of texts in subsidiary canon
Upavasa	Fasting for 36 hours or more
Uvajjhaya	Those monks who teach scriptures
Vrata	Vows
Vyavahara	Pragmatic
Yapaniya	An extinct sub-sect trying to unite Digambara and Svetambara sects

Index

L

M